SPIRAL GUIDES

Travel With Someone You Trust®

LONDON

Contents

the magazine 5

Finding Your Feet 31

St James's, Mayfair and Piccadilly 45

The City 67

Written by Lesley Reader
Magazine by Fiona Dunlop
Where to sections by Elizabeth Carter
Captions and additional writing by Tim Jepson

Copy edited by Lodestone Publishing Limited
Page layout by Amanda Chauhan, Tony Truscott
Verified by Paul Murphy
Indexed by Marie Lorimer

Updated by Paul Murphy
Update managed by Lodestone Publishing Limited

American editor Sharon Picone

Edited, designed and produced by AA Publishing
© Automobile Association Developments Limited 2006

Published in the United States by AAA Publishing,
1000 AAA Drive, Heathrow, Florida 32746
Published in the United Kingdom by AA Publishing

ISBN-13: 978-1-59508-110-0
ISBN-10: 1-59508-110-0

Cover design and binding style by permission of AA Publishing

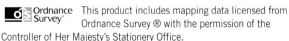 This product includes mapping data licensed from
Ordnance Survey ® with the permission of the
Controller of Her Majesty's Stationery Office.
© Crown copyright 2006. All rights reserved. License number
399221.

Mapping produced by the Cartographic Department of
the Automobile Association

Color separation by Keenes, Andover
Printed and bound in China by Leo Paper Products

10 9 8 7 6 5 4 3 2

A03214

London
the magazine

Double Destruction

London's two infernal nightmares, the Great Fire and the Blitz, albeit three centuries apart, both left smouldering ruins. Yet, phoenix-like, out of the ashes arose new approaches to urban living that transformed the face of the capital.

London's Burning!

The flames crackled and cinders whirled into the night sky: it was 2 September, 1666, the king's bakery in Pudding Lane was on fire and 80 per cent of the city of London was about to go up in smoke. It was not the first time this medieval town had seen a fire, but this one was to be by far the most destructive. As the flames raged, the Lord Mayor dithered, unwilling to rouse himself, and announced dismissively that "a woman might piss it out". That woman unfortunately did not materialise, and the fire soon spread to riverside warehouses filled with combustible materials. The blaze took hold.

Even the efforts of King Charles II, his brother the Duke of York and armies of fire-fighters were to little avail and four nights later, when the wind

The Great Fire of London, 1666

abated and the fire finally died down, over 13,000 houses had bitten the dust, along with 76 churches, 44 livery company halls, the Guildhall, the Royal Exchange and St Paul's Cathedral. Remarkably, there were only nine deaths, but 100,000 became homeless.

It didn't take long for the king to issue new building regulations: all new construction was to be in brick or stone and all streets were to be wide enough for carriages to pass along them. This Rebuilding Act was the first of much legislation over the next two centuries designed to regulate the standard of housing. Although architect Sir Christopher Wren's plan for a model urban layout was rejected, on grounds of practicality, some improvements were made, notably a continuous quay between the Tower of London and London Bridge.

Rebuilding took about ten years – not counting St Paul's and 50 or so churches, all designed by Wren – but the most important spin-off was the accelerated drift to the suburbs, either across the river to Southwark or west to Westminster. The old City of London thus lost its hold, its population plummeted, and the embryo of suburban London took shape.

Survivors

Not every City church succumbed to the flames of the Great Fire. Among the survivors in the Bishopsgate area were St-Botolph-without-Bishopsgate, the tiny St Ethelburga and above all the remarkable St Helen's, once part of a 12th-century Benedictine nunnery. However, all three were to suffer extensive damage in 1993 when an IRA bomb blasted out Bishopsgate. To the west, the beautiful medieval church of St-Bartholomew-the-Great, much restored in the 19th century, also escaped the fire, together with London's oldest hospital, St Bartholomew's ("Barts").

Sir Christopher Wren, architect of St Paul's Cathedral and some 50 London churches

Although thousands of steel bomb shelters were issued to Londoners who had gardens, many East Enders used the public shelters. The largest was an underground goods yard in Stepney, where 16,000 people would spend their nights in overcrowded conditions. Far better in terms of facilities was a network of caverns at Chislehurst, Kent, where electric light, bunk-beds, lavatories and an old piano all added to the rousing atmosphere of solidarity. But top of the popularity stakes were the Underground stations. Tickets were issued for regulars, bunk-beds set up and impromptu sing-songs took place. At times, around 177,000 people came here each night.

London Blitz

Blackouts and wailing sirens were the prelude to London's World War II drama: the Blitz. The aerial assault of the city began on 7 September, 1940, when some 320 Luftwaffe bombers flew up the Thames to unleash their devastation on the East End. The bombing continued mercilessly for 57 consecutive nights, then intermittently for a further six months, with more than 27,000 bombs and countless incendiaries dropped on the city. By November more than 11,000 people had been killed and 250,000 were homeless. Initially the East End, Docklands and the City were the targets, but attacks on central London soon followed. The last raid came on 10 May, 1941, when 550 bombers hammered the capital for five hours, destroying the Chamber of the House of Commons (among other buildings) and killing more than 1,400 people.

After the war, priority was given to planning new satellite towns and filling the craters that pockmarked the urban landscape. The late 1950s and 1960s witnessed a building bonanza of offices and public housing, with tower blocks often overshadowing a Wren church or a Regency terrace. Slum clearance, too, gave way to highrises, but it took two decades and inner city riots during the 1980s before these concrete jungles were recognised as non-viable. Like them or not, they're part of London's history and have created a social patchwork across the capital.

In the last-ditch Nazi assault of 1944 terrifying V1 doodlebugs (flying bombs) were launched from northern France, soon followed by the even faster and more devastating V2 rockets. It was impossible to mount a defence against these rockets and they killed more than 2,000 Londoners.

St Paul's Cathedral, a miraculous survivor of the London Blitz

In 1999 a memorial to the 30,000 Londoners who died in the Blitz was unveiled by the late Queen Mother in the courtyard of St Paul's Cathedral. She was an appropriate choice to dedicate the memorial. At the height of wartime bombing, she had tirelessly toured the city's bombsites. When Buckingham Palace received a direct hit, she wrote: "I'm glad we've been bombed. It makes me feel I can look the East End in the face".

THE FACTS OF LONDON LIFE

London, Europe's largest city, covers more than 610sq miles (1,580sq km).

The city attracts 29 million visitors each year. Despite the 95,000 hotel rooms, it is estimated that 20,000 more beds are needed to satisfy demand.

Despite the introduction of a congestion charge for vehicles in the city centre, daytime traffic still crawls at a snail's pace. No wonder every day around 5 million people opt to use the Underground (Tube).

Westminster, the most visited part of the capital, has around 90 tonnes of rubbish collected from its streets each day.

London's population today, hovering around the 7 million mark, is the same as it was in 1900 when it was the world's most populated city.

The city's financial institutions process about £200 billion in foreign exchange daily and manage half the world's ship brokering, company mergers and acquisitions.

The Millennium Dome, the largest structure of its kind in the world, could accommodate Nelson's Column standing upright and the Eiffel Tower placed horizontally.

The city has 1,700 parks and it's possible to walk from Westminster to Notting Hill, a distance of 2 miles (3.2km), through parkland alone.

The Millennium Bridge connecting Tate Modern with St Paul's Cathedral is the first pedestrian bridge to be built across the Thames since 1900.

At the height of the recession in 1992, the freshly completed but unoccupied Canary Wharf was losing £38 million per day.

There are 40,000 tulips planted each year in front of Buckingham Palace and 250,000 more at Hampton Court.

The 1,020-feet (311m) length of Canary Wharf station is enough to accommodate the next-door Canary Wharf Tower, Britain's tallest building, placed horizontally.

Battersea Dogs Home is the world's oldest rescue centre for lost or unwanted dogs.

Canary Wharf Tower, at the heart of the Docklands redevelopment, is nowadays fully occupied

Tracking down the glitterati

Above: Richard
Branson chooses
to live in Holland
Park, near
Notting Hill

Literary, Arty, Musical, Political or Thinking London... the metropolis bristles with blue plaques posted on the former residences of its illustrious inhabitants. Today, with well-defined areas still attracting high-profile personalities, you may just bump into a living legend. London is constantly evolving, so you are unlikely still to see cutting-edge artists in stylish Hampstead or Chelsea. Increasing property values have sent them running to Hackney, whose lofts house the greatest concentration of artists in Europe. Hang out in the "cool" new bars of Shoreditch and spot tomorrow's star, then move on to that haven of affluent bohemia, Notting Hill, to shadow entrepreneur Richard Branson, singer Robbie Williams, writer Martin Amis or designer Stella McCartney.

Creative Londoners

London has inspired thousands of writers over the centuries. Top areas for the today's literati are the northern districts of Hampstead, Camden Town and Islington (chosen pre-*fatwa* by author Salman Rushdie, and by composer Michael Nyman and actress Cate Blanchett), reflecting a remarkable continuity with the past. Some houses have even been home to more than one famous inhabitant, as at 23 Fitzroy Road, Primrose Hill (Tube: Chalk Farm), once occupied by the Irish poet W B Yeats and later by the American poet Sylvia Plath. Plath was drawn to Yeats's blue plaque when on her way to visit her doctor and decided that it was "the street and the house" for her. Within minutes of persuading some builders to let her in, she was at the agents, negotiating the lease for the top-floor apartment.

George Orwell (1903–50), in keeping with his socio-political concerns, lived closer to the pulse of less erudite streets, gravitating between Camden Town and rent-free rooms above a bookshop in South End Green where he worked. He later moved to 27 Canonbury Square in Islington (Tube: Highbury and Islington) – at the time a far from gentrified address. Another socially concerned writer, H G Wells (1866–1946), meanwhile lived in style overlooking Regent's Park from 13 Hanover Terrace (Tube: Baker Street). When negotiating the lease he said, "I'm looking for a house to die in". This he did ten years later, having survived the world war that he had so grimly predicted.

Chelsea has seen a stream of luminaries ever since Sir Thomas More, Henry VIII's Lord Chancellor, built his stately house in Cheyne Walk in the 16th century, though this is now long gone. Exoticism and scandal always went hand in hand here, but Chelsea's notoriety really took off in Victorian times when custom-built artists' studios became the rage. At this time, Oscar Wilde (1854–1900) penned plays at 34 Tite Street (Tube: Sloane Square). Though Wilde's wife and children lived here, he was partying madly with his boyfriend "Bosie", a double life perfectly reflected in his novel *The Picture of Dorian Gray*.

Before the American John Singer Sargent (1856–1925) became London's most fashionable portraitist from his

Tite Street home, his compatriot James Whistler (1834–1903) was painting Chelsea's riverscapes from 96 Cheyne Walk. He was not the first, however, as the great landscape painter J M W Turner (1775–1851) had already been inspired into abstraction from windows at No 119.

In the 20th century Chelsea continued to attract creative souls and it was in Cheyne Row that Ian Fleming pounded out his first James Bond novel, *Casino Royale*, on a gold-plated typewriter while T S Eliot lived below. The latter's checkered marital life was exposed at 24 Russell Square in Bloomsbury, where for 40 years he worked for the publishers Faber & Faber (Tube: Russell Square). Literary hopefuls who mounted the steps often spotted Eliot's first wife, Vivienne, who would arrive wearing placards saying "I am the wife he abandoned".

Money is now everything in Chelsea; gone are the bearded bohemians, royal mistresses and struggling actors, today replaced by the likes of former prime minister Margaret Thatcher (Chester Square), actress Joan Collins (Eaton Square), architect Sir Richard Rogers (Turks Row) and everyone's favourite foppish Englishman, actor Hugh Grant.

ENGLISH HERITAGE
T. S. ELIOT, O.M.
1888-1965
Poet
lived and died here

Both T S Eliot and Ian Fleming (left), the creator of James Bond, were residents of exclusive Cheyne Row in Chelsea

Actress Joan Collins has a home in Eaton Square

Blue plaques of Hampstead

John Keats (1795–1821), Wentworth Place, Keats Grove
Katherine Mansfield (1888–1923), 17 East Heath Road
D H Lawrence (1885–1930), 1 Byron Villas
John Constable (1776–1837), 40 Well Walk
George Romney (1734–1802), Holly Bush Hill
Anna Pavlova (1885–1931), Ivy House, North End Road
Sigmund Freud (1856–1939), 20 Maresfield Gardens

Virginia Woolf, novelist and leading light of the Bloomsbury Group

Political exiles

With democracy stamped on the nation's psyche, it is hardly surprising that numerous politicos on the run made London their base. Napoleon III (1808–73), Bonaparte's nephew, found himself exiled in London twice over and in 1848 lived at 1 King Street, in the gentlemanly heart of St James's (Tube: Green Park). He became so inspired by the parks of the English capital that on his subsequent coronation as emperor he ordered his city architect to set about copying them in Paris. Nearly a century later, another Gallic exile, General Charles De Gaulle (1890–1970), was notoriously less of an anglophile, despite an equally salubrious address at 4 Carlton Gardens (Tube: Charing Cross). This was his base for organising the Free French forces while broadcasting to resistance fighters before a triumphal return at liberation.

At the other end of the spectrum was Karl Marx (1818–83) who, after expulsion from Germany, settled in London to pursue a rocky, often impecunious existence. From 1851 to 1856 he lived in what was then a seedy Soho, at 28 Dean Street (Tube:

Tottenham Court Road), later writing much of *Das Kapital* in the British Museum's Reading Room. He was buried in Highgate Cemetery beneath a gigantic bust bearing the words "Workers of the World Unite".

Marx's wealthier compatriot, supporter and fellow thinker, Friedrich Engels (1820–95), was also buried in Highgate Cemetery after spending much of his life in London. From 1870 to 1892 he lived at 121 Regent's Park Road, a desirable address overlooking the park (Tube: Camden Town). Communist theoreticians continued to be inspired by no less a figure than Vladimir Ilyich Lenin (1870–1924), who in 1905 lived at 16 Percy Circus, near King's Cross (now the Royal Scot Hotel), within walking distance of the London Patriotic Society in Clerkenwell where he worked. This neo-classical 1737 building now houses the Marx Memorial Library (37a Clerkenwell Green, Tube: Farringdon).

This stern image of Karl Marx tops his burial place in Highgate Cemetery

London's rural retreats

Visit London in winter and it looks colourless. Visit in summer and you'll be greeted by huge splashes of green, from perfectly manicured lawns to towering plane or lime trees lining streets and avenues. The great British love for all things rural is undeniable and the fact that the capital, despite rising pollution and traffic, manages to preserve this aspect must stem from some psychic feat of collective will-power. The squares of central London are bucolic havens carved out of the general mayhem. With a break in the clouds, Londoners are out there, on deck-chairs, bikini-clad on the grass or striding across the parks.

Holland Park

One of London's prettiest and most secluded parks is a favourite getaway for residents of Kensington and Notting Hill. In 54 acres (22ha) of grounds, wilderness and order are juxtaposed, although only the east wing of the Jacobean mansion survived a bomb in 1941. The park's intrinsic leafiness attracted a colony of wealthy artists to its fringes in

Urban Green

Victorian days; these included Frederic, Lord Leighton. His house, now a museum, includes an extraordinary arabesque hall and beautiful Pre-Raphaelite paintings. Today's well-heeled park *habitués* take in art exhibitions at the Ice House or the Orangery Gallery, or indulge in summer evening concerts in a tent on the lawn. Meanwhile, well-spoken families gather at the tea-house, squirrels and peacocks roam in the woods of the northern half, and nannies and childminders watch over their charges in the playground of the formal gardens. The Kyoto Japanese Garden offers a meditative retreat to the northwest of Holland House. Tube: Holland Regent's Park.

A statue of Lord Holland presides over the park to which he gave his name

residences within which lies the Inner Circle of botanical glories, with their fantastically diverse and fragrant rose-gardens (including a Japanese-style waterfall, a favourite for Chinese wedding photos) and an open-air theatre that optimistically stages Shakespeare productions on summer evenings. The open, northern section is where players of ball games vie with the zoo's mountain goats for attention. On the western perimeter looms the copper dome of the London Central Mosque, and cosmopolitan strollers include Gulf Arabs, members of the orthodox Jewish community, and Chinese or Americans (the residence of the US ambassador stands in the park). Tube: Regent's Park.

Islington Squares

The liberal intelligentsia of Islington's gentrified squares have been dubbed the "chattering classes", although they are now joined by bankers eager to live within spitting distance of the City. Unlike Kensington and Chelsea, the essentially Georgian and Regency squares of Islington are mainly public and surprisingly well maintained, despite the regular onslaught of office workers' picnics, local children and, at times, the homeless.

Southern Islington offers the intimacy of Wilmington Square and its crumbling

The Kyoto Japanese Garden in Holland Park

The most northerly of the royal parks is the work of John Nash, "a thick squat dwarf with round head, snub nose and little eyes" (his own self-appraisal). Appearances aside, this visionary architect came up with the prototype for England's garden suburbs and cities, combining urban and rural in one fell swoop in order to lure the nobility to what was then considered far north of the fashionable West End.

The 494-acre (200-ha) circular park is edged by the Outer Circle of highly desirable, white stuccoed

Parklife

In summer, the northern side of Hyde Park's Serpentine (► 130–131) sees Londoners out in force. Some picnic on the grass, but for the more energetic there is roller-blading or boating.

1920s garden kiosk, the harmonious Palladian-style Lloyd Square (unusually private, because it is part of an estate) and vast, church-dominated Myddelton Square. Barnsbury, to the north, is home to elegant Gibson Square with its curious brick folly – in reality a ventilation shaft for the London Underground's Victoria line – and Milner Square, unique for its neo-classical architecture. In contrast are Lonsdale Square's unexpected grey-brick neo-Gothic houses. Tube: Angel.

Battersea Park

On 198 acres (80ha) of land where the Duke of Wellington and Lord Winchelsea once fought an uneventful pistol duel (they both deliberately missed), Battersea Park was created in 1858. It catered for "tens of thousands of mechanics, little tradesmen,

apprentices, and their wives and sweethearts". Today, its location directly across the river from Chelsea (earning Battersea the sobriquet "south Chelsea"), makes it an obvious escape for the people who live and work there, among others, interior decorators or antiques dealers from the King's Road musing on potential deals.

On the park's eastern edge loom the stacks of Battersea Power Station, closed since 1983 and now being redeveloped as a huge leisure complex. At the other end of the entertainment spectrum is the charming children's zoo. The park's big surprise, however, is the Peace Pagoda, a two-tier building by the Thames erected in 1985 by Japanese Buddhists. Queenstown Road rail station is the nearest to the park.

Left: The Buddhist Peace Pagoda in Battersea Park

RIDING HIGH

RIDING HIGH

Triathlon in Hyde Park? Beach volleyball on Horse Guards Parade? Yes, London will be staging the 2012 Olympic Games. The countdown to the Games began on 6 July 2005 when International Olympic Committee members voted in favour of London over Paris in a hard-fought battle to host the 30th Olympiad.

Check out budding designers' clothes at markets such as Portobello (in stalls under the overpass) and Camden Lock. Then cruise down Monmouth Street for emerging talent, and Bond Street and Brompton Cross for the big labels.

It will mean big changes as the city redevelops its East End with a vast new sports complex and athletes' village in Stratford.

Fashion from Vivienne Westwood (below)

But the rest of London won't miss out, and there will be memorable backdrops to many of the sporting dramas. Cyclists will speed past the capital's landmarks, and archers will take to Lord's cricket pitch. Some venues are obvious – tennis matches will be settled at Wimbledon – while some require a little imagination: beach volleyball will be played on Horse Guards Parade. Despite the tremendous boost to London, there is a lot of work to be done, and it is an Olympic tradition for the city's initial budget of £2.5 billion to be exceeded. But Londoners' nascent enthusiasm for the Games bodes well.

Trend-setting London

No other European capital can claim the same buzz, flair and above all hype that London generates as it rides high on a

The London Eye

The British Airways London Eye (➤ 104) has become one of the city's most iconic landmarks. Londoners may initially have been wary of a massive observation wheel, 443 feet (135m) in diameter, directly opposite the Houses of Parliament, but the superb structure, and the fantastic views from its capsules (below), are, in every sense, one of the capital's highlights.

wave of prosperity and self-confidence. Fashion, art, architecture, design, music and film are the main ingredients of this heady mix.

It is not the first time that London has been swinging. The 1960s also saw a tidal wave of inventiveness, spearheaded by pop groups who did not necessarily originate in the capital but who just had to be there; The Beatles came from Liverpool, but their Abbey Road recording studios were the focus of the nation's music. London was the uncontested pulse of the nation with Carnaby Street, Kensington Market and the King's Road setting the tone for fashion victims, while Mary Quant, Biba, Ossie Clark or Mr Freedom cut the patterns to match. Carnaby Street isn't a cutting-edge fashion centre any more and the King's Road is drifting into mainstream, but homegrown designers have matured into realism. Some, such as Alexander McQueen, John Galliano and Stella McCartney, have even steered the fortunes of top couture houses in France, while London's grande dame,

Vivienne Westwood, continues to stun. Above all, street fashion is still big. Even Parisian couturiers such as Jean-Paul Gaultier and Christian Lacroix admit to pillaging ideas from London's trend-setting young clubbers.

Facelifting

London's innovative architects are chiselling the capital's facelifted image and great stylish swathes of glass and steel are now slotting into the

Norman Foster's Swiss Re Tower

Below right: The striking Millennium Bridge links Tate Modern with St Paul's Cathedral

Below: Spotted in all the right places – Damien Hirst, *enfant terrible* of the British art scene

city fabric. Many of these new buildings were designed by Norman Foster (now Lord Foster of Thames Bank) and Richard Rogers (now Lord Rogers of Riverside), originally partners in the 1960s before working separately on major projects in Europe and the Far East. Rogers' earliest landmark is the towering high-tech Lloyd's Building in the financial heart of London, which opened its doors in 1986, just before the yuppie

most eye-catching project since the British Airways London Eye (▶ panel 17) is the Swiss Re Tower – a stunning 590-foot (180m) rounded skyscraper, known as The Gherkin, completed in 2004. It stands on the site of the old Baltic Exchange in the heart of the City of London. On the opposite bank of the river is City Hall, another striking, rounded, glass building, home to the Greater London Authority.

bubble burst and recession set in. Foster's most recent contribution, and the capital's

The Millennium Bridge is also a stylish Foster creation, the first pedestrian bridge to be built over the river since 1900. Conceived as a purist "blade of light", the bridge connects Tate Modern with St Paul's and marks the general shift eastwards of the city's cultural focus. Early construction problems meant that opening was delayed to 2002.

Another Millennium project, the Underground Jubilee Line extension, is a showcase for architectural audacity with each station the work of a

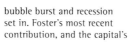

Best Contemporary Art Galleries

The **Saatchi Gallery** (▶ 104) is *the* place in the city to see cutting-edge contemporary art but there are other interesting venues, including the **Serpentine Gallery** (▶ 131), **Camden Arts Centre** (Arkwright Road, NW3, tel: 020 7472 5500) and the **Hayward** (▶ 110). One of the best private galleries is the **Lisson Gallery** (52–54 Bell Street, NW1, tel: 020 7724 2739, Tube: Edgware Road).

Art for art's sake

Provocative, even scandalous, the Britpack (a label for the youngest generation of British artists) is a fixture in London's galleries. Much of the impetus for the Britpack came from advertising mogul Charles Saatchi who bought the work of, among others, Hirst, the Chapman brothers and Gary Hume. In 2003 the opening of the Saatchi Galley (▶ 104) made Saatchi's collection accessible to a wider audience.

different designer, from Foster at Canary Wharf, to Will Alsop at North Greenwich, Ian Ritchie at Bermondsey and Chris Wilkinson at Stratford.

Maturer London-based artists include Rachel Whiteread, Anish Kapoor, Richard Deacon and the doyens of the East End, Gilbert and George.

Above: Foster's design for Canary Wharf Underground station

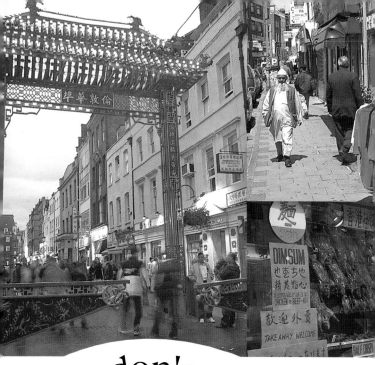

London's global
villages

The Tower of Babel? London's tapestry of cultures has had far-reaching influences on its character, its music, its literature, its streetlife and, not least, its eating habits. Ever since London's founders arrived in AD 43, namely the Roman army of Emperor Claudius, its citizens have descended from a variety of cultures, whether Angles, Saxons or Normans, all adding to a rich cosmopolitan flavour. Religious persecution later brought French Huguenots and members of the European Jewish community, while economic necessity brought Italians, Irish and Chinese. Large-scale immigration, however, really began after World War II, with a huge influx of people from newly independent Commonwealth countries. These new citizens became a much exploited cheap workforce.

Today, inner city areas encapsulate a kaleidoscope of around 40 different cultures, making up 20 per cent of the population. Tension between communities has in the past exploded in street riots (Notting Hill in 1958, Whitechapel in the 1970s and

A taste of Italy

The annual Italian festival takes place every year on the Sunday closest to 16 July. A procession leaves St Peter's, on Clerkenwell Road, and food-stalls set up in Warner Street.

as MP Oona King and broadcaster and journalist Trevor Phillips.

The East End Jewish community has a lengthy list of rags-to-riches tales, whether hairdresser Vidal Sassoon or playwrights Harold Pinter and Steven Berkoff.

Whitechapel

Walking down Brick Lane, you'll hear the wail from the mosque or the beat of *bhangra* music, see traditionally dressed Bangladeshi men and women, and smell the pungent aromas of a string of budget curry restaurants. The heart of this East End garment district, where street-name plaques are written in Bengali, beats in the shadow of the Jamme Masjid, once a Huguenot church, in 1897 a synagogue and, since 1976, the Great Mosque, each reincarnation pointing to the dominant culture of the time. In 1700, London absorbed around 25,000 Huguenots

Brixton in 1981). But as integration develops, it is increasingly difficult to separate the immigrants of yesteryear from those who were born and bred in London.

Young Asians have an increasingly high profile in the music world, alongside more traditional roles in business, finance, law and restaurants. Just one example of a first-generation success story is that of millionaire Muquim Amed (born in 1963 in Bangladesh) who, starting from nothing in Brick Lane, now owns a chain of restaurants and is on first name terms with Prime Minister Tony Blair. Writers Salman Rushdie and Hanif Kureishi have also both imposed their global mark.

The black community has produced one of England's most popular news presenters, Trevor McDonald, as well as endless sportspeople, actors, musicians and politicians such

London's streets reflect its ethnic diversity

Don't miss the 24-hour bagel shop, Beigel Bake, at the top of Brick Lane (No 159), an East End institution popular with taxi-drivers. The place is bustling at all times and on Sunday mornings, when Brick Lane's junk market is in full swing, queues stretch down the street

escaping persecution in France, and many set up silk-weaving businesses here, some with outlets in Petticoat Lane market. By the 1880s came another wave, this time from the Eastern European Jewish community who worked in the shoe and clothing industries. As they prospered and moved out, Bengalis replaced them to set up, in their turn, leather-clothes workshops.

Clerkenwell

Hip Clerkenwell, inner London's epicentre of loft lifestyles, is shaking off its history of crafts-people and immigrants. Huguenots, again, were the first, joined in the 19th century by Italians who peaked at around 10,000 between the world wars, living parallel to the Hasidic Jewish community which still runs London's diamond trade from Hatton Garden.

Although prosperity has scattered the Italian community, Little Italy preserves some trusty relics: restaurants such as Carlo's, at 7 St John Street, and churches (St Peter's is the official Italian church, but the Holy Redeemer in Exmouth Market truly

echoes Italianate style) are steeped in Italian character and chatter.

Soho

Soho's Gerrard Street is London's Chinatown, lavishly announced by pagoda-style gateways and phone boxes, at night joined by flashing neon ideograms. London's Chinese community dates back to the late 18th century, when East India Company ships bringing goods from the Far East disgorged sailors into the docklands. Some settled there to open shops, restaurants or opium dens, but it was after World War II that Chinese (mainly Cantonese) fleeing the Communist regime focused on the labyrinth of streets south of Shaftesbury Avenue. Few of London's 60,000 Chinese now live here but this area is the best window on Chinese culture. You can pick up that much-prized giant fruit, the stinking durian, a wok, a newspaper fresh off the presses of Beijing, an embroidered *cheong san* dress or devour a Peking duck in one of the many restaurants.

Notting Hill

The first group of 500 immigrants from the Caribbean shivered in the cold of Tilbury docks in 1948 but since then have made their exuberant presence felt. The Notting Hill Carnival (every August bank holiday) is the zenith of Caribbean culture in Britain, with technicolour floats and costumes, throbbing reggae, steel bands, impromptu food-stands and cavorting crowds making it the world's second largest carnival after Rio de Janeiro.

Ongoing gentrification is changing this area, however, and the unofficial clubs and relaxed cafés of the Afro-Caribbean community are slowly disappearing.

Two types of watering-hole exemplify the often eccentric social traditions of London. By their very essence, gentlemen's clubs are reserved for the privileged few who pay annual dues to relax in the hushed atmosphere while traditionally perusing *The Times* over a Scotch. Pubs, meanwhile, are open to all comers, male and female alike, rich or poor, their often warm, smoky, jostling atmospheres a welcoming retreat for downing pints of beer while chatting to friends or strangers. On warmer days, customers at popular pubs will overflow on to the street.

Pubs & Clubs

Gentlemen's Clubs

There is no doubt about it, St James's Street and Pall Mall are the epicentre of London's most distinguished and discreetly ageing gentlemen's clubs. You won't be allowed in but their stately façades betray just a hint of what goes on inside. These are the bastions of upper-class England where new members are admitted only on personal recommendation. Business deals, networking, introductions and society gossip are the bottom line, while in the background Reuters spews out the latest on international stock markets.

When first established as gambling dens, these clubs saw a string of scandals in the fine upper-class tradition of waywardness and eccentricity. Money was rarely a problem and vast amounts were lost or gained on the most trivial of bets – although in extreme cases this inspired bankruptcy and even suicide.

At the oldest club, White's (1693), the diarist Horace Walpole recorded a typical incident: "A man dropped down dead at the door, was carried in and the club immediately made bets on whether he was dead or not". Brooks's and Boodle's were established soon after White's, setting a similar standard of excellence, and even today these three clubs remain top of the list for those in the upper echelons of British society.

Opposite: A taste for tradition – the Wig and Pen Club and Restaurant in Fleet Street

The Reform Club, founded by reformist Liberals in 1841, was a haunt of author Henry James and a hole was bored in the door of his favourite room so that the valet knew whether or not to disturb him. It was from the club's drawing room that Phileas Fogg, Jules Verne's

The RAC Club in Pall Mall

Since the 1970s, some clubs have relaxed the ban on women members although the Carlton Club, a bastion of the Conservative Party, had to make a special case to admit Margaret Thatcher. In others, women will be admitted only as guests or, as at the Athenaeum, just to a basement restaurant.

fictional hero, bet that he could travel round the world in just 80 days.

At the nearby Athenaeum, easily recognisable for its neo-Grecian frieze and dazzling gilt statue of Pallas, writers William Thackeray and Anthony Trollope both laboured away in the library, while Charles Dickens was another pen-pushing member.

Members-only clubs continue to proliferate, above all in Soho, but the new generation is a far cry from its predecessors in St James's. Women are accepted on an equal footing with men and it's the thirty-somethings who dominate. But the bottom line is the same: you are allowed entry only if signed in by a member. Today's most high-profile club is Groucho's, on Dean Street, home to the media and film *cognoscenti* who graduate from bar to restaurant.

Victoriana rules

Many pubs still preserve the etched glass screens (known as snob screens), mirrors, tiles, wood panelling and lofty boarded ceilings of Victorian times. Track down these classics:

Red Lion
(2 Duke of York Street, SW1
Tube: St James's Park, Green Park 197 E1)
Dog & Duck
(18 Bateman Street, W1
Tube: Tottenham Court Road ✚ 197 E2)
The Lamb
(94 Lamb's Conduit Street, WC1
Tube: Russell Square ✚ off map 200 B5)
Paxton's Head
(153 Knightsbridge, SW1
Tube: Knightsbridge ✚ 195 F2)

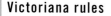

Pubs operate a system of first-come, first-served, so be prepared to elbow your way to the bar to order your drinks. Beware of theme pubs and brewery chains: the true sense of a "free house" is that the pub sells beers from different breweries and the decor reflects the landlord's or landlady's taste. You cannot buy alcohol in a pub (or anywhere in Britain) unless you are at least 18 years old, and it is an offence to buy it for anyone under 18 (although 16 and 17 year olds accompanied by an adult may consume beer, wine or cider with a table meal in a pub or restaurant). Many pubs allow children into their premises though they may be restricted to certain areas; children should always be kept away from the bar. If you think you may be challenged about your age, carry legal ID (for example, your passport).

Pubs

Pubs are moving with the times too. Some now produce cuisine that easily compares with top restaurants (see panel "Upgraded pubs") making for hazy distinctions between the two. Others have opted for satellite television on a big screen to boost pub crowds, with rousing atmospheres during major sporting events. But whatever the changes, pubs are still the mainstay for neighbourhood or after-work socialising. They may have gone a long way from their origins, but the aim is the same – drinking and conversation.

It was the Victorian era that saw pubs multiply but in the more egalitarian late 20th century the classic division between unadorned "public bar" (where the serious drinking was done) and carpeted "saloon bar" (for couples and the middle social classes) has virtually vanished. Changes in licensing hours too have encouraged long afternoons that are spent continental-style at outdoor tables, and the cloistered atmosphere of Victorian times is fast disappearing.

Standards of comfort and decor vary wildly, as does pub food, but if you find the right one you may have the bonus of an upstairs fringe theatre, art gallery or live music.

Traditional London pubs like the Dog and Duck are under threat from bland theme pubs

"Time please!"

For some years, many pubs have opened throughout the day, usually closing at 11 pm (10:30 on Sunday). However, effective from November 2005, the "24-hour drinking laws" will allow the country's pubs, clubs and bars to apply for longer opening hours. In reality, few, if any, will want to stay open around the clock, but many venues may extend their licences to close at 1 am on Thursday, Friday and Saturday.

Upgraded pubs

The Engineer (65 Gloucester Avenue, NW1, Tube: Camden Town) has a bar serving light meals and also a full-blown restaurant. A patio garden and mirrored upstairs rooms add to its charms.

Market Bar (240a Portobello Road, W11. Tube: Notting Hill Gate, Ladbroke Grove, ✚ off map 194 A4) draws the market crowds and local bohemia to its neo-Gothic bar and restaurant.

The Peasant (240 St John Street, EC1. Tube: Angel, ✚ off map 201 E5) has an ornate bar with a tiled mural of St George and a designer restaurant upstairs.

LONDON'S BEST . . .

BEST FREE MUSIC
• In **Covent Garden's Piazza** (➤ 150–151) on a sunny day you'll hear anything from Vietnamese xylophones to Peruvian flutes or a homegrown electric guitar – or all at once.
• **The Barbican Centre** (➤ 88) on Sunday lunchtime holds free jazz concerts in the bar.

BEST BUS ROUTES
• **No 7** – be spirited past the Oxford Street shoppers to Marble Arch, the Middle Eastern enclave of Edgware Road, Paddington station, hip Westbourne Grove and, through the backstreets of Notting Hill, end at Portobello Road.
• **No 15** – from the shopping hub of Oxford Circus to Piccadilly Circus, Trafalgar Square, the Strand and Aldwych, along Fleet Street, and up Ludgate Hill to St Paul's, the Monument and the Tower of London (➤ 184–186).
• **No 38** – from Victoria through Belgravia, passing Buckingham Palace gardens, then along Piccadilly to Soho, the bookstores of Charing Cross Road and Bloomsbury – a few steps from the British Museum. Stay on longer for Clerkenwell and Islington.

• **RV1** – this new route (operated by First, tel: 020 7222 1234) links the South Bank arts and cultural venues to the West End shopping and theatre district, and the City of London from Tower Gateway railway station, near the Tower of London, to the lively entertainment and shopping area of Covent Garden via London Bridge railway station and Tate Modern gallery.

BEST ANTIQUES AND JUNK MARKETS
• **Bermondsey Market** (Bermondsey Square, SE1, ✚ 202 B1) glitters with silverware, paintings, odd furniture and obsolete objects. Go at dawn on Friday to jostle with sharp-eyed professional antiques dealers for bargains.
• **Camden Markets** (➤ 152) is for anyone hankering after London street fashions, crafts, jewellery, ethnic nick-nacks, design objects or furniture. Fight your way through teeming youth for fortification from countless drink and snack vendors. Thursday to Sunday.
• **Portobello** (➤ 131) for anything and everything, from fruit and veg to specialist bric-à-brac, young designer fantasies or antiques – fake or sublimely real. Best on Saturday.

BEST BRIDGE VIEWS
• **Albert Bridge** (Tube: Sloane Square). Not just another of Queen Victoria's odes to her deceased husband, but a

Top: The Oxo Tower Restaurant

Above: Street
performers in
Covent Garden

Right: All that
glitters... a stall
in Portobello
Road market

magically illuminated suspension bridge between Battersea Park and Chelsea. Take in views of the exclusive Chelsea Harbour development and Cheyne Walk to the north and monumental Battersea Power Station to the east.

• **Blackfriar's Bridge** (Tube: Blackfriars, ✚ 201 D3). The widest bridge on the Thames offers views of the expanding skyline of Southwark to the south – including Tate Modern, St Paul's Cathedral and the spires, highrises in the City to the north, the South Bank Centre, Waterloo Bridge and Westminster to the west

• **Tower Bridge** (► 76–77). From this symbol of London you can see burgeoning waterside lofts replacing wharves as well as HMS *Belfast* on the south bank, and the dwarfed turrets and walls of the Tower of London alongside St Katharine's Dock to the north. It opens for river traffic about 500 times a year.

If you go to only one...

...stand-up comedy show, head for the Comedy Store (► 66) with impromptu amateur acts or sets by polished professional comedians. Beware of hard-hitting audience participation.

...continental coffee-shop, indulge at Soho's Pâtisserie Valerie (► 158) or its offshoots on Marylebone High Street and King's Road, Chelsea.

...bar with a view, you should hit the terrace of the Oxo Tower restaurant towards sunset (► 109).

For and against

London is the only place in which the child grows completely up into the man.
William Hazlitt (1778–1830)

London is a modern Babylon.
Benjamin Disraeli (1804-81)

Town life nourishes and perfects all the civilized elements in man. Shakespeare wrote nothing but doggerel verse before he came to London and never penned a line after he left.
Oscar Wilde (1854–1900)

London, that great cesspool into which all the loungers and idlers of the Empire are irresistibly drained.
Sir Arthur Conan Doyle (1859-1930)

I've learned to accept London as my muse. Initially, there I was, sitting on the tube, when she came in: filthy, raddled, smelly, old and drunk. But now we're inseparable, going round and round the Circle Line, arm in arm, perhaps for eternity.
Will Self, 'Granta 65: London', 1999

Of course I got lost: for London is laid out as haphazardly as a warren. It is a myriad of Streets High and Low, of Courts and Cloisters and Crescents and full Circles, Paths and Parks and Parkways, and Yards, and Mews, and Quays, Palace and Castles and Mansions and Halls and mere Houses...there are Ways to go and Ends to be arrived at... London is, in other words, a maze, but I was simply amazed, surprised that it had taken me so long to realize I was lost.
Dale Peck, ' Granta 65: London' 1999

I hate this daily ten-minute walk, along the outlines of the cold squares, past dark shopfronts where cats claw at the window panes, then into the tingling strip of Queensway, through shuddering traffic and the sweet smell of yesterday's trash.
Martin Amis 'Success', 1978

London hates to let you go... If you drive out of London towards Brighton, there are seventy-five sets of traffic lights before you reach the motorway, and a dozen false dawns.
Ian Parker, 'Granta 65: London', 1999

It is not a pleasant place; it is not agreable or cheerful or easy or exempt from reproach. It is only magnificent.
Henry James (1843-1916)

The vast town is always in movement night and day, wide as an ocean, with the grind and howl of machinery..., commercial adventure..., the Thames befouled, the atmosphere packed with coal dust; the superb parks and squares...the city with its vast moneybags.
Dostoevsky (1821–81)

A wet Sunday in London: shops closed, streets almost empty; the aspect of a vast and well-kept graveyard. The few people in this desert of squares and streets, hurrying beneath their umbrellas, look like unquiet ghosts; it is horrible.
Hippolyte Taine (1828–93)

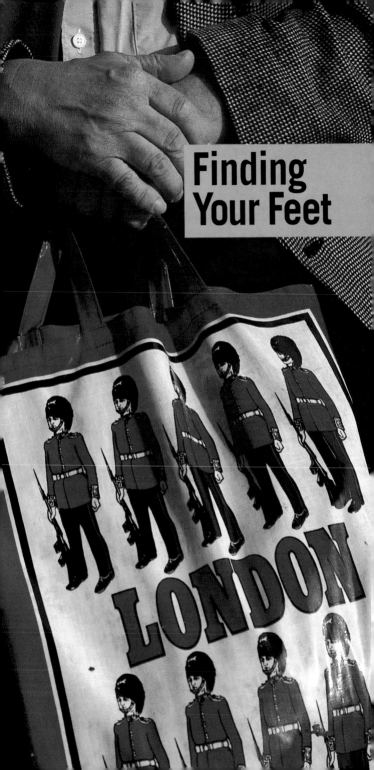

Finding Your Feet

First Two Hours

Heathrow and Gatwick are the principal airports serving London. However, Stansted and London City Airport are increasingly busy with traffic from continental Europe.

From Heathrow

Heathrow (code LHR) lies 15 miles (24km) west of central London and is served by good road and rail connections. All the services below go from all four terminals and are well signposted. A fifth terminal (T5) is under construction.

- The **London Underground** (tel: 020 7222 1234), Piccadilly line, serves Heathrow from 4:58 am to 11:54 pm (Monday to Saturday) and 5:50 am to 10:50 pm (on Sunday). The journey to central London takes about an hour and can get very crowded in the rush hour but is the most convenient, best-value option. From January 2005 to September 2006, Terminal 4 Underground station is closed and passengers have to take the replacement bus service to Hatton Cross station.
- The **Heathrow Express** (tel: 0845 600 1515; www.heathrowexpress.com) is a high-speed train to Paddington station. It runs from 5:10 am to 11:25 pm every 15 minutes and the journey takes 15 minutes – it's fast but expensive.
- Pick up a black metered **taxi** outside any terminal. Expect around an hour's journey time and £46 to £50 on the meter by the time you get to central London. Don't forget to allow for a 10 per cent tip for the driver.

From Gatwick

Public transport from Gatwick (code LGW), which lies 27 miles (43km) south of the city centre, includes an express train service.

- **Gatwick Express** (tel: 0845 850 1530) train service runs to Victoria Station in central London. It runs every 15 minutes most of the day and hourly most of the night with the last train at 1:35 am and service resuming at 4:35 am; journey time is 30 to 35 minutes. An alternative train service is provided by Thameslink, which goes to King's Cross and Euston (tel: 020 7222 1234).
- **National Express** (tel: 08705 747777) operates on the hour, every hour, from 7 am to 11 pm to Victoria Coach station. The journey takes up to 1 hour 15 minutes.
- **Taxis** operate from outside the terminal – journey time to central London is usually more than 1 hour 15 minutes and prices are around £80.

From Stansted

Stansted (code STN), small and modern, lies 35 miles (48km) northeast of the city centre.

- **Stansted Express** (tel: 0845 600 7245) train service runs to Liverpool Street station, every 15 to 30 minutes, from 5:30 am to midnight.
- **Stansted A6 Airbus** (tel: 08705 747777) to Victoria bus station operates 24 hours a day. The service runs every 30 minutes and takes around 1 hour 30 minutes.
- There's a **taxi** booking desk inside the terminal and a taxi costs around £86 into central London. The journey takes between 1 and 2 hours.

From London City Airport

London City Airport (code LCY) is the most central of the capital's airports, lying just 9 miles (14.5km) east of the city centre.

- The best option is the **Airport Shuttle Bus** (tel: 020 7646 0088). Buses run to Liverpool Street station every 10 minutes Monday to Friday from 6:50 am to 9:10 pm, Saturday 6:50 am to 1:10 pm and Sunday 11:56 am to 9:10 pm. The journey takes 25 minutes and costs around £7 one way.
- Black metered **taxis** wait outside the terminal – journey time is about 30 minutes into Liverpool Street and the cost will be around £16. Expect to pay around £25 for journeys to central London, depending on traffic.

Train Arrivals

International train services (Eurostar, tel: 08705 186186) from France (Lille and Paris) and Belgium (Brussels) arrive at Waterloo International Terminal where you connect with the Underground system. In 2007, the international terminal will move to King's Cross.

Getting Around

Buses and the Underground (London's metro system) operate from 5:30 am until just after midnight, after which a network of night buses operates until early morning. The system is divided into zones – six for the Underground and four for the bus system. These are marked on bus and Underground maps and displayed at stations. On both buses and the Underground you must have a ticket valid for the zone you are in or you are liable for an on-the-spot fine. For all London transport enquiries visit the excellent website www.tfl.gov.uk

Travelcards and Bus Passes

If you are going to do a lot of travelling over a day or a week, buy a pass that gives you unlimited travel in that period. Make sure it covers all the zones you need – most of the places in the main part of this guide are in Zones 1 and 2.

- **Travelcards** are valid on buses, the Underground, the Docklands Light Railway and National Railways' services in the London area off peak (after 9:30 am during the week and any time at weekends or on public holidays). Travelcards and other off-peak tickets are much cheaper than peak tickets. **Weekend Travelcards** and **Family Travelcards** are also good value. All Travelcards can be purchased at Underground stations, London Travel Information Centres and National Railways' stations, or newsagents shops displaying a London Transport logo.
- For a weekly or monthly pass, you'll need a passport-size photograph.

The Underground

The Underground (or Tube) is easy to use, though travellers with disabilities or those with baby strollers may find it less convenient. The system operates on 12 lines, which are colour-coded on maps and signs. Follow signs for the line you need and the direction you want to travel (north, south, east or west).

- Tickets and Travelcards can be purchased from machines or ticket offices in Underground stations.
- If you are going to make three or more Underground trips in one day, or a mix of bus and Underground trips, then **consider buying a Travelcard** (▶ 33).
- A **pack of 10** Zone 1 Underground tickets is a cheaper option if you will be making a number of trips in central London spread over several days. They are available from Zone 1 Underground stations or designated newsagents.

Buses

An extensive bus network operates in London. Though good for travelling short distances, buses tend to be slower on longer journeys.

- The older style of buses, which have a back entrance (with no doors) and a conductor to take fares, are rare and will be phased out completely by 2017; find a seat and pay when the conductor comes along.
- On all other buses you enter via the door at the front to pay the driver or show your pass and get off through the doors nearer the back.
- You need to know your destination and have change to pay for the fare.

Docklands Light Railway (DLR)

Docklands Light Railway is an above-ground train system operating from Bank Underground station to Lewisham in the south, Stratford in the north, Beckton in the east. Most visitors to London use it to get to Greenwich. For all ticketing purposes the DLR is part of London Underground, and Travelcards are valid.

Taxis

Black cabs (many now painted in gaudy colours) are available from outside stations and hotels but you can also hail them from the roadside.

- Cabs **available for hire** will have the yellow "For Hire" sign lit.
- All taxis are metered and the fare will depend on journey time; there are surcharges in the evenings. Drivers expect a 10 per cent tip.
- To ring for a taxi, **Radio Taxis** (tel: 020 7272 0272) and **Dial-a-Cab** (tel: 020 7426 3420) are both 24-hour services.
- **Black Taxi Tours of London** (tel: 020 7935 9363) offer a 2-hour tailor-made sightseeing tour.

Sightseeing Buses

Several companies operate private bus routes that cover the main tourist sights. The tour is usually in open-topped buses with a commentary in several languages. It's a hop-on, hop-off service. For more information contact:

Big Bus Company (tel: 020 7233 9533)
The Original London Sightseeing Tour (tel: 020 8877 1722)

Car Hire (Rental)

A car can be a liability in London; traffic is congested and parking expensive and elusive. Parking illegally can result in a parking ticket or having your car immobilised by a wheel clamp. It's only really worth renting a car for an excursion from the city. All the main international car rental companies have branches in central London.

Alamo (tel: 0870 400 4562)   **Europcar** (tel: 0870 607 5000)
Avis (tel: 0870 010 0287)   **Hertz** (tel: 0870 844 8844)

Driving

To drive in the United Kingdom, you need a full driving licence or an International Driver's Permit (available from national motoring organisations in your own country).

- Traffic in the United Kingdom drives on the **left**.
- It is obligatory to wear **seat belts**.
- The **speed limit** in built-up areas is 30 mph (48 kph); 60 mph (97 kph) on single carriageways; and 70 mph (113 kph) on dual carriageways (divided highways) and motorways (expressways).
- There are stringent laws against drinking and driving.

■ Private cars are banned from **bus lanes** – watch out for signs informing you when they are in operation.

Congestion Charging

A congestion charge was introduced in central London in February 2003. Every private car in the zone is charged £8 between 7 am and 6:30 pm Monday to Friday, excluding public holidays. You can pay online (www.cclondon.com), by phone 24 hours a day (tel: 0845 900 1234), in person at various outlets throughout the UK, including fuel stations and shops, or by credit or debit card at self-service machines at car parks inside the zone and other selected locations. When you pay, you need your vehicle registration. You can pay before midnight on the day or up to 90 days before your journey into the zone. The charge rises after 10 pm on the day of travel. Digital cameras check licence plates and those in breach of regulations are fined at least £80.

City Centre Tourist Offices

London Tourist Board (LTB) runs a recorded information system, charged at premium call rate (tel: 09068 663344) or visit the website: www.londontown.com

Britain and London Visitor Centre
⊠ 1 Regent Street
☎ 0870 156 6366
🕙 Mon 9:30–6:30, Tue–Fri 9–6:30,
Sat–Sun 10–4 (summer 10–5)

London Information Centre
⊠ Leicester Square
☎ 020 7292 2333
🕙 Daily 8 am–midnight

Prices
The cost of admission for museums and places of interest mentioned in the text is indicated by the following price categories
Inexpensive up to £3   **Moderate** £3–£6
Expensive £7–£10   **Very expensive** more than £10

Accommodation

London is an expensive city and its hotels reflect this. The capital is simply too popular, and with not enough beds to go round, prices for hotel rooms are forced ever higher.

Hotels

The hotels listed below are the pick of the bunch: what they offer in terms of service, character, charm and standard of facilities is second to none. More hotel and B&B listings can be found by clicking the Hotels and B&B link at the AA website: www.theAA.com

Bed and Breakfasts

Bed and breakfasts (B&Bs) can be a less expensive alternative to hotels. At their simplest, B&Bs offer a bedroom in a private house with a shared bathroom, but further up the scale are rooms with private bathrooms in beautiful old houses.

Budget Accommodation

For travellers on a budget, London can present something of a challenge.
■ **Youth hostels** run by the Youth Hostel Association (YHA) are a good starting point if you don't mind sleeping in bunks in a single-sex dormitory, though family rooms are also available in some hostels.

You need to be a member of the Association (tel: 0870 770 8868 in UK; 00 44 1629 592700 outside UK; www.yha.org.uk). For details of London hostels visit the website (www.yhalondon.org.uk). Membership costs around £14 (£7 for under 18s).

■ During the summer, usually from the end of June to mid-September, **university halls of residence** are rented to non-students. These are slightly more expensive than youth hostels but you get a single room (and even a few doubles) with shared facilities. The **Imperial College of Science and Technology** (15 Prince's Gardens, SW7, tel: 020 7594 9494. Tube: South Kensington) is one of the best located, being close to South Kensington museums.

Seasonal Discounts

July, August and September are the capital's busiest months, though Easter and pre-Christmas are also popular periods, when room prices and availability are at a premium. In the winter months, especially November, January and February, rooms may be discounted. The period between Christmas and New Year is also relatively quiet (many hotels offer special rates after Boxing Day and before New Year's Eve – but you have to ask for them).

Prices
Prices are per night for a double room
£ up to £75   **££** £75–£150   **£££** £150–£250   **££££** more than £250

Abbey Court Hotel ££–£££

Located in Notting Hill and within easy reach of Kensington, this elegant town house is in a quiet side road. Rooms are individually decorated and furnished to a high standard and there is room service of light snacks. Breakfast is taken in the conservatory.

🗓 194 A4 ✉ 20 Pembridge Gardens, Kensington, W2 ☎ 020 7221 7518; fax: 020 7792 0858; www.abbeycourthotel.co.uk Ⓜ Notting Hill Gate

The Academy £££

This cosy, light, Bloomsbury hotel – not far from the British Museum – has been carved out of four Georgian town houses. Bedrooms in particular have been thoroughly updated and are now fully air conditioned; studio rooms are the most spacious and the best equipped. Food is good too: the breakfast buffet is a cornucopia of fresh fruits, compotes, warm rolls and croissants, while the various lunch and dinner menus offer food with a Mediterranean slant.

🗓 197 E3 ✉ 17–21 Gower Street, WC1 ☎ 020 7631 4115; fax: 020 7636 3442; www.theetoncollection.com Ⓜ Goodge Street

The Amsterdam Hotel ££

Although just a couple of minutes from Earl's Court Underground station, this town house is set in a peaceful street. The hotel retains the house's original character while providing every modern comfort. Walls in the lobby and stairs are crowded with modern prints and a stylish use of pastel colour and fabrics distinguishes the 28 bedrooms. Guests have the use of a kitchenette.

🗓 off map 194 A1 ✉ 7 Trebovir Road, SW5 ☎ 020 7370 5084; fax: 020 7244 7608; www.amsterdam-hotel.com Ⓜ Earl's Court

Basil Street Hotel £££

This hotel, whose location just behind Harrods could not be bettered, is one of the more characterful and old-fashioned London hotels. It wears a genteelly faded air, boosted by the charm of the grand staircase, antiques, tapestries and well-proportioned public rooms. Bedrooms are individually styled and vary in size.

🔲 198 A4 ✉ Basil Street, SW3
☎ 020 7581 3311; fax: 020 7581 3693;
www.thebasil.com 🚇 Knightsbridge

Bryanston Court ££

Look for the smart blue awning that distinguishes this well-run hotel in a Georgian terrace not far from Marble Arch. The bar looks like a gentlemen's club, with leather chairs and old portraits; breakfast is served in the basement restaurant where evening snacks are available in the week. Bedrooms are modern, but vary in size.

🔲 196 A2 ✉ 60 Great Cumberland Place, W1 ☎ 020 7262 3141; fax: 020 7262 7248; www.bryanstonhotel.com

Claridge's £££–££££

Claridge's has, for more than a century, enjoyed the patronage of visiting royalty, heads of state and dignitaries. A major refurbishment has brought the hotel's facilities right up to date, though outwardly little appears to have changed. Bedrooms now have the latest service systems and tele-communications, as well as a privacy button alongside those for maid, valet and floor waiter. Suites and de luxe rooms are outstanding.

🔲 196 C2 ✉ Brook Street, W1
☎ 020 7629 8860; fax 020 7499 2210;
www.claridgeshotel.com
🚇 Bond Street

Five Sumner Place £££

Entering this Victorian townhouse feels like walking into someone's very smart home. The personal service is second to none and there are just a dozen bedrooms, all of which have a traditional feel and are well equipped. Breakfast is served in the huge airy conservatory, which doubles as a lounge. The South Kensington location is surprisingly quiet.

🔲 Off map 195 E1 ✉ 5 Sumner Place, SW7 ☎ 020 7584 7586; fax: 020 7823 9962; www.sumnerplace.com
🚇 South Kensington

Gate Hotel ££

The Georgian house is set in one of the trendiest streets in one of the most fashionable parts of the capital. Portobello Road antiques market (held on Saturdays) is on the doorstep. Although bedrooms are small, they lack for nothing, with a refrigerator, TV, radio, phone, minibar and bathroom. Continental breakfast only is served in the bedrooms.

🔲 194 A4 ✉ 6 Portobello Road, W11 ☎ 020 7221 0707; fax: 020 7221 9128; www.gatehotel.com
🚇 Notting Hill Gate

Goring Hotel £££–££££

One of the few top hotels in the capital to be independently run, the Goring is a wonderful example of a good old-fashioned British hotel and, as such, is deservedly very popular. Guests are drawn by the blue-blooded appeal of the classic décor, the exemplary staff (many of whom have worked there for years) and the excellent facilities, which run to fully air-conditioned bedrooms and power showers.

🔲 198 C3 ✉ Beeston Place, Grosvenor Gardens, SW1
☎ 020 7396 9000; fax: 020 7834 4393;
www.goringhotel.co.uk
🚇 Victoria

Hampstead Village Guesthouse £–££

Antiques, bric-à-brac and family memorabilia clutter, albeit in a charming manner, this detached Victorian house just off Hampstead High Street. Most rooms have attached bathrooms, and all have welcome trays. Breakfast is served in the garden (weather permitting). Hampstead Underground station is just minutes away so the place is handy for central London.

🔲 Off map 197 D5 ✉ 2 Kemplay Road, NW3 ☎ 020 7435 8679; fax: 020 7794 0254;
www.hampsteadguesthouse.com
🚇 Hampstead

Hotel 167 ££

This well-kept small hotel, not far from Harrods and the South Kensington museums, has 19 bedrooms all with their own bathrooms, mini-refrigerators and in-house video. Breakfast is served at a few tables in the charming lobby. The hotel's modest prices and good, central location make it essential to reserve well in advance.

➕ Off map 195 E1 ✉ 167 Old Brompton Road, SW5 ☎ 020 7373 3221; fax: 020 7373 3360; www.hotel167.com
🚇 South Kensington

London County Hall Premier Travel Inn Metro ££

The rooms here are simple but functional, neatly designed and quite comfortable. All have bathrooms and will accommodate up to two adults and two children (under 15). So, if all you really want is a bed for the night in the heart of central London (right next to the London Eye and opposite the Houses of Parliament, though sadly with no views in this direction) then you can't beat the value–location equation that this chain hotel offers. It occupies the modern part of the old County Hall, formerly the headquarters of the Greater London Authority.

➕ 200 B2 ✉ County Hall, SE1
☎ 0870 238 3300; fax: 020 7902 1619; www.travelinn.co.uk 🚇 Westminster

London Marriott County Hall £££–££££

Like its neighbour, the Premier Travel Inn Metro (► above) the Marriott occupies part of the old County Hall, and has a great location next to the London Eye. Housed in the grand older wing of the building, it has an unbeatable view across the River Thames to the Houses of Parliament. Rooms are smartly laid out and thoughtfully equipped with the business traveller in mind. The hotel spa will revive you after a day of business or leisure around town.

➕ 200 B2 ✉ County Hall, SE1
☎ 020 7928 5200; fax: 020 7928 5300; www.marriott.com 🚇 Westminster

The Ritz ££££

César Ritz opened the hotel in 1906 following the success of the Hotel Ritz in Paris. It remains one of London's most fashionable hotels, distinguished by an exterior that is pure Parisian elegance and an interior that has been restored in *belle époque* style. French period furniture, colourful chintzes and gilt detailing to the moulded-plaster walls, together with modern facilities like VCRs, provide exceptional levels of comfort in the bedrooms.

➕ 199 D5 ✉ 150 Piccadilly, WI ☎ 020 7493 8181; fax: 020 7493 2687; www.theritzlondon.com
🚇 Green Park

Thanet Hotel ££

This family owned and run Georgian town house is right in the heart of Bloomsbury, with the British Museum a short walk away. The 16 bedrooms are pleasantly decorated and each has a shower room. Back rooms are quieter. The price includes a hot English breakfast, which is served in the cheerful breakfast room. Thanet Hotel is tremendous value for money in an area not noted for good, individual places to stay.

➕ 197 D3 ✉ 8 Bedford Place, WC1
☎ 020 7636 2869; fax: 020 7323 6676; www.thanethotel.co.uk
🚇 Russell Square

Vicarage Private Hotel ££

Located in one of London's most exclusive areas, this hotel is a real bargain. The 18 bedrooms are a good size and the tall Victorian house retains a strong period feel and many original features. The down side, if there has to be one, is that only two of the bedrooms have attached bathrooms, the others share the spotlessly maintained shower room and lavatory located on each floor. However, the price includes a traditional hot English breakfast.

➕ 194 B3 ✉ 10 Vicarage Gate, Kensington, W8 ☎ 020 7229 4030; fax: 020 7792 5989; www.londonvicarage hotel.com
🚇 Kensington High Street

Food and Drink

London is regarded as one of the restaurant capitals of the world, boasting food styles and chefs from all corners of the globe, and finding a restaurant table in London on a Saturday night is no easy task.

New Trends

The explosion of new restaurants, even pubs, serving excellent food means that there is a wider choice of places to eat than ever before. Fusion cooking, incorporating ideas from all over the world, plus an entirely new school of modern Italian cooking, and the reworking of traditional British dishes into lighter cuisine have all made their mark. And to crown it all, some of the finest French cuisine to be found in the capital is being created by British chefs. For the food lover there has never been a better time to visit London.

Movers and Shakers

In the 1990s, two men from widely different backgrounds influenced the London dining scene more than anyone else. Businessman Sir Terence Conran blazed the way with the Blue Print Café at the Design Museum and the stylish **Bibendum** on the Fulham Road (➤ 132). With the South Bank's **Gastrodome**, which also includes **Le Pont de la Tour, Cantina del Ponte** (➤ 108) and **Butler's Wharf Chop House**, and the mega-restaurants **Quaglino's** (➤ 64), **Floridita** (➤ 156) and **Bluebird** (➤ 132) at the King's Road **Gastrodome**, he has transformed dining habits in fashionable districts.

For a long time Marco Pierre White was considered the *enfant terrible* of the London restaurant scene. He has retired from the stove to build a restaurant empire that includes the **Mirabelle** (➤ 63), in Mayfair. His brand of complex modern British cooking still has many fans in the capital.

But both restaurateurs have been eclipsed by the success of a chef who once worked with Marco Pierre White: Gordon Ramsey. The Scot opened his first restaurant, **Gordon Ramsey Restaurant** (➤ 133) in 1998 and has since developed some of the most highly regarded eateries in London, including the Boxwood Café in the Berkeley Hotel and the restaurant at **Claridge's** (➤ 37). His protégés have revitalized some of London's finest (and most expensive) restaurants: Angela Hartnett at The Connaught and Marcus Wareing at Petrus.

As well as Ramsey, any list of homegrown talent should include celebrity chef Jamie Oliver, founder of the restaurant Fifteen, and Fergus Henderson of **St John** (➤ 87). Jamie Oliver has successfully influenced government policy on school food, while Fergus Henderson has reintroduced traditional, even if unfamiliar, British dishes – roast marrow bone is a signature dish – to the London palate.

Up and Coming

With big bucks dominating the West End, the burgeoning restaurant scene has pushed out the boundaries of fashionable London. To check on the latest openings, look in the *Evening Standard* newspaper every Tuesday when formidable restaurant critic Fay Maschler digests the pick of the crop. Saturday and Sunday editions of *The Times* and *The Independent* newspapers also carry good reviews of restaurants, which are generally London based.

Be prepared to travel out of the centre in search of the latest hit restaurant – Clerkenwell and Farringdon, for example, are rich hunting grounds. These areas were once deserted after dark but are now booming, with stylish bars, shops and galleries jostling for the available space. Ethnic restaurants, such as **Moro** (➤ 87) and **Tas** (➤ 109), do particularly well outside the West End.

The Drinking Scene

One of the sharpest features of **Quaglino's** (➤ 64) and **Floridita** (➤ 156) are the smart American-style bars that attract some of London's coolest inhabitants. Popularity bred success, so much so that both **Bank** (➤ 156) and Oliver Peyton's acclaimed **Atlantic Bar & Grill** (➤ 62) made a real feature of their bars. Their door policies retain an exclusive feel but do not apply if you have a reservation for dinner and the dress code is not strict.

All across London, gastropubs – pubs where eating good food is as much of a priority as drinking – are going from strength to strength. Pioneers, such as **The Eagle** (➤ 86), introduced inventive menus to the pub environment, and new gastropubs now open regularly. Many make a point of offering exciting wine lists and beers from independent brewers.

Drinkers will find that each London neighbourhood has its own character: traditional pubs line old-fashioned Borough High Street, south of the Thames, while trendy bars have followed nightclubs into the East End's Brick Lane. On both sides of Oxford Street, in Soho especially, there are hundreds of pubs and bars to choose from.

Budget Eating

In general, you would be lucky to get a decent meal and a glass of wine for less than £15 a head in London. But inexpensive eateries do exist. Pizza and pasta places can be good value. The well-distributed **Pizza Express** group is always a good choice. The **Pret-à-Manger** chain has captured Londoners' hearts with its sandwiches, wraps, salads, pastries, and even sushi, made freshly each day.

Ethnic restaurants are also a good bet. If you head for Chinatown (➤ 159) there are many noodle bars and cafés serving inexpensive one-plate meals. Of the many Japanese restaurants in central London, an increasing number now offer great value set-lunch deals – there are no hidden extras if you stay away from alcohol. The South Indian restaurants in Drummond Street (Tube: Warren Street/Euston Square) are particularly good for vegetarians.

Afternoon Tea

Afternoon tea in a grand hotel is the ultimate treat. It's an excuse to dress up (nearly all the hotels listed here adhere to a jacket-and-tie code) and partake in a very British institution. Beware: it is also expensive and the bill for two people will be somewhere between £40 and £70, more if you choose the "Champagne Tea" option. On the plus side, the quality is high and the portions are generous. It is advisable to make reservations at the establishments listed below.

Brown's Hotel

Tea in the Drawing Room of Brown's Hotel is a cosy experience; it's like spending the afternoon in an English country house. There is a splendid Victoria sponge cake, as well as delicate sandwiches and freshly made scones served with jam and cream. If you indulge yourself in the whole tea be prepared to forgo dinner. Reservations essential.

➕ 197 D1 ✉ 33–4 Albemarle Street, W1 ☎ 020 7493 6020; www.brownshotel.com ⊕ Daily 2, 3:45, 5:30 Ⓖ Green Park

The Dorchester

The Promenade, where tea is served, is soothing and luxurious, with deeply comfortable armchairs and thick carpets. A piano plays in the background and tea brings mouthwatering pâtisserie. Reservations advisable.

➕ 198 B5 ✉ 54 Park Lane, W1 ☎ 020 7629 8888; www.dorchesterhotel.com ⊕ Daily 2:30–8 Ⓖ Hyde Park Corner

The Ritz

The Palm Court, with its opulent Louis XVI décor, is the quintessential location for tea at the Ritz. This very touristy afternoon tea is an unforgettable experience. Reservations for any of the sittings is required six weeks in advance (three months for weekends).

➕ 199 D5 ✉ Piccadilly, W1 ☎ 020 7493 8181; www.theritzlondon.com
🕐 Noon, 1:30, 3:30, 5:30, 7:30
🚇 Green Park

The Savoy

The Savoy is the most accessible of the capital's grand hotels, with tea served in the stately Thames Foyer. To the sound of a tinkling piano, an exquisite array of food is served, including miniature sandwiches, scones with jam and cream, and a selection of cakes and pastries.

➕ 200 B3 ✉ The Strand, WC2 ☎ 020 7836 4343; www.savoygroup.co.uk
🕐 Mon–Fri 2–3:30, 4–6, Sat–Sun noon–1:30, 2–3:30, 4–6 🚇 Charing Cross, Embankment

The Waldorf Hilton

It's no longer possible to take tea in the hotel's famous Palm Court but the original restored 1930s Waring & Gillow panelling in the new Homage Pâtisserie provides an equally stunning backdrop. Among the rich fabrics and period furniture the focal point is a "jewel box" counter displaying fine pastries by day and serving champagne cocktails by night.

➕ 200 B4 ✉ Aldwych, WC2
☎ 020 7836 2400 🕐 Daily 2:30–5:30
🚇 Covent Garden

Fish and Chips

Fish and chips (french fries) is the one dish tourists to London want to try most. Forget fusion, modern British cooking and the rest of the food revolution, here are four top-quality "chippies".

Expect to pay around £10 per main course if you dine in, around £6 for a fish-and-chips take-away (take-out).

Fish Central

Regarded by many as the capital's best fish-and-chip shop, all manner of piscine delights are listed here, from sea bass to sole. Make a reservation to be sure of a table.

➕ Off map 201 D5 ✉ King Square, 151 Central Street, EC1 ☎ 020 7253 4970 🕐 Mon–Sat 11–2:30, 5–10:30
🚇 Angel, Old Street

North Sea Fish Restaurant

This is where the cabbies (taxi drivers) come for their fish and chips. They usually occupy the back room, while the rest of the clientele sit in the front, among the pink velvet upholstery and stuffed fish. Portions are gigantic, and the fish is very fresh. Reservations are recommended for dinner.

➕ 197 F5 ✉ 7–8 Leigh Street, WC1
☎ 020 7387 5892 🕐 Mon–Sat noon–2:30, 5:30–10:30
🚇 Russell Square

Rock and Sole Plaice

This claims to be the oldest surviving chippie in London, opened in 1871. The Covent Garden location draws a pre-theatre crowd to the restaurant and reservations are recommended for dinner. A take-away (take-out) service is also available until midnight.

➕ 200 A4 ✉ 47 Endell Street, WC2
☎ 020 7836 3785 🕐 Daily 11:30–10:30, Sun noon–10
🚇 Covent Garden

Sea Shell

Sea Shell is probably the most famous of London's fish and chip shops. It is certainly very popular with visitors to the city – you should be prepared to wait as reservations are not taken for parties that are fewer than six people.

➕ Off map 195 F5 ✉ 49–51 Lisson Grove, NW1 ☎ 020 7224 9000
🕐 Mon–Fri noon–3, 5–10:30, Sat noon–10:30
🚇 Marylebone

Shopping

A wave of change has swept through the city's retailers, and you will find an enthusiastic mood and glimpse a new modernism in London's shopping streets. Traditional institutions and long-established stores, however, continue to provide top-quality goods and deserve time on any visit.

Fashion

The capital's shops cater for a wide variety of tastes and pockets, whether you are looking for designer labels, a top-quality made-to-measure suit, or moderately priced high-street fashion.

- High street chain stores sell good quality clothes at moderate prices. **Oxford Street** (➤ 66), **Covent Garden** (➤ 159) and **Chelsea** and **Kensington** (➤ 134) have the best choice.
- Boutiques and smart department stores are the best bet for **designer names** and lovers of international designer labels will have fun finding their favourite names on either **Bond Street** (➤ 65) or **Sloane Street** (➤ 134).
- For those who favour a classical approach, **Burberry** have two locations, one in Haymarket, the other in Regent Street. **Savile Row** (➤ 65), a shrine to pinstriped cloth and made-to-measure gentlemen's wear, also contains new-wave tailors such as Ozwald Boateng.
- To find everything under one roof try the fashion-orientated department stores: **Harrods** (➤ 116), **Harvey Nichols** (➤ 134), **Liberty** (➤ 65) and **Selfridges** (➤ 66).

Art and Antiques

A thriving commercial art scene has both antiques and art from the London of a bygone age, as well as pictures so fresh the paint is still drying. London caters for every visual taste.

- The **galleries of Mayfair**, primarily Cork Street and Bond Street, show established names and sure-fire investments, with plenty of late 20th-century work.
- Many young artists have warehouse studios in the East End and a number of galleries here show exciting work at attractive prices. Listings magazines contain weekly updates of exhibitions and studio shows.
- If antiques are your passion the auction houses of **Sotheby's** on New Bond Street (Tube: Bond Street), **Christie's** in South Kensington (Tube: South Kensington) and, to a lesser extent, **Bonham's** in Chelsea (Tube: Knightsbridge) provide the best hunting grounds.
- The **King's Road** (➤ 135) in Chelsea and **Kensington Church Street** (➤ 134–135) are two long stretches of road lined by shops stuffed with furniture, ceramics, memorabilia and jewellery – eye-catching displays make for interesting window shopping.

Contemporary Furniture

Habitat, **Heal's** and **Conran** are still popular for furniture but are definitely resting on their design laurels; these days they are generally considered to be middle-of-the-road, disguised as modernist. Two places selling furniture designs that are bang up-to-date are **Purves & Purves** (80–81 and 83 Tottenham Court Road, W1, tel: 020 7580 8223. Tube: Goodge Street) and **Viaduct** (1–10 Summers Street, EC1, tel: 020 7278 8456. Tube: Farringdon).

Specialist Food Shops

■ The **Conran Shop** at Brompton Cross (Tube: South Kensington) and Conran's **Bluebird** in the King's Road (► 132) are terrific for stylish food purchases.

■ Historic **Fortnum & Mason** (► 65) stocks a fabulous range of teas and a choice of 50 types of marmalade among other luxury foods.

■ **Harrods** food hall, with its lush displays and own-brand comestibles, is irresistible to Londoners and tourists alike (► 116).

Markets

■ Antiques hunters have to be at **Portobello Road Market** (► 131) at the crack of dawn, but if you're hunting for clothes or are just plain curious you can afford to visit at a more leisurely hour.

■ **Portobello Road Market** (► 131) and **Camden markets** (► 152) are probably the best places for second-hand and unusual designer clothes, and are fun just for browsing.

Department Stores

■ For general gift ideas, household goods and clothes, try the following department stores: **Debenhams** and **John Lewis** (both on Oxford Street); **Peter Jones** on Sloane Square (also part of the John Lewis group); **Marks & Spencer**, in particular its flagship store at 458 Oxford Street. At the luxury end of the market are **Harrods** (► 116), **Harvey Nichols** (► 134) and **Liberty** (► 65).

Entertainment

The choice of entertainment in London is vast and listings magazines are invaluable for detailing what's on, whether it's theatre, movies, art exhibitions or gigs. *Time Out*, published every Tuesday, covers the whole spectrum of entertainment and is the best buy. Thursday editions of the *Evening Standard* (London's evening newspaper) and Saturday editions of national newspapers such as *The Times* and *The Independent* also have listings magazines.

Music

Diversity sums up the London music scene, and supports a serious claim to the title of music capital of Europe. Classical music is celebrated by five symphony orchestras as well as various smaller outfits, several first-rate concert halls and high standards of performance. The ever-changing pop music culture that is the driving force behind London fashion and stylish restaurants and bars can feature more than a hundred gigs on a Saturday night alone, from pub bands to big rock venues.

■ If you enjoy classical music, the **Proms**, an annual festival at the Royal Albert Hall, is held from mid-July to mid-September (► 136).

■ In summer, informal **open-air concerts** are held at Kenwood House (tel: 020 8233 7435. Tube: Hampstead) and in Holland Park (► 13, 136).

■ The **Royal Opera** at Covent Garden (Floral Street, WC2, tel: 020 7304 4000. Tube: Covent Garden), stages elaborate productions with performances by the major stars. Alternatively, try the **English National Opera** (London Coliseum, St Martin's Lane, WC2, tel: 020 7632 8300. Tube: Leicester Square), where works are sung in English.

Dance

Dance can mean anything from classical to flamenco and jazz tap, with London playing host to top international performers throughout the year.

- London's premier venue, the **Royal Festival Hall** is closed until 2007; productions which would have been staged there will move to smaller theatres (see *Time Out* dance listings page for details). **Sadler's Wells** (tel: 020 7863 8000. Tube: Angel) in Islington has an eclectic mix of dance programmes, although it is better known for ballet. The **Royal Ballet** is based at the Royal Opera House, Covent Garden (Tube: Covent Garden).
- **Dance Umbrella**, an international festival of contemporary dance, is held at various venues around London during October and November (tel: 020 8741 5881 for information).

Theatre

Theatre in the capital is diverse, ranging from popular West End (Broadway-style) musicals to avant-garde productions in small independent theatres.

- The **Royal National Theatre** (➤ 110) at the South Bank Centre (tel: 020 7452 3000. Tube: Waterloo) and **Barbican Centre** (➤ 88) produce all manner of drama. Also worth visiting is **Shakespeare's Globe** at Bankside (➤ 106). The **Royal Court** (➤ 136) and the **Old Vic** (tel: 0870 060 6628; www.oldvictheatre.com) are the most dynamic theatres promoting the works of young unknowns as well as major new plays by avant-garde writers.
- "Off-West End" and fringe theatre has a healthy reputation. The **Almeida** (Almeida Street, Box office tel: 020 7359 4404; www.almeida.co.uk. Tube: Angel) and **Donmar Warehouse** (Earlham Street, Box office: 0870 060 6624; www.donmar-warehouse.com. Tube: Covent Garden) are the major players, but theatres such as **The Gate** (11 Pembridge Road, tel: 020 7229 0706; www.gatehouse.co.uk. Tube: Notting Hill) and **King's Head** (115 Upper Street, N1, tel: 020 7226 1916; www.kingsheadtheatre.org. Tube: Angel, Highbury and Islington) are also worth checking out.

Buying Tickets

The best way to buy a ticket for any London theatre production is to contact the venue direct (so avoiding agency commissions). However, tickets for hit plays and musicals are hard to come by, particularly at short notice, and often are only obtainable through ticket agencies. **First Call/Keith Prowse Ticketing** (tel: 0870 906 3838; www.firstcalltickets.com) and **TicketMaster** (tel: 0870 534 4444; www.ticketmaster.co.uk) are the most reliable. Credit card bookings made through these agencies are subject to a hefty booking fee.

- Buy your tickets directly from the concert or theatre venue, from ticket agencies or on-line. **Never buy from ticket touts (scalpers)**– the practice is illegal and you may well end up with forgeries.
- If you are flexible about which production you want to see, try **tkts**, a reduced-price ticket booth at Leicester Square (➤ 160). Expect a fairly long wait and remember that tickets are limited to two pairs per person.
- The lowest-price seats are always at the top of the theatre, known as the "gods", but you will probably need binoculars.
- **Matinées** cost less than evening performances and tickets are easier to obtain.
- Some theatres offer **restricted-view seats** at a reduced rate.

Cinema

For movie-goers, The Odeon, Leicester Square, is recommended for the most modern and up-to-date movie experience the capital can offer.

St James's, Mayfair and Piccadilly

Getting Your Bearings

The area between Buckingham Palace and Trafalgar Square is one of London's quintessential quarters, and if you have time for only a day in the city, you should consider spending it here.

A district of considerable wealth and architectural grandeur, this area contains the leafy squares and prestigious residential buildings of Mayfair, the exclusive gentlemen's clubs of St James's, and the long-established shops and hotels of Piccadilly, one of London's great thoroughfares.

Previous page and above: Pomp and ceremony: the Horse Guards on parade

Here, too, is Buckingham Palace, the monarch's official residence, which since 1993 has thrown open its doors, in part at least, to the general public during most of August and September.

The area owes its original development to St James's Palace, built by Henry VIII in the 1530s and subsequently the home of several later sovereigns, including Elizabeth I and Charles I. Charles, the current Prince of Wales, lived here too from 1992 to 2003 after which he moved to the adjacent Clarence House. The royal palace lent the area considerable social cachet, particularly after the 17th century, when King Charles II opened beautiful St James's Park to the public for the first time. By the 18th century, members of the aristocracy who wished to be close to court had built fine mansions in the area. In time, sumptuous arcades and exclusive Piccadilly shops sprang up to serve the area's high-spending visitors and residents. In the 19th century Queen Victoria moved the court to Buckingham Palace, and the 20th century, saw the building of the present grand ceremonial route along The Mall between Buckingham Palace and Trafalgar Square.

Today, the area's elegance and refinement make it unique in the capital. You can enjoy the parks and grand walkways, the fine old houses, the shops and galleries (notably the Royal Academy, scene of major art exhibitions), and the principal sights at either end of The Mall: Buckingham Palace, with its famous ceremonial Changing of the Guard, and Trafalgar Square with the National Gallery, home to the country's premier art collection.

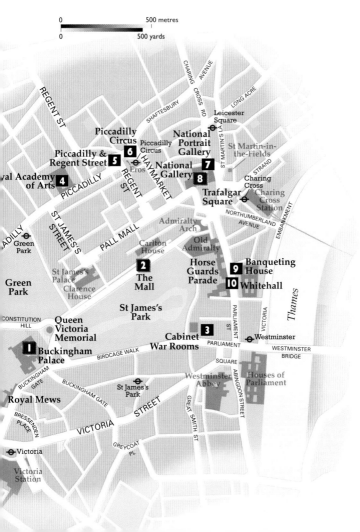

Enjoy a couple of royal palaces, some of the best-known sights of London, countless artistic masterpieces and the capital's prettiest park, right in the heart of the city.

St James's, Mayfair and Piccadilly in a Day

One of the recommended highlights is the State Rooms in Buckingham Palace (➤ 50–51), but they're open only for around six weeks every year (August to September, dates vary) – and if you do visit them then it's unlikely you'll be

able to find a good vantage point afterwards to watch the Changing of the Guard (or have the time to walk to Horse Guards Parade to see it there ➤ 53). Come back another day if you have your heart set on seeing the ceremony. You can still follow the plan below after visiting the palace, however – you'll just be doing everything a couple of hours later.

9:00 am

Start at **1 Buckingham Palace** (left, ➤ 50–51) – either ogle the grand façade through the railings or, if you are in London at the right time of year, visit the magnificent State Rooms. To avoid waiting on the day see Top tips (➤ 51).

10:00 am

Stroll through **St James's Park**, a tranquil oasis, and then walk along the broad, majestic, tree-lined **2 Mall** (➤ 52–53) to Horse Guards Parade to see the **Changing of the Guard**, one of London's most famous ceremonies. Be in place by 11 to 11:15 am to find a good vantage point.

12:15 pm

The Changing of the Guard over, walk through to **3 Trafalgar Square** (above right ➤ 53). Since the post-Millennium reconstruction of the square, involving new pedestrian areas and crossings, a new traffic layout, landscaping and new facilities, it is once again a natural and enjoyable meeting place.

1:00 pm

Time for lunch. St Martin-in-the-Fields (above), adjacent to the National Gallery on Trafalgar Square, has an inexpensive café in its crypt, and the gallery itself has a coffee bar and brasserie.

2:00 pm

While away the afternoon viewing the gems of the superlative art collection at the 8 National Gallery (➤ 54–57). If you're here on a Wednesday, the gallery doesn't close until 9 pm.

4:00 pm

Drop into the 7 National Portrait Gallery (➤ 60–61) for a quick look at its appealing collection of portraits of famous Brits. Alternatively, make your way to 6 Piccadilly Circus (➤ 60). From here it's a short stroll to some of Mayfair's squares and back lanes, or the exclusive shops of Piccadilly (right ➤ 58–59). You're also just around the corner from Leicester Square, the heart of Theatreland, with sleazy, flamboyant Soho and exotic Chinatown near by (➤ 155).

❶ Buckingham Palace

The British sovereign's grandiose London home was built between 1701 and 1705 by the 1st Duke of Buckingham, but was redeveloped as a palace by King George IV in the 1820s, and became the official royal residence in the reign of Queen Victoria in 1837. Although it's a must-see for all visitors to London, at first glance it doesn't look terribly impressive – its stolid lines appear plain, solid and dependable rather than an exuberant celebration of majesty in stone.

While the palace is nothing special from the outside, its interior is sumptuous. The **State Rooms** were first opened to the public in 1993, a move prompted by changing attitudes within the Royal Family, and a desire to contribute funds towards the restoration of Windsor Castle (▶ 164–166). They shouldn't be missed if you're in London at the right time.

Above: The white marble Queen Victoria Memorial in front of the palace

➕ 199 D4 ☎ Enquiries 020 7766 7324; www.royal.gov.uk Credit card bookings: 020 7766 7300 🕓 Tickets on the day from the Green Park ticket office, near the palace: Daily 9:30–4:15 (last admission), Aug–Sep. State Rooms: Daily 9:30–4:15 (last admission), early Aug–Sep. Royal Mews: Daily 11–3:15, Mar–Oct 🚇 Green Park, St James's Park, Victoria 🚌 Piccadilly 3, 8, 9, 14, 19, 22; Victoria Street 11, 24, 211; Grosvenor Place 2, 8, 16, 36, 38, 52, 73, 82 💷 Palace: very expensive; Mews: moderate; Queen's Gallery: expensive

Right: Buckingham Palace, The Mall, Queen Victoria Memorial and St James's Park

The State Rooms are where the real work of royalty goes on, providing a stage for state entertaining, investitures, receptions and official banquets. Their sheer richness and decorative theatricality are mesmerising, from the grand marble staircase and the brightly furnished drawing rooms to the Throne Room and the elaborate red-and-gilt State Dining Room. Your feet sink softly into plush red carpets, wall coverings are almost works of art in themselves, and balustrades, doors, chandeliers and windows all display spellbinding and unforgettable detail. Equally compelling are the paintings that hang in the Picture Gallery, including works by Van Dyck, Rembrandt and Rubens, the classical sculptures and exquisite furniture. Look out in particular for the thrones and the fabulously ornamental ceilings which are some of the most elaborate imaginable. Don't expect to meet any of the Royal Family – they move elsewhere when the general public come to call.

BUCKINGHAM PALACE: INSIDE INFO

Top tips To avoid waiting for tickets, **reserve tickets in advance** by credit card and collect them on the day from the Green Park ticket office. Arrangements can be made to have tickets sent out by mail. Allow seven days for United Kingdom and two to three weeks for overseas addresses.
• You don't need to buy an **official guide** as an audio guide (available in six languages) is included in the ticket price.
• The **Changing of the Guard** ceremony (▶ 53) with bands and standard bearers takes place at 11:30 am in the palace forecourt and lasts 40 minutes. Get there by 11–11:15 am to get a good position – by the front railings between the gates is best.

In more detail Visit the **Royal Mews** to see the state carriages and coaches together with their horses. The collection's gem is the Gold State Coach.
• **The Queen's Gallery** is one of the finest private collections of art in the world. Exhibitions change every six months or so. For opening times and prices tel: 020 7766 7324 or visit the website (www.royal.gov.uk).

❷ The Mall to Trafalgar Square

The Mall is the grand, tree-lined processional avenue between Buckingham Palace and Trafalgar Square, a thoroughfare that comes into its own on ceremonial occasions such as the State Opening of Parliament in November and Trooping the Colour in June. Near the Mall are two royal parks: Green Park, which is at its best in spring when the daffodils are in flower, and St James's Park, which is a delight at any time of year.

To start your exploration, turn your back on Buckingham Palace and cross the road to the **Queen Victoria Memorial**. This white marble statue, the Mall and Admiralty Arch were laid out in the early 20th century as a memorial to Queen Victoria who died in 1901. The statue depicts a rather dour-looking Victoria surrounded by figures representing the glories of the British Empire.

These days the Mall is a busy, traffic-filled thoroughfare, albeit one whose grandeur and dignity remain majestically intact. Until the 17th century, however, it was a small country lane, its confines used by King James I to play a French game known as *palle-maille* (anglicised to pell mell). A hybrid of golf and croquet, the game has long gone out of fashion, but it is remembered in the names of the Mall and Pall Mall, one of Piccadilly's main streets. Later, King Charles II improved the area, most notably by opening St James's Park and Green Park to the public, a move that made this *the* fashionable spot in the capital to take a daily walk.

Above: Changing the Guard at Buckingham Palace

Right: The sweeping façade of Admiralty Arch

Top right: Nelson's Column dominates Trafalgar Square

Looking down the Mall on the left you can see 19th-century Clarence House, named after its first resident, the Duke of Clarence, who became King William IV in 1830. In 1953, when Queen Elizabeth II acceded to the throne, it became the London home of the late Queen Mother. After her death in 2002, Prince Charles, current heir to the throne, moved here. Behind Clarence House rise the red-brick Tudor turrets of St James's Palace, built in the 1530s by Henry VIII (who died here).

From the Queen Victoria Memorial you may want to enter **St James's Park**, following shady paths towards the lake; at the bridge you have a choice: one route takes you back to the Mall and a right turn past Carlton House Terrace, distinguished by its early 19th-century white stucco façade, leads you along the Mall to Admiralty Arch.

Either way, you should take in **Horse Guards**, the huge parade ground at the park's eastern end that provides the stage for the **Changing of the Guard** (➤ Inside Info, below). Then walk through Admiralty Arch to **Trafalgar Square**, laid out in 1820 as a memorial to British naval hero Admiral Horatio Nelson, who stands three times life-size on the 170-foot (52m) column at the square's heart. Reliefs at the column's base depict four of his greatest naval victories, of which the Battle of Trafalgar against the French in 1805 – where Nelson died – was the most famous. The square's celebrated lion statues were added in the late 1860s.

The square's northern flank is dominated by the National Gallery (➤ 54–57), and – to its right – the fine spire of St Martin-in-the-Fields, a lovely church famous for its concerts and with a first-rate café and brass-rubbing centre.

TAKING A BREAK

The **Café in the Crypt** at St Martin-in-the-Fields church is a relaxed spot for lunch (tel: 020 7766 1129). You can enjoy a coffee, a glass of wine, a full meal or treat yourself to an afternoon tea.

THE MALL TO TRAFALGAR SQUARE: INSIDE INFO

Top tips The **Changing of the Guard**, where the mounted guards change over their duties, takes place in Horse Guards Parade, off Whitehall (Mon–Sat 11 am, Sun 10 am). The same ceremony for foot soldiers proceeds in the forecourt of Buckingham Palace (➤ 50–51). If the weather is bad, the ceremony may be cancelled at short notice. (Daily 11:30, Apr–Jul; alternate days 11:30, Aug–Dec, tel: 020 7414 2357).

• **Clarence House** is normally open to the public from August to mid-October (tel: 020 7766 7303; www.royal.gov.uk. Admission: moderate). Visitors are given a guided tour of the ground floor where official engagements are conducted.

• In **St Martin-in-the-Fields** church free lunchtime concerts are given at 1 pm on Monday, Tuesday and Friday.

🇸 National Gallery

The National Gallery has one of the world's greatest collections of paintings. Covering the years from around 1250 to 1900, it presents the cream of the nation's art collection, including some 2,200 works of European art hung in a succession of light, well-proportioned rooms. Pick a famous painter from almost any era – Botticelli, Canaletto, Cézanne, Constable, Leonardo da Vinci, Monet, Rembrandt, Renoir, Raphael, Titian, Turner, Van Gogh – and the chances are they'll be represented here.

Suggested Route

The gallery is divided into **four wings**, each covering a chronological period: it makes sense to visit the wings in this order:

- **Sainsbury Wing** 1250 to 1500 Rooms 51–66
- **West Wing** 1500 to 1600 Rooms 2–14
- **North Wing** 1600 to 1700 Rooms 15–32
- **East Wing** 1700 to 1900 Rooms 33–45

The National Gallery was designed as the architectural focus of Trafalgar Square

🔆 197 F1
✉ Trafalgar Square, WC2
☎ 020 7747 2885;
www.nationalgallery.org.uk
🕐 Daily 10–6 (Wed 10–9). Closed 1 Jan and 24–26 Dec

🚇 Charing Cross, Leicester Square
🚌 3, 6, 9, 11, 12, 13, 15, 23, 24, 29, 53, 77A, 88, 91, 139, 159, 176, 453
🎫 Free; charge for special exhibitions

An allegory of motherhood – the celebrated Leonardo da Vinci cartoon in the National Gallery depicts the Madonna and Child with a young John the Baptist and St Anne, the mother of the Virgin Mary

Sainsbury Wing

The wonderfully airy Sainsbury Wing (named after the supermarket dynasty that sponsored it) was designed by architect Robert Venturi and opened in 1991. Although it is the newest part of the gallery, it displays the oldest paintings, in particular the masterpieces of the various Italian schools after about 1300. Two of its loveliest works are by Leonardo da Vinci (Room 51). The unfinished *The Virgin of the Rock* (1508) depicts Mary, John the Baptist and Christ with an angel in a rocky landscape. Some of the work may be by pupils, but the sublime expression on the angel's face suggests pure Leonardo. In a specially darkened room near by, da Vinci's cartoon of *The Virgin and Child with St Anne and St John the Baptist* (1508) is an exquisitely beautiful depiction of a meeting never mentioned in the Bible – Christ and his maternal grandmother.

Be certain to see *The Wilton Diptych* (Room 53), a late 14th-century altarpiece commissioned by Richard II for his private prayers: it shows the king kneeling on the left and being presented to the Madonna and Child. Both the artist and his nationality remain a mystery. Less tantalising but no less beautiful are two portraits, Van Eyck's *Arnolfini Portrait* (Room 56) and Giovanni Bellini's matchless *Doge Leonardo Loredan* (Room 61).

West Wing

Turn round as you cross from the Sainsbury to the West Wing for the gallery's most remarkable view – a series of receding archways designed to frame a Renaissance altarpiece on a distant wall. In the West Wing are mostly French, Italian and Dutch works from the High Renaissance. Perhaps the most memorable is Hans Holbein the Younger's *The Ambassadors* (1533) – almost life-size portraits of Jean de Dinteville and Georges de Selve (Room 4). The picture is crammed with symbol and allusion, mostly aimed at underlining the fleeting nature of earthly life. In the middle foreground of the picture is a clever *trompe l'oeil* of what appears face on to be simply a white disc; move to the right side of the painting (foot marks on the floor indicate the correct position) and it's revealed as a human skull.

North Wing

Painters who challenged the primacy of the Italians during the 16th and 17th centuries are the stars of the North Wing – Rubens, Rembrandt, Van Dyck, Velázquez, Vermeer and Claude, to name but a handful. Velázquez's *The Toilet of Venus* (also known as *The Rokeby Venus* after Rokeby Hall where it once hung) is one of the best-known paintings (Room 29). It is an unusual work, firstly because it shows a back view of the goddess (with an extraordinary face captured in a mirror), and secondly because it is a nude, a genre frowned upon by the Inquisition in Spain when the work was completed in 1651.

East Wing

The East Wing is often the busiest in the gallery, mainly because it contains some of the best-known of all British paintings. Chief among these is John Constable's *The Hay Wain* (Room 34), first exhibited in 1821 when the fashion was for blended brushwork and smooth painted texture: contemporary critics disapproved of what they saw as the painting's rough and unfinished nature. Today it represents an archetype of an all-but-vanished English rural landscape. More works by Constable are on display in Tate Britain (➤ 102) and the Victoria and Albert Museum (➤ 117–120).

J M W Turner, though a contemporary of Constable, developed a radically different style. In his day he was considered madly eccentric, particularly in his later works, yet it is these mature paintings that have the most profound modern-day resonance. Two of the greatest, *The Fighting Téméraire* (1838) and *Rain, Steam and Speed* (1844), display the powerful and almost hallucinatory effects of light on air and water characteristic of the painter (Room 34). More of the same can be seen in Tate Britain's Clore Gallery (➤ 102).

Equally as popular as the Turners and Constables are the National's numerous Impressionist masterpieces (Rooms 43 and 46), including a wealth of instantly recognisable paintings such as Van Gogh's *Sunflowers* (1889) and Seurat's *The Bathers at Asnières* (1884), the latter's shimmering clarity a fitting memory to take with you back onto Trafalgar Square.

TAKING A BREAK

You can get light refreshments or a full meal at **Crivelli's Garden** (➤ 62), in the Sainsbury Wing of the gallery.

The splendid interior of the National Gallery provides a suitably grand setting for one of the greatest collections of paintings in Europe

The Bathers at Asnières by Georges Seurat is among the best known of the National Gallery's many Impressionist masterpieces

NATIONAL GALLERY: INSIDE INFO

Top tips The gallery displays many British artists, but many more, especially modern British painters, are better represented in Tate Britain's collection (➤ 102).
• Two types of **audio guide** are available. You can choose one of the Themed Audio Guides, which follow themed tours, each looking at about 20 paintings or the Gallery Audio Guide, with commentaries on more than 1,000 paintings. A highlights tour is available in six languages. These are nominally free (though a voluntary contribution is expected and some form of security or deposit is requested).

In more detail ArtStart in the Sainsbury Wing contains a computerised system with information on every painting and artist in the collection.

Hidden gem Most of the pictures owned by the National Gallery are on display – those not in the main galleries are in the **lower floor galleries** in the main building. Telephone before visiting to make sure that these lower galleries are open.

At Your Leisure

❸ Cabinet War Rooms

You can almost feel Churchill's presence and smell his cigar smoke and, thanks to the audio guides, you can hear his rasping voice for real as the bombs drop and the air raid sirens sound outside. This underground warren provided secure accommodation for the War Cabinet and their military advisers during World War II and was used on more than 100 occasions. Today it is a time capsule, with the clocks stopped at 16:58 on15 October, 1940. You can visit the Map Rooms, the Transatlantic Telephone Room, the Cabinet Room, Churchill's bedroom and a museum devoted specifically to the great British leader.

➕ 199 4F ✉ Clive Steps, King Charles Street, SW1 ☎ 020 7930 6961 ⏰ Daily 9:30–6 🚇 Westminster, St James's Park 🚌 3,11,12, 24, 53, 77a, 88, 109, 159, 184, 211 💷 Expensive

❹ Royal Academy of Arts

Burlington House is one of the few remaining 18th-century Piccadilly mansions. Today it houses one of London's most illustrious art galleries, the Royal Academy, which stages a variety of high-profile exhibitions. June to August sees its annual Summer Exhibition, for which every aspiring artist in the country hopes to have a piece selected. In March 2004, the Royal Academy opened its splendid 18th-century neo-Palladian suite of John Madejski Fine Rooms to provide a permanent display space for major works by Reynolds, Gainsborough,

Constable, Spencer and Hockney, as well as the outstanding *Taddei Tondo*, one of only four marble sculptures by Michelangelo outside Italy.

➕ 197 D1 ✉ Burlington House, Piccadilly, W1 ☎ 020 7300 8000; www.royalacademy.org.uk ⏰ Daily 10–6 (Fri–Sat 10–10). Fine Rooms: Tue–Fri 1–4:30, Sat–Sun 10–6 🍴 Café and restaurant 🚇 Piccadilly Circus, Green Park 🚌 9, 14, 19, 22, 38 💷 Admission charge depends on the exhibition

❺ Piccadilly and Regent Street shopping

If you need a change from sightseeing, take time off to visit some of London's most exclusive stores: Piccadilly, St James's and Regent Street (▶ 65–66) are home to some of London's finest.

The best of the Piccadilly shops are the old-fashioned bookstore, **Hatchards**, the high-class grocery turned department store, **Fortnum & Mason** (▶ 65), and the covered arcades of prestigious shops that lead off to left and right. **Burlington Arcade**, where top-hatted

Piccadilly Circus

Piccadilly & Regent Street ❺ Eros ❻

Royal Academy ❹ of Arts PICCADILLY

HAYMARKET REGENT ST

ST JAMES'S STREET

PALL MALL

Carlton House

THE MALL

St James's Palace

Clarence House

Admiralty Arch

Old Admiralty

Horse Guards Parade

WHITEHALL

Cabinet War Rooms ❸

PARLIAMENT ST

officials ensure shoppers act with due decorum (there are regulations against singing and hurrying), is the best known. Piccadilly itself was named in honour of a 17th-century tailor who made his fortune from collars known as "picadils". The mansion he built became known as Piccadilly Hall, in time lending its name to the entire street. These days much of the tailoring has moved north of Piccadilly to **Savile Row** and south to **Jermyn Street** (► 65). **Liberty** in Regent Street is a department store of class and character, with plush carpets, wood panelling and a balconied hall hung with glorious fabrics (► 65).

✚ 197 E1

☎ www.regentstreetonline.com

FORTNUM & MASON

Piccadilly and Regent Street are home to exclusive stores such as Fortnum & Mason (above), famed for its sumptuous food, and Liberty, whose interior (right) is an Aladdin's Cave of luxury goods. At elegant Burlington Arcade, beadles (top right) have the power to enforce regulations against singing and hurrying!

Regent Street is one of the capital's premier shopping streets

introduced in the early 20th century, and have become something of a London icon – come after dark for the best effects.

For all its faults, the Circus is useful as a jumping-off point to other sights; along Shaftesbury Avenue towards Chinatown or Soho, along Coventry Street to Leicester Square, or to Regent Street and Piccadilly.

✚ 197 E1

❼ National Portrait Gallery

The gallery houses a fascinating and strangely beguiling collection of paintings, sculptures and photographs of eminent Britons past and present. The material dates from the early 16th century to the modern era, and includes many of the country's most famous faces. Whatever your fields of interest, you'll almost certainly find something here to interest you.

The monarchs represented include Richard III, Henry VII, Henry VIII, Elizabeth I (depicted several times) and many members of the present Royal Family. However, it is the portraits of non-royals that are most memorable. There is a supposed portrait of Shakespeare, a drawing of Jane Austen by her sister, the Brontë sisters by their brother Patrick and striking photographs of Oscar Wilde, Virginia Woolf and Alfred, Lord Tennyson.

❻ Piccadilly Circus

While Piccadilly Circus features large in the minds of visitors to the city (a photograph in front of the statue at its heart is almost obligatory), most Londoners dismiss it as a tacky mêlée of tourists, traffic and noise.

The Eros statue, which actually represents the Angel of Christian Charity not the Greek god of love, was erected in 1893 to commemorate Antony Cooper, 7th Earl of Shaftesbury (1801–85), a tireless campaigner for workers, the poor and the mentally ill. The neon advertisements were

Eros and the bright lights of Piccadilly Circus are best seen at night

Among recent literary stars are Salman Rushdie and Dame Iris Murdoch.

Politicians and figures from the arts, sciences, sport and media are also well represented. Look for the portraits of British prime ministers Margaret Thatcher and Tony Blair, scientist Stephen Hawking, film director Alfred Hitchcock and soccer player David Beckham.

🔲 197 F1 ☒ St Martin's Place, WC2 ☎ 020 7312 2463; www.npg.org.uk 🕐 Mon–Sat 10–6 (also Thu–Fri 6–8:50); closed 1 Jan, Good Friday, May Day bank holiday and 25–26 Dec 🚇 Charing Cross, Leicester Square 🍴 Café in the basement 🚌 3, 6, 9, 11, 12, 13, 15, 23, 24, 29, 53, 77A, 88, 91, 139, 159, 176 🎟 Admission free (charge for some exhibitions)

🟨 Banqueting House

The Banqueting House is the only remaining part of the old Palace of Whitehall, formerly the monarch's official home, which was destroyed by fire in 1698. It was built by the great architect Inigo Jones in the early 17th century, and includes a painted ceiling by Flemish artist Peter Paul Rubens as its decorative centrepiece. The ceiling was commissioned in 1635 by the king, Charles I, who paid the artist £3,000, an astronomical sum at that time. This, and other paintings were all conceived as paeans to Charles's father, James I.

It was from a window of the Banqueting House that, on 30 January, 1649, Charles I, tried and convicted of high treason following the defeat of Royalist forces in the English Civil War, stepped on to the scaffold and faced his executioner. As he went to his death, branded an enemy of state, he remarked, "I have a good cause and a gracious God on my side".

🔲 200 A2 ☒ Whitehall ☎ 0870 751 5178; www.hrp.org.uk 🕐 Mon–Sat 10–5; closed public holidays, and for special functions 🚇 Westminster, Charing Cross 🚌 3, 11, 12, 24, 53, 77A, 88, 109, 159, X53 🎟 Moderate; audio guide included

🔟 Whitehall

This busy but undistinguished street lined by the bland façades of government offices takes you south from Trafalgar Square through the heart of British Government. Downing Street, a side turning blocked off by a large gate, is where the British prime minister has his (or her) official residence. Traditionally this is at No 10, while No 11 plays host to the Chancellor of the Exchequer, though the present prime minister Tony Blair and his family reside at the larger No 11. The only real patch of colour is provided by the mounted soldiers at Horse Guards.

At the centre of Whitehall is the Cenotaph, a memorial to the war dead and the solemn focus of the annual Remembrance Day Ceremony in November.

🔲 200 A2

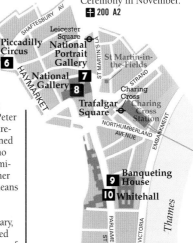

For Kids

• The colourful Changing of the Guard ceremony at Buckingham Palace and/or Horse Guards (▶ 51).
• A visit to Hamleys toy shop (▶ 65) and the Disney Store, both in Regent Street.
• Feeding the ducks in St James's Park (▶ 53).

Where to...
Eat and Drink

Prices
Expect to pay per person for a meal excluding drinks and service
£ up to £25   ££ £25–£50   £££ more than £50

Atlantic Bar & Grill ££

Sweep down the grand staircase into a noisy, atmospherically lit cavernous space, filled with a cosmopolitan crowd. Some are here just for a drink at the clamorous bar, but the food is worth investigation. There's a Modern European, French and Italian twist on the whole menu, but the classics are equally pleasing. Dinner reservations are essential.

✚ 197 E1 ◻ 20 Glasshouse Street, W1 ☎ 020 7734 4888;
www.atlanticbarandgrill.com
◑ Mon–Sat noon–3, 6–midnight (also Fri–Sat 6–12.30 am)
◉ Piccadilly Circus

Le Caprice ££

This famous restaurant, tucked neatly behind the Ritz hotel, attracts a smart celebrity crowd. Despite the stark white walls and black-and-chrome furniture, the atmosphere is far from intimidating, and the fast-paced service remains friendly at all times. The menu is a great mix of classic brasserie dishes balanced by some more lively up-to-date ideas.

✚ 199 D5 ◻ Arlington Street, SW1 ☎ 020 7629 2239; www.caprice-holdings.co.uk ◑ Mon–Sat noon–3, 5.30–midnight, Sun noon–4, 5.30–midnight ◉ Green Park

Chor Bizarre ££

This overseas branch of the New Delhi restaurant embraces its name (which means "thieves' market") with gusto, displaying a crowded and exotic collection of Indian antiques and artefacts. The menu explores the regions of India with some imagination, and provides a good choice of vegetarian dishes and tandoori favourites. Wines have been carefully chosen.

✚ 197 D1 ◻ 16 Albemarle Street, W1 ☎ 020 7629 9802/7629 8542; www.chorbizarrerestaurant.com
◑ Mon–Sat noon–3, 6–11.30, Sun noon–2.30, 6–10.30 ◉ Green Park

Crivelli's Garden £–££

Climb the wide, stone staircase of the National Gallery's Sainsbury Wing, take a sharp left turn, and enter what appears to be a high-class bar and cafeteria. In the bar, there's a good choice of snacks, including *bruschetta* and *panini*, each with a recommended glass of wine, plus salads and pizza. In the restaurant, the menu provides a mixture of Provençale and northern Italian cooking. You can choose from a good selection of wines by the glass, as well as moderately priced bottles of wine.

✚ 197 F1 ◻ The National Gallery, WC2 ☎ 020 7747 2869; fax: 020 7747 2438 ◑ Mon, Tue, Thu–Sun 10–6, Wed 10–8.30
◉ Charing Cross

Le Gavroche £££

Le Gavroche, London's longest-running French restaurant, is comfortable rather than opulent, with tables that are generous in size and service that is smoothly, soothingly efficient. For many years Albert Roux's classic French cooking was the solid rock on which the restaurant's seasonally changing menus were built, but now that son Michel has taken over, ideas, although firmly rooted in that same classic tradition, have moved with the times. The cooking is still confident and skilled, but with a lighter touch. The wine list is aristocratic, with prices to match.

➕ 196 B1 ☒ 43 Upper Brook Street, W1 ☎ 020 7408 0881/7499 1826; www.le-gavroche.co.uk ⓒ Mon–Fri noon–2, 7–11, Sat 7–11 ⓖ Marble Arch

La Madeleine £

This truly French café lies just off Regent Street. Kick-start the day with a buttery croissant and make a light lunch of a *croque monsieur* or a range of salads. At any time of the day a vast array of tarts, pastries and all sorts of cream-filled delights will be appropriate. The staff are charming and there is limited seating on the pavement outside.

➕ 197 D1 ☒ 5 Vigo Street, W1 ☎ 020 7734 8353 ⓒ Mon–Sat 8–7, Sun 11–6 ⓖ Green Park, Piccadilly

Mirabelle ££

Thanks to Marco Pierre White (▲39), Mirabelle is one of the most glamorous places to eat in London, serving MPW's trademark first-class classic French-style cooking. The restaurant's revamped décor matches an easier, less formal style, though tables are perhaps a little too close together. Lunch is especially good value, with the reasonably priced menu ensuring that the place is packed. Get a reservation for a patio table in fine weather.

➕ 198 C5 ☒ 56 Curzon Street, W1 ☎ 020 7499 4636; www.whitestarline.org.uk ⓒ Lunch: Daily noon–2.30 (also Sat–Sun 2.30–3). Dinner: Mon–Sat 6–11.30, Sun 6–10.30 ⓖ Green Park

Mitsukoshi ££

This smart, comfortable restaurant is on the lower level of a Japanese department store. The à la carte selection includes classic Japanese dishes, but choosing one of the many set meals will give an excellent introduction to the cuisine. Go for a simple *hana*, which includes an appetiser, tempura, grilled fish, rice, miso soup and pickles; the ten-course *kaiseki* feasts (ordered in advance) or the sushi menu.

➕ 197 E1 ☒ Dorland House, 14–20 Lower Regent Street, SW1 ☎ 020 7930 0317; www.mitsukoshi-restaurant.co.uk ⓒ Mon–Sat noon–2, 6–10, Sun noon–3.30 ⓖ Piccadilly Circus

Nicole's ££

This is a fashionable place in every respect, from the chic setting in the basement of Nicole Farhi's Bond Street store to the ladies-that-lunch who come to toy with the light, ultra-modish food. The restaurant's less figure-conscious clientele will be equally satisfied – an earthier approach can be discerned with such rustic fare as duck confit appearing on the menu. Breakfast is served from 10 to 11.

➕ 196 C2 ☒ 158 New Bond Street, W1 ☎ 020 7499 8408; fax: 020 7409 0381 ⓒ Lunch: Mon–Fri noon–3.30, Sat noon–4. Dinner: Mon–Fri 6:30–10:45 ⓖ Green Park, Bond Street

Noble Rot ££

The restaurant takes its name from the mould that forms on over-ripe grapes and produces the characteristic richness of certain sweet wines. Not surprising, then, that it claims to feature one of the largest selections of sweet wines in the UK. The environment is chic and appealing, the stone floor contrasting with contemporary furnishings. Expect Modern British and European dishes such as halibut with lobster, smoked eel risotto and pinot noir, and wild mushroom lasagne.

➕ 197 D2 ☒ 3–5 Mill Street, W1 ☎ 020 7629 8877; www.noblerot.com ⓒ Lunch: Mon–Fri noon–3. Dinner: Mon–Sat 6:30–10:30 ⓖ Oxford Circus

Nobu £££

Nobuyuki Matsuhisa brings the full force of his pan-American experience (which ranges from restaurants in the United States to travels in South America) to bear on the first floor of the seriously chic Metropolitan Hotel. This is the ultimate place to see-and-be-seen. The combination of the ultra-modern interior and the trendy clientele add up to an irresistible package, especially when New York-style service and spiced-up Japanese cooking are thrown into the equation. Reservations essential.

✚ 198 C5 ⊠ Metropolitan Hotel, 19 Old Park Lane, W1 ☎ 020 7447 4747; www.noburestaurants.com 🕒 Lunch: Mon–Fri noon–2:15, Sat–Sun 12:30–3. Dinner: Mon–Thu 6–10:15, Fri–Sat 6–11 🚇 Hyde Park Corner, Green Park

Quaglino's ££

Make an entrance down the sweeping staircase, feel the buzz and experience a bit of Hollywood glitz. This is the most glamorous of the Conran mega-restaurants and it's a slick operation. Just go for a drink in the bar or try out a menu that has a strong French bistro feel. If you prefer, traditional English classics such as fish and chips with

tartare sauce are on offer. The crustacea bar is a major feature.

✚ 199 D5 ⊠ 16 Bury Street, St James's, SW1 ☎ 020 7930 6767; www.conran.com 🕒 Lunch: daily noon–3. Dinner: Mon–Thu 5:30–11:30, Fri–Sat 5:30–1, Sun 5:30–11 🚇 Green Park

Rasa W1 £–££

Das Sreedharan opened this lavish, spacious restaurant after the huge success of his first restaurant in East London. His exquisite vegetarian food from the Kerala region is considered some of the best Indian cooking in town and meat dishes are also available. The menu offers a wide range of poppadums, stuffed pastries, curries, dosas, lentil patties, and some excellent breads.

✚ 196 C2 ⊠ 6 Dering Street, W1 ☎ 020 7629 1346; www.rasarestaurants.com 🕒 Lunch: Mon–Sat noon–3. Dinner: Mon–Sat 6–11 🚇 Oxford Circus

Sotheby's Café ££

One of Bond Street's best-kept secrets is tucked away in the lobby of Sotheby's auction house. Join the café's cosmopolitan clientele for stylish lunches and afternoon tea.

✚ 196 C2 ⊠ 34 Bond Street, W1 ☎ 020 7293 5077 🕒 Lunch: Mon–Fri noon–3. Tea: 3–4:45 🚇 Bond Street

The Square £££

Nigel Platts-Martin's exceptional restaurant combines the allure of chic, spacious premises with a prestigious setting – just a short distance from Berkeley Square. His highly regarded chef and partner, Philip Howard, offers imaginative, yet classically based, Modern French cooking. Dishes are prepared with great attention to detail and champion free-range and organic produce.

✚ 196 C1 ⊠ 6 Bruton Street, W1 ☎ 020 7495 7100; www.squarerestaurant.com 🕒 Lunch: Mon–Fri noon–2:45. Dinner: Mon–Sat 6:30–10:45, Sun 6:30–9:45 🚇 Bond Street

Tamarind ££

This prestigious Indian restaurant serves an imaginative interpretation of Indian regional cooking in its discreetly designed basement dining room. Dishes are prepared with imported herbs and spices to create some truly memorable flavours.

✚ 198 C5 ⊠ 20 Queen Street, W1 ☎ 020 7629 3561; www.tamarindrestaurant.com 🕒 Lunch: Mon–Fri, Sun noon–3. Dinner: Mon–Sat 6–11:30, Sun 6–10:30 🚇 Green Park

The Wolseley £–££

The award-winning Wolseley is housed in an opulent art deco building, once home to a bank, resplendent with chandeliers and marble pillars. Despite its grandeur it is friendly, serves excellent Modern British café-style food throughout the day and is perfect for afternoon tea or breakfast.

✚ 199 5D ⊠ 160 Piccadilly, W1 ☎ 020 7499 6996; www.thewolseley.com 🕒 Mon–Fri 7 am–midnight, Sat 9 am–midnight, Sun 9 am–11 pm. Closed 1 Jan, 24–25 Dec 🚇 Green Park

Where to...
Shop

SAVILE ROW AND JERMYN STREET

Savile Row (Tube: Piccadilly Circus) is synonymous with bespoke men's clothes. There are several long-established tailors here: try either **Henry Poole** (15 Savile Row, W1, tel: 020 7734 5985), established in 1806, or **Kilgour, French & Stanbury** (8 Savile Row, W1, tel: 020 7734 6905), dating from 1882.

Jermyn Street (Tube: Piccadilly Circus) has the monopoly on men's shirt makers. Try **Turnbull & Asser** (71–2 Jermyn Street, W1, tel: 020 7808 3000), **Harvie & Hudson** (77 Jermyn Street, W1, tel: 020 7930 3949), and **Hilditch & Key** (73 Jermyn Street, W1, tel: 020 7930 5336).

REGENT STREET

Regent Street (Tube: Piccadilly Circus) is home to stores on a grand scale. **Aquascutum** (100 Regent Street, W1, tel: 020 7675 8200) is *the* place to buy the classic English raincoat and tailored, tweedy jackets for both men and women, **Burberry** (165 Regent Street, W1, tel: 020 7839 5222) is the home of the distinctive English trenchcoat, and **Austin Reed** (103–13 Regent Street, W1, tel: 020 7734 6789) is good for Savile Row-style clothes at rather lower prices.

At the Oxford Circus end of Regent Street is the famed department store **Liberty** (210–20 Regent Street, W1, tel: 020 7734 1234. Tube: Oxford Circus). Even the façade, a mock-Tudor extravaganza, exudes great character. Within, the shop is a treasure trove of antiques, oriental carpets, furnishings, dress fabrics and leather goods, as well as cutting-edge fashion, luxury cosmetics and wonderful accessories.

Regent Street is also home to **Hamleys** (188–96 Regent Street, W1, tel: 0870 333 2450. Tube: Piccadilly Circus), one of the world's largest toy stores, suitable for kids of all ages. Prices here are higher than elsewhere and at weekends it's packed, but there are magic tricks and demonstrations galore.

PICCADILLY

Fortnum & Mason is a London institution (tel: 020 7734 8040. Tube: Piccadilly Circus). Its internationally renowned food emporium sells everything from own-brand marmalades, teas and condiments to hams, pâtés, cheeses, bread and fresh fruit. It is less well known as an excellent department store with up-to-date women's designer fashions and a splendid stationery and gift section. The Piccadilly branch of **Waterstones** (203–6 Piccadilly, tel: 020 7851 2400. Tube: Piccadilly Circus), is the bookstore to go if you are looking for a good holiday read.

BOND STREET

Bond Street is a showcase for fast-paced, high fashion major international designers and their innovative stores, none more so than **Donna Karan** (19 New Bond Street, W1, tel: 020 7495 3100. Tube: Bond Street), **Gucci** (32–3 Old Bond Street, W1, tel: 020 7629 2716. Tube: Piccadilly Circus) and **Versace** (113–15 New Bond Street, W1, tel: 020 7355 2700. Tube: Piccadilly Circus).

Formerly a jeweller, **Asprey** (167 New Bond Street, W1, tel: 020 7493 6767. Tube: Bond Street) relaunched itself in 2004 as a luxury lifestyle emporium. Also setting out their wares are jewellers such as **Tiffany & Co** (25 Old Bond Street, W1, tel: 020 7409 2790. Tube: Piccadilly Circus) and **Cartier** (175 New Bond Street, W1, tel: 020 7408 5700. Tube: Bond Street), two great auction houses, **Sotheby's** (34–5 New Bond Street, W1, tel: 020 7293 5000. Tube: Bond Street) and **Bonhams** (101 New Bond Street,

Where to...
Be Entertained

W1, tel: 020 7447 7447. Tube: Bond Street), and major representatives of the art and antiques dealing world, notably the **Fine Art Society** (148 New Bond Street, W1, tel: 020 7629 5116. Tube: Bond Street). Here too is **Fenwick** (63 New Bond Street, W1, tel: 020 7629 9161. Tube: Bond Street), a charming, fashion-orientated department store. The ground floor is given over to one of the best accessory collections in town, the basement to a dazzling selection of gifts at less-than-Bond Street prices.

SOUTH MOLTON STREET

On South Molton Street there are smaller, quirkier boutiques, among them **Browns** (23–7 South Molton Street, W1, tel: 020 7514 0000. Tube: Bond Street) – a series of interconnected little shops at the knife-edge of fashion.

Gray's Antique Market (58 Davies Street, W1, tel: 020 7629 7034. Tube: Bond Street) hosts an impressive collection of stalls run by

knowledgeable people. It's noted for antique jewellery and oriental artefacts, but there is much more.

OXFORD STREET

Oxford Street, big, brash and noisy, with unceasing crowds, is where you'll find most of the big department stores. **John Lewis** (278–306 Oxford Street, W1, tel: 020 7629 7711. Tube: Oxford Circus) sells everything from dress fabrics to computers, **Marks & Spencer**, at both Marble Arch (458 Oxford Street, W1, tel: 020 7935 7954. Tube: Marble Arch) and north of Oxford Circus (173 Oxford Street, W1, tel: 020 7437 7722. Tube: Bond Street) for basic wardrobe staples. **Selfridges** (400 Oxford Street, W1, tel: 0870 837 7377. Tube: Bond Street) has Europe's largest perfumery department and a massive cosmetics section, two vast floors of current women's fashions, and a good food hall with various cafés.

You'll find major cinemas (movie houses) and some splendid theatres in the area around Haymarket and Piccadilly Circus. For advice on how to obtain theatre tickets ▶ 160.

CINEMA

The **Curzon Mayfair** (38 Curzon Street, W1, tel: 020 7495 0500. Tube: Green Park) shows art-house, foreign and some mainstream movies. **The Institute of Contemporary Arts (ICA)** (Nash House, The Mall, W1, tel: 020 7930 3647. Tube: Charing Cross) has a small cinema and hosts groupings of films linked by director, style or theme.

CLUBS

100 Club (100 Oxford Street, W1, tel: 020 7636 0933. Tube: Oxford Circus), where The Rolling Stones, The Kinks, The Sex Pistols and The Clash have all played, follows an eclectic booking policy that also takes in traditional jazz, blues, jive and many other styles.

COMEDY

If you enjoy hard-hitting stand-up comedy, head for **The Comedy Store** (1a Oxendon Street, W1, recorded information tel: 0870 060 2340. Tube: Piccadilly Circus). Shows start at 8 pm, but to get the best seats get to the venue when doors open at 6.30 pm.

The City

Getting Your Bearings

The City of London, the commercial heart of the capital, is one of the busiest financial centres in the world, with banks, corporate headquarters and insurance companies occupying dramatic showcases of modern architecture. Yet alongside the glass-and-steel office buildings, you find beautiful 17th-century churches, cobbled alleyways, historic markets, and even fragments of the original Roman city wall.

The modern City stands on the site of the Roman settlement of *Londinium*, and has long been a centre of finance and government. Historically, it had an identity separate to that of the rest of the capital. When Edward the Confessor moved his palace from the City of London to Westminster in 1042, the area retained some of its ancient privileges, and later in the 14th century secured charters granting it the

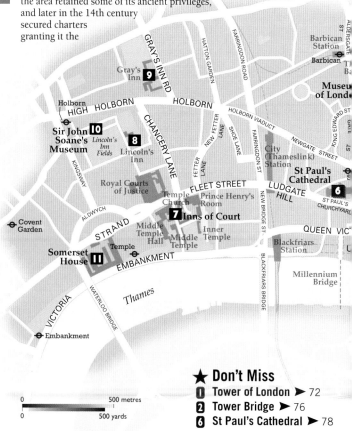

★ **Don't Miss**

right to elect its own mayor and council. Even the sovereign could not enter the City without formal permission. Today, the legacy of these privileges still survives. The Corporation of London, the successor to the original council, which is overseen by the Lord Mayor, administers the City through council meetings held in the Guildhall.

Much of the medieval City was destroyed by the Great Fire of 1666 (➤ 6), although the Tower of London survived. In the construction boom that followed, architect Sir Christopher Wren was commissioned to build more than 50 churches, the most prominent and well-known of which is St Paul's Cathedral. Many of the lesser-known Wren churches survived the severe bombing of World War II, and remain tucked away in quiet streets.

The City is also home to the modern Barbican Centre, a performing arts complex, as well as the acclaimed Museum of London, where the story of the capital is brought to life. On the western boundary of the City lie the four historic Inns of Court, the heart of legal London. Next to Lincoln's Inn is Sir John Soane's Museum, a wonderful 19th-century time capsule, while back on the river Somerset House is now home not only to the stunning Courtauld Gallery but also to the glittering treasures of the Gilbert Collection and Hermitage Rooms.

At Your Leisure

Previous page: The distinctive dome of St Paul's Cathedral

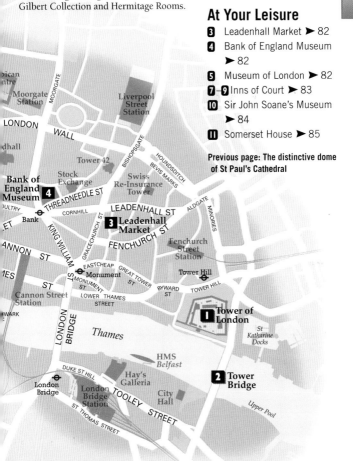

Three of London's most iconic sights – St Paul's Cathedral, the Tower of London and Tower Bridge – are the day's highlights. Some magnificent views over the city are in store.

The City in a Day

9:00 am

Try to be at the **1 Tower of London** (➤ 72–75) as it opens (10 am on Sunday and Monday) to beat the worst of the crowds, even if this means you may get caught up in the morning rush hour. The rewards are jewels, ravens, Beefeaters (left), and an insight into the long and often bloody history of London from the perspective of its famous fortress. You can buy your entrance ticket in advance from any Underground station.

11:30 am

Walk up on to nearby **2 Tower Bridge** (below, ➤ 76–77) and visit the Tower Bridge Exhibition for an excellent history of the structure. Stunning views of the River Thames make the climb to the top worthwhile.

1:00 pm

Take a break for lunch. For top-quality fare head across to the south bank of the river to Cantina del Ponte (► 108). Reservations are recommended.

2:15 pm

Walk back across the bridge and catch the No 15 bus from Tower Hill, the main road to the north of the Tower, which will deliver you outside St Paul's Cathedral.

3:00 pm

Climb up to the galleries at the top of the dome of **6 St Paul's Cathedral** (below, ► 78–81) for magnificent views of the city. Stop for a coffee in the café in the crypt. Then soak up the magnificence of the architecture and artefacts around you.

5:00 pm

If possible, stay on in St Paul's for evensong – the times of services are posted inside and outside the cathedral (or visit their website).

To move on from St Paul's catch the No 15 bus back to Trafalgar Square or use St Paul's Underground station, which is just beside the cathedral.

◨ Tower of London

The Tower of London has always fascinated visitors – even 300 years ago it was a popular attraction – and today it is one of the country's top tourist sights. Begun by William the Conqueror shortly after the 1066 conquest, it has survived for more than 900 years as a palace, prison, place of execution, arsenal, royal mint and jewel house. Throughout this time it has remained woven into the fabric of London and its history, while maintaining its essential character as a fortress and self-contained world within the defensive walls.

St Edward's Crown, one of the many priceless treasures making up the Crown Jewels

The Crown Jewels

Begin your exploration of the Tower by visiting Waterloo Barracks, where the Crown Jewels are on display. You may have a long wait to see the collection, one of the richest in the world, but there is archive footage of the Coronation of Queen Elizabeth II to put you in the mood while you wait, providing a prelude to and preview of the exhibition. The most dazzling piece in the collection is the **Imperial State Crown**, used by the monarch at the State Opening of Parliament in October or November, and crusted with 2,868 diamonds, 273 pearls, 17 sapphires, 11 emeralds and 5 rubies. Among the collection's other treasures is the **Sovereign's Sceptre**, which contains the world's largest cut diamond, Cullinan I. Also worth a look is the crown of the late Queen Elizabeth the Queen Mother. It contains the fabulous Koh-i-Noor diamond, which is only ever used in a woman's crown as it is believed to bring bad luck to men.

For fascinating background on the Crown Jewels, visit the "Crowns and Diamonds" display in the Martin Tower, accessed via the Salt Tower, whose walls bear graffiti carved by prisoners.

✚ 202 C3
✉ Tower Hill, EC3   ☎ 0870 756 6060, www.hrp.org.uk
🕐 Tue–Sat 9–6, Sun–Mon 10–6, Mar–Oct; Tue–Sat 9–5, Sun–Mon 10–5, rest of year. Last admission one hour before closing. Closed 1 Jan and 24–26 Dec
🍴 Café and restaurant
🚇 Tower Hill   🚌 15, 25 (weekends), 42, 78, 100, D1   💷 Very expensive

Tower Green

This benign-looking spot was the place of execution of seven high-ranking prisoners, the most notable of whom were Anne Boleyn and Catherine Howard, Henry VIII's second and fifth wives (both beheaded following charges of adultery). Execution here was an option reserved for the illustrious – less socially elevated prisoners met a much slower, more painful end on nearby Tower Hill. The executioner's axe and block are on display in the White Tower.

The White Tower

The Tower's oldest and most striking feature is the White Tower, begun around 1078, its basic form having remained unchanged for more than 900 years. Today its highlight is a superlative collection of armour, a display that manages to be awe-inspiring and strangely beautiful at the same time. Henry VIII's personal armour is the main attraction, but smaller

The Tower of London was begun in 1066, its position affording clear views of any enemy forces that might approach up the Thames

pieces, such as the suits crafted for young boys, are equally interesting. Be sure to see the evocative St John's Chapel on the first floor, one of England's earliest remaining church interiors, and also take a peep into some of the tower's "garderobes" – 11th-century lavatories.

The Tower Ravens

Ravens have been associated with the Tower throughout its history. Legend tells how King Charles II wanted to get rid of the birds, but was told that if they ever left the White Tower the kingdom would fall and disaster would strike. No chances are taken these days – one wing of each raven is clipped.

The White Tower (1078) is one of the oldest parts of the Tower of London. It took its name after Henry III had its exterior whitewashed in 1241

The Bloody Tower

Not all prisoners in the Tower lived – and died – in terrible conditions. Some passed their time in more humane lodgings. One such prisoner was Sir Walter Ralegh, explorer, philosopher and scientist, who was imprisoned in the Bloody Tower from 1603 to 1616, accused of plotting against James I. The Tower's most notorious incumbents, partly the reason for its name, were the "Princes in the Tower". Following the death of King Edward IV in 1483, the princes – the King's sons Edward (the heir to the throne) and his younger brother Richard – were put in the Tower under the "protection" of their uncle, Richard,

The forbidding walls of the Tower, built to keep attackers out, were later used to confine those perceived to be enemies of the Crown

Beefeaters

The Tower's guards, or Yeoman Warders, are commonly known as Beefeaters, though how they came by the name is not known for certain. About 38 in number, they all have a military background, and perform ceremonial duties around the Tower – they'll also answer your questions and give you directions.

Duke of Gloucester. However, the boys mysteriously vanished and, in their absence, their uncle was crowned King Richard III. The skeletons of two boys, presumed to be those of the princes, were found hidden in the White Tower 200 years later. Richard's involvement, or otherwise, in the boys' death has been much debated since, but never proved one way or the other.

Traitors' Gate was the Tower of London's entrance from the river

The Medieval Palace

The entrance to the Medieval Palace lies just beside the infamous Traitors' Gate, the river entrance to the Tower through which many prisoners arrived for their execution. The palace is laid out as it would have been in Edward I's reign (1272–1307), and staffed by costumed guides.

From the palace you should stroll along the Wall Walk on the Tower's south side, a route that offers fine views of Tower Bridge (► 76–77). This route also takes you through the Wakefield Tower in whose upper chamber Edward I's throne room has been dramatically reconstructed.

TAKING A BREAK

The cafés of nearby **Leadenhall Market** (► 82) are a great place to stop for a coffee or a light lunch. Alternatively, the Tower has its own restaurant and café.

TOWER OF LONDON: INSIDE INFO

Top tips Come **early** in the morning to avoid the crowds.
- Buy admission tickets at one of the nearby Tube stations to **avoid a long wait** at the main ticket office.
- On arrival, head straight for the Waterloo Barracks and visit the **Crown Jewels** – this is the Tower's most popular attraction and soon becomes crowded.
- Be **flexible** in your approach to what you visit and when: if one part of the Tower is busy, give it a miss and return later.
- If you have time, the Yeoman Warders (Beefeaters) lead free, hour-long **guided tours** throughout the day. Most of the guides are great characters and bring the history of the Tower wonderfully alive.

② Tower Bridge

Tower Bridge is one of London's most familiar landmarks and the views from its upper walkway are some of the city's best, yet it has occupied its prominent place on the capital's skyline for only a little over a hundred years.

By the late 1800s, crossing the River Thames had become a major problem. London Bridge was then the city's most easterly crossing, but more than a third of the population lived even further east. Building a new bridge, however, posed a dilemma for architects and planners. Any construction had to allow tall-masted ships to reach the Upper Pool, one of the busiest stretches of river in the world, handling ships and goods from all corners of the British Empire. It also needed to be strong and adaptable enough to allow for the passage of motor and horse-drawn vehicles. Though designs had been submitted to Parliament since the 1850s (more than 50 were rejected), it wasn't until 1886 that one was finally approved. The plan for a remarkable lifting roadway (known as a "bascule" bridge after

Top: The floodlit bridge is a prominent feature of the capital's night-time skyline

➕ 202 C2
☎ 020 7403 3761, www.towerbridge.org.uk
🕐 Daily 10–6:30, Apr–Sep; 9:30–6, rest of year. Closed 24–25 Dec.
Last entry 60 minutes before closing time
🚇 Tower Hill, London Bridge
🚌 15, 25, 40, 42, 47, 78, 100, D1, P11, RV1 💷 Moderate

VITAL STATISTICS

- ❏ The bridge took eight years to build.
- ❏ Its structure is brick and steel, but it is clad in Portland stone and granite to complement the nearby Tower of London.
- ❏ Tower Bridge is made up of more than 27,000 tonnes of bricks, enough to build around 350 detached homes.
- ❏ Each moving bascule weighs 1,200 tonnes.
- ❏ The height from the road to the upper walkways is 108 feet (33m).

the French word for see-saw), was the brainchild of architect Horace Jones and engineer John Wolfe Barry.

Access to the bridge's towers and walkways is via the **Tower Bridge Exhibition**, a display of film, artefacts and photographs explaining the history, construction and operation of the bridge. You also get to visit the original Victorian engine rooms, which were used to power the bridge right up until 1976. The highlight of your visit, however, is the view from the upper walkway, where there are also some fascinating archive photographs, as well as interactive computers offering more detail on Tower Bridge and the surrounding area.

TAKING A BREAK

If you fancy a treat, head across to the south bank of the river for lunch at **Cantina del Ponte** (► 108). The food is great, as are views of the bridge.

Opened in 1894, Tower Bridge is one of the most recognisable bridges in the world

TOWER BRIDGE: INSIDE INFO

Top tips Try to see the **bridge lifting**; telephone (020 7940 3984) for times.

- Make a return visit to see the bridge at **night-time** – it looks fabulous when spot-lit.
- Even if you choose not to visit the Exhibition, don't miss the magnificent view from either of the bridge's piers.

6 St Paul's Cathedral

The towering dome of St Paul's Cathedral has stood sentinel over London for almost 300 years, a lasting testament to the revolutionary genius of its architect, Sir Christopher Wren. Innovative and controversial, the cathedral rose from the ashes of the Great Fire of London in the 17th century, making it a positive youngster when compared with the medieval cathedrals of most European countries. Centuries later it became a symbol of London's unbeatable spirit, standing proud throughout the wartime Blitz of 1940–1, while more recently it has been the scene of national events such as the wedding of Prince Charles to Diana, Princess of Wales (then Lady Diana Spencer) in 1981.

The present cathedral, completed in 1710, is the fourth on this site

The entrance to the cathedral is in the **West Front** between the towers. Be prepared for noise and crowds, and remember the cathedral is enormous.

On first entering the cathedral, take a few moments to just stand and soak up something

✚ 201 E4
☎ 020 7236 4128, www.stpauls.co.uk
✉ Ludgate Hill, EC4
🕐 Mon–Sat 8:30–4:30 (last admission 4 pm) 🍴 Café and restaurant
Ⓢ St Paul's 🚌 4, 11, 15, 23, 25, 26, 100, 242
💷 Expensive; free for Sun service

VITAL STATISTICS

- ❏ The cathedral's largest bell, Great Paul, which weighs 17 tonnes, is rung at 1 pm every day for 5 minutes.

- ❏ The distance from ground level to the very top of the cross on the cathedral's roof measures just short of 368 feet (112m).

- ❏ The clock, Big Tom, on the right-hand tower on the cathedral's West Front, is 16 feet (5m) in diameter and the minute hand 10 feet (3m) in length.

Monochrome frescoes depicting the life of St Paul decorate the interior of the dome

of the building's grandeur. Soaring arches lead the eye towards the huge open space below the main dome, and on to a series of smaller, brilliantly decorated domes that rise above the choir and distant high altar.

Then move to the centre of the nave, marked by an intricate black-and-white compass pattern and a memorial to Wren which includes the line "Reader, if you seek his monument, look around you". Looking up into the **dome** from here you

can admire the Whispering Gallery, the monochrome frescoes by 18th-century architectural painter Sir James Thornhill (1716–19) of the life of St Paul, and the windows in the upper lantern. Wren was 75 years old by the time the upper lantern was underway, but still insisted on being hauled up to the galleries in a basket several times a week to check on progress. What he wouldn't have seen are the ceiling's shimmering mosaics, completed in the 1890s, and made from an estimated 30 million or more pieces of glass. They depict biblical scenes and figures such as Evangelists, prophets, the Creation, the Garden of Eden and the Crucifixion.

Then take in the area around the **altar,** a part of the cathedral filled with exquisite works of art. Master woodcarver Grinling Gibbons, noted for his high relief carvings, designed the limewood choir stalls – the cherubs are especially fine – and Jean Tijou, a Huguenot refugee, created the intricate ironwork gates (both were completed in 1720). The canopy is based on a similar bronze canopy in St Peter's, Rome, designed by the 16th-century baroque architect Bernini. In St Paul's, however, the canopy is made of English oak and dates from as recently as 1958.

The Galleries

The dome has three galleries, all of them open to the public and all unmissable if you've the time, energy and a head for heights. The views of the cathedral's interior and of London are breathtaking – but there are more than 500 steps to climb to the top before you can enjoy them. The best interior views come from the **Whispering Gallery** (259 steps), where the building's patterned floor and sheer scale can be enjoyed to the full. The gallery's name describes the strange acoustic effect that allows something said on one side of the gallery to be heard on the other. For panoramas of London you'll need to climb to the top two galleries, the **Stone Gallery** (378 steps from the bottom) and the **Golden Gallery** (a further 172 steps).

At the other extreme, downstairs, is the crypt, a peaceful and atmospheric space supported by massive piers and redoubtable vaulting. This is the largest such crypt in Europe, and contains around 200 graves and memorials, the grandest of which belong to national heroes such as Admiral Lord Nelson and the Duke of Wellington, who defeated Napoleon at the battle of Waterloo in 1815.

The Whispering Gallery, where whispers on one side of the gallery can be heard on the other

TAKING A BREAK

St Paul's offers two options: the Refectory restaurant (tel: 020 7246 8358, open 11–5:30); and the Crypt Café, an ideal place for a light lunch or afternoon tea.

ST PAUL'S CATHEDRAL: INSIDE INFO

Top tips Guided tours (90 min–120 min; additional charge) run at 11, 11:30, 1:30 and 2. Audio tours are also available.

Hidden gem The choir, one of the finest in the world, sing on Sunday at 11:30 am (Eucharist) and 3:15 pm (evensong). **Evensong** on weekdays is usually at 5 pm, but check on the lists posted at the cathedral or visit the website.

At Your Leisure

3 Leadenhall Market

This iron-and-glass Victorian food hall, built on the site of an ancient medieval market, now caters for the needs of City workers, with plenty of eating places, tailors, shoe shops, bookshops, chemists and grocers. The huge glass roof and finely renovated and painted iron work, plus the bustle of the crowds, make this one of the best places in the City to browse, grab a snack or linger over lunch.

🚇 202 B4 ✉ Whittington Avenue, EC3 🕙 Mon–Fri 7–4 🚇 Monument 🚌 25, 40

4 Bank of England Museum

You won't see mountains of gold, but the material that is on display is surprisingly interesting – and is helped along by an excellent audio-guide. There are a couple of gold ingots on show which always draw a big crowd, but more fascinating are the displays explaining how bank notes are printed and the complex security devices employed to beat counterfeiters. If you fancy yourself as a financial whizz-kid, there are interactive computer programmes that allow you to simulate trading on the foreign exchange markets – after a few minutes trying to get to grips with the processes you can see how real City superstars begin to justify their huge salaries.

🚇 202 A4 ✉ Bartholomew Lane, EC2 ☎ 020 7601 5545; www.bankofengland. co.uk 🕙 Mon–Fri 10–5 🚇 Bank 🚌 8, 11, 21, 23, 25, 26, 47, 48, 76, 133, 141, 149, 242 🎟 Free

5 Museum of London

This fascinating museum details the story of London from prehistoric times to the present day, its magnificent array of exhibits laid out chronologically to present a cogent and colourful account of the city's evolution.

The Roman Gallery is particularly well illustrated, and includes excellent reconstructions of Roman-era rooms. Look also for the panelled 17th-century interior of a prosperous merchant's home, complete with appropriate music, and the streets of Victorian shops, with the requisite fittings and goods.

On a smaller scale, the working model of the Great Fire of London, accompanied by the words of contemporary diarist Samuel Pepys, is an excellent illustration of the drama of this cataclysmic event (➤ 6–7). Perhaps the most gorgeous exhibit, however, is the Lord Mayor's Coach, commissioned in 1757. A confection of colour and ornament, it is covered in magnificent carvings and sculptures and has panels by the Florentine artist Cipriani decorating its sides. The coach is still used during the annual Lord Mayor's Parade in November and the coronation of a new sovereign.

🚇 201 F5 ✉ London Wall ☎ 0870 444 3852; www.museum oflondon.org.uk

The elaborately carved and gilded Lord Mayor's Coach, one of the exhibits at the Museum of London

🕙 Mon–Sat 10–6, Sun noon–6; last admission 5:30. Closed 1 Jan and 24–26 Dec 🍴 Café 🚇 St Paul's, Barbican 🚌 4, 8, 25, 56, 100, 172, 242, 521 🎟 Free

7–9 Inns of Court

Entered through narrow, easy-to-miss gateways, the four Inns of Court are a world away from the busy city outside. Their ancient buildings, well-kept gardens and hushed atmosphere create an aura of quiet industry. Home to London's legal profession, the Inns began life in the 14th century as hostels where lawyers stayed. Until the 19th century, the only way to obtain legal qualifications was to serve an apprenticeship at the Inns, and even today barristers must be members of an Inn.

While most of the buildings are private, some are open to the public; even if you don't see inside any of the august institutions it is enough simply to wander the small lanes and cobbled alleyways, stumbling upon unexpected courtyards and gardens and breathing the rarefied legal air.

The way to see the Inns is to start at the Temple and then walk to Lincoln's Inn and Gray's Inn.

For Kids
- Tower of London (➤ 72–75)
- St Paul's Cathedral galleries (➤ 78–81)
- Museum of London (➤ 82)

Inner and Middle Temple

Consecrated in 1185, Temple Church originally had links with the Knights Templar, a confraternity of soldier monks established to protect pilgrims travelling to the Holy Land. This may account for the building's unusual circular plan, which mirrors that of the Church of the Holy Sepulchre in Jerusalem. The floor of the church has ancient effigies of the Knights' patrons, though few date from after the 13th century as the Knights fell out of favour and the Order was abolished in 1312. The church is a tranquil oasis in a busy part of the city.

The imposing **Middle Temple Hall**, where it is said Queen Elizabeth I attended the first performance of Shakespeare's *Twelfth Night*, retains its 16th-century oak-panelled interior.

✚ 200 C4 ✉ Access from Fleet Street, just opposite end of Chancery Lane, EC4 🕙 Temple Church: Wed–Sun 11–4; Middle Temple Hall: usually Mon–Fri 10–11, 3–4. Ring in advance to confirm ☎ 020 7427 4800

Prince Henry's Room

This remarkable little building – above the Fleet Street entrance to the Temple – was built in 1610 as part of a Fleet Street tavern. The room, decorated to commemorate the investiture of Henry, eldest son of James I, as Prince of Wales, retains the ceiling inscribed with the Prince of Wales' feathers and part of its original oak panelling. It houses memorabilia associated with the diarist Samuel Pepys (1633–1703), who lived locally but who was not directly associated with the building.

✚ 200 C4 ✉ 17 Fleet Street, EC4 🕙 Mon–Sat 11–2

Lincoln's Inn

Lincoln's Inn is large, well maintained and spacious, and its red-brick buildings are constructed on a grand scale, particularly the four-storeyed mansions, New Hall and library of New Square (begun in 1680). Many illustrious British politicians studied here, among them Pitt the Younger, Walpole, Disraeli, Gladstone and Asquith. Other former students include William Penn, founder of Pennsylvania, and 17th-century poet John Donne. Make a special point of seeing the Inn's chapel (Mon–Fri noon–2:30), built above a beautiful undercroft with massive pillars and dramatic vaulting.

✚ 200 C4 ✉ Entrances off Chancery Lane and Lincoln's Inn Fields, WC2
🕐 Mon–Fri 7–7

Gray's Inn

Entrances off High Holborn, Gray's Inn Road, Theobald's Road, WC1. This Inn dates from the 14th century, but was much restored after damage during World War II. Famous names to have passed through its portals include the writer Charles Dickens, who was a clerk here between 1827 and 1828. Its highlights are the extensive gardens or "Walks" as they are commonly known (Mon–Fri noon– 2:30), once the setting for some infamous duels and where diarist Samuel Pepys used to admire the ladies promenading. The chapel is also open to the public (Mon–Fri 10–6), but lacks the charm of its Lincoln's Inn equivalent (see above).

✚ 200 C5

🔟 Sir John Soane's Museum

When 19th-century gentleman, architect and art collector Sir John Soane died in 1837, he left his home and its contents to the nation. The only condition of his bequest, the terms of which were enshrined in a special Act of Parliament, was that nothing in his home was altered. The resulting museum, a charming artistic and social showcase, has remained unchanged for 150 years.

Soane's passion was for collecting; a passion that seems to have been more or less unchecked or unguided – he simply bought whatever caught his eye. As a result, the house is packed with a miscellany of beautiful but eclectic objects, with ceramics, books, paintings, statues, even a skeleton, jostling for space. One of the collection's highlights is the ancient Egyptian sarcophagus of Pharaoh Seti I, carved from a single block of limestone and engraved with scenes from the afterlife to guide the soul of the deceased. When the sarcophagus was delivered, Soane, totally enraptured with his new treasure, greeted its arrival with a three-day reception party.

For many years this jewel was known only to the well-informed few. Now that the secret is out, you can expect more people; come early or late on weekdays to avoid the worst crowds.

A beautiful miscellany – just some of the treasures in Sir John Soane's eclectic collection

➕ 200 B4 ✉ 13 Lincoln's Inn Fields, WC2 ☎ 020 7405 2107; www.soane.org ⏰ Tue–Sat 10–5 (also first Tue of month 6–9 pm with some rooms candlelit). Groups of six or more must book in advance 🚇 Holborn 🚌 1, 8, 25, 68, 91, 168, 171, 188, 242 ♿ Free

⑪ Somerset House

Once the repository of British citizens' birth, marriage and death records, this majestic riverside building is now home to three superb art collections.

The most famous is the long-established **Courtauld Institute Gallery**, whose reputation rests largely on its collection of Impressionist and Post-Impressionist paintings, which includes works by Cézanne, Seurat, Gauguin, Renoir, Monet, Manet (*Bar at the Folies-Bergère*), Toulouse-Lautrec and Van Gogh (including his famous 1889 work, *Self-Portrait with a Bandaged Ear*). Rooms on the lower floors contain earlier paintings, many of them religious works. The 15th-century *Triptych* by the Master of Flemalle (Room 1) and *Adam and Eve*

by Lucas Cranach the Elder (1526) are among the highlights.

The **Gilbert Collection**, a beautiful exhibition of decorative arts, focuses in particular on snuff boxes and micro-mosaics. The subject matter may not seem overly promising, but many of the exhibits are breathtaking in the degree of technical virtuosity. Huge gold and silver items, jewelled chalices and a pair of quite amazing golden church gates are among the collection's other highlights.

The **Hermitage Rooms** display rotating exhibitions of world-class paintings and other objects on loan from the famous St Petersburg museum in Russia.

➕ 200 B3 ✉ Strand WC2 ☎ 020 7845 4600 (recorded information), 020 7836 8686; www.somerset-house.org.uk ⏰ Daily 10–6 🍴 Café, Admiralty restaurant 🚇 Temple (closed Sun), Embankment or Covent Garden 🚌 1, 4, 6, 9, 11, 13, 15, 23, 26, 76, 77A, 91, 168, 171, 171A, 176, 188 ♿ Courtauld Institute Gallery and Gilbert Collection: moderate, free to under18s, free Mon 10–2, joint ticket available. Hermitage Rooms: moderate, under 18s free. Tickets sold for timed slots on the hour and half-hour

Where to...
Eat and Drink

Prices

Expect to pay per person for a meal excluding drinks and service

£ up to £25   ££ £25–£50   £££ more than £50

Alba £

This smart, modern Italian restaurant, just a short walk from the Barbican Centre, provides excellent value for money and is deservedly popular. It is filled with business people at lunchtime and theatre-goers in the evening.

The menu is sensibly short, encouraging some serious cooking. Fish or meat dishes, such as Trentino lamb stew, and classics like chicken *cacciatore* are prepared with first-rate ingredients. The annotated wine list gives an impressive selection of wines from the best Italian vineyards.

✚ Off map 201 F5 ✉ 107 Whitecross Street, EC1 ☎ 020 7588 1798; www.albarestaurant.com 🕐 Mon–Fri noon–3, 6–11; closed 10 days Christmas, bank holidays 🚇 Barbican

Club Gascon ££

Pascal Aussignac, from Toulouse in Southwest France, has rapidly established a name for himself in this gastronomically evolving part of London. He offers top-class Gascon cooking with the emphasis on *joie gras* and duck, ingredients which are supplied direct by French farmers and producers in Gascony. Although traditionally prepared dishes are Aussignac's specialities, he is not afraid to experiment. Tables may be cramped but the atmosphere at Club Gascon is vibrant. Highly recommended. Booking is essential.

✚ 201 E5 ✉ 57 West Smithfield, EC1 ☎ 020 7796 0600 🕐 Lunch: Mon–Fri noon–1.45. Dinner: Mon–Thu 7–9.45, Fri 7–10.15, Sat 7:30–10:30 🚇 Farringdon

The Eagle £

The Eagle was one of the pioneers of converted pubs specialising in very good food and still leads the field. Choose from a short, but mouth-watering selection of Mediterranean and Asian-influenced dishes; all are great value for money. Reservations are not taken and as this establishment is lively and often crowded, you need to arrive early to secure a table and have the best choice from the blackboard. You order and pay for your food and drink at the bar.

✚ Off map 201 D5 ✉ 159 Farringdon Road, EC1 ☎ 020 7837 1353 🕐 Lunch: Mon–Fri 12:30–3, Sat–Sun 12:30–3.30. Dinner: Mon–Sat 6:30–10:30 🚇 Farringdon

Lanes ££

This elegant but friendly dining room in the heart of the City of London breaks the mould of formal dining in the City. The Modern European menu under head chef Hayden Smith (who learned his trade under Marco Pierre White) is refreshingly New World edge which reflects influences he has brought from his home country of New Zealand.

✚ 202 C5 ✉ East India House, 109–117 Middlesex Street, E1 ☎ 020 7247 5050; www.lanesrestaurant.com 🕐 Mon–Fri noon–3, 5:30–10 🚇 Liverpool Street

Medcalf £

Housed in a former butcher's shop in buzzing Exmouth Market in trendy Clerkenwell, Medcalf serves the best of Modern British cooking into the early evening and is a popular bar later on, with DJs on Friday and Saturday nights. The cooking draws from a seasonal and often organic menu featuring classic British dishes such as oxtail, scallops and oysters, but the chic young crowd that is drawn here is anything but traditional.

✚ Off map 201 D5 ✉ 40 Exmouth Market, EC1 ☎ 020 7833 3533
🕒 Food served: Mon-Thu 10-8.45, Fri 10-7.45, Sun noon-5.
Bar: daily 10 am-11 pm
Ⓕ Farringdon

Moro ££

The standard of cooking at this buzzing, critically acclaimed Spanish/North African restaurant is consistently excellent, with good raw materials simply cooked in a wood-burning oven or chargrilled. The minimalist décor with a long zinc bar down one wall, an open-plan kitchen along another, and plain, close-packed wooden tables creates an informal setting. Reservations need to be made well in advance.

✚ Off map 201 D5 ✉ 34-6 Exmouth Market, EC1 ☎ 020 7833 8336;
www.moro.co.uk 🕒 Lunch: Mon-Fri 12:30-2.30. Dinner: Mon-Sat 7-10.30
Ⓕ Farringdon

Novelli in the City ££

The latest venture for the celebrated chef Jean-Christophe Novelli is located in the brasserie of an exclusive private members club in the heart of the City. Expect the likes of Langoustine bisque, lobster oil and ricard foam, warm galette of Andalusia plum tomatoes, sun-blushed tomato pesto and goats cheese panna cotta, roasted confit shoulder of Welsh lamb, braised quince, snake beans and cous cous.

✚ 202 A3/4 ✉ London Capital Club, 15 Abchurch Lane, EC4 ☎ 020 7717 0088; www.londoncapitalclub.com
🕒 Mon-Fri 5:30-9.30 (members only for breakfast and lunch) Ⓕ Cannon Street, Monument, Bank

Quality Chop House £-££

Much of the original character of this informal former Victorian chop house has been preserved, including high-backed mahogany booths. The food is a fashionable mix of updated traditional English dishes and French brasserie classics, with eggs, bacon and french fries, fish soup with *rouille*, confit of duck, and Toulouse sausage with mash and onion gravy never off the menu.

✚ Off map 201 D5 ✉ 94 Farringdon Road, EC1 ☎ 020 7837 5093
🕒 Lunch: Mon-Fri noon-3, Sun noon-4. Dinner: Mon-Sat 6:30-11, Sun 7-11 Ⓕ Farringdon, King's Cross

St John ££

Back-to-basics eating is the principle behind this Clerkenwell hotspot close to Smithfield. The décor of the former smokehouse is starkly white and minimalist, and an open-plan kitchen adds to the general informality. Traditional old English recipes are reworked – offal (organ meats) is greatly favoured – and sit happily alongside modern Mediterranean dishes on the short menu. The kitchen adopts a simple approach, using some fresh produce.

✚ 201 E5 ✉ 26 St John Street, EE1
☎ 020 7251 0848;
www.stjohnrestaurant.com
🕒 Lunch: Mon-Fri noon-3.
Dinner: Mon-Sat 6-11
Ⓕ Farringdon

BARS

Cicada £

At this stylish bar/restaurant, drinkers frequently outnumber those eating in the evening. The young, clientele create an atmosphere that is lively, noisy and fun. The food, should you wish to eat here, is oriental in style, backed up by some excellent, inexpensive wines from a list that includes chilled *sake* by the flask.

✚ Off map ✉ 132-6 St John Street, EC1 ☎ 020 7608 1550;
www.cicada.nu 🕒 Mon-Fri noon-3, 6-11, Sat 6-10.30 Ⓕ Farringdon

Where to... Shop

The City of London is not a significant shopping area, particularly when compared with other parts of the capital.

Shops in the City are geared to the needs of office workers, and sandwich bars, wine bars and pubs dominate, with a few tourist gift shops near the City sights. However, the few **markets** that remain in this part of London have strong historic and social roots and make an enjoyable outing.

Columbia Road Flower Market
(Columbia Road, E2, open Sun 8–2. Tube: Old Street) is where many Londoners come to stock up with plants for their patios and window boxes. Even if you don't want to

buy a massive yucca or tray of begonias, it's worth a visit.

Petticoat Lane market
(Middlesex Street and beyond, E1, open Mon–Fri 10–2, Sun 9–2. Tube: Aldgate) is an East London institution. It's *the* place to buy inexpensive clothes and shoes. However, bus loads of tourists add to the crush on Sunday, which is the main day, and make browsing difficult. The end of the market by Aldgate East Underground station is devoted to leather jackets. Take cash not credit cards to get the best deal.

The giant Victorian covered marketplace at **Spitalfields Market** (Commercial Street between Lamb Street and Brushfield Street, E1, open Mon–Fri 10–5, Sun 10–5. Tube: Liverpool Street) is filled with interesting crafts and has an array of food outlets selling a wide range of comestibles from crêpes to sushi and tandoori. The market has a very good organic food section, which operates every Wednesday and Sunday 10–5.

Where to... Be Entertained

Much of the City remains quiet in the evenings. The Barbican Centre and Broadgate Centre are the area's focal points.

When the **Barbican Centre** (Silk Street, EC2. Box Office tel: 020 7638 8891; general information tel: 020 7638 4141) first opened, journalists wrote critical reviews about how difficult it was for concert-goers to find their way around this behemoth in a featureless part of the City. Music and theatre-lovers crowd in, however, lured by the centre's proximity to Clerkenwell, London's latest culinary hotspot, as well as by the cultural programme.

The Barbican is the home of the London Symphony Orchestra, who offer about 85 concerts a year with

performances by some of the world's top musicians, as well as two theatres and two cinema screens, where you can see the latest movies.

It's well worth dropping by the Barbican, especially at weekends when a variety of free entertainment is on offer. There are also various cafés on the different levels.

The Barbican is best reached by Underground. Barbican and Moorgate stations are the closest, and have the bonus of clearly marked directions to the complex.

At the **Broadgate Centre** (Broadgate Circus, Eldon Street, EC2. Tube: Moorgate) tiers of shops and restaurants line an impressive amphitheatre, where you can go ice-skating in winter and enjoy open-air entertainment in summer.

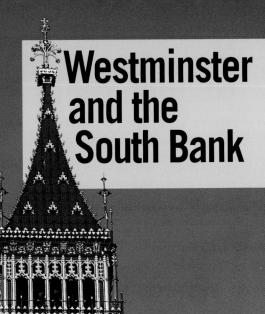

Westminster and the South Bank

DOMINE·SALVAM·FAC·REGINAM·NOSTRAM·VICTORIAM·PRIMAM

Getting Your Bearings

Stand on one of the bridges or embankments and as you gaze at the slowly flowing River Thames you can't help but notice the contrast between the water's stately progress and the noise and drama of the surrounding city.

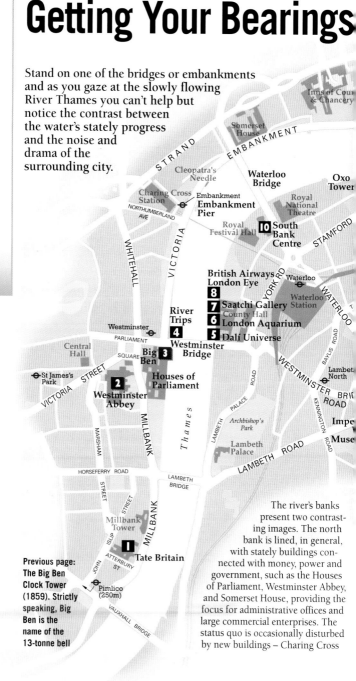

STRAND

EMBANKMENT

Somerset House

Inns of Court & Chancery

Cleopatra's Needle

Charing Cross Station

Embankment

Embankment Pier

NORTHUMBERLAND AVE

Waterloo Bridge

Oxo Tower

Royal National Theatre

Royal Festival Hall

10 South Bank Centre

STAMFORD

WHITEHALL

VICTORIA

British Airways London Eye

8

Waterloo

YORK RD

Waterloo Station

WATERLOO

7 Saatchi Gallery

County Hall

6 London Aquarium

5 Dalí Universe

River Trips

4

Westminster

PARLIAMENT

Westminster Bridge

Central Hall

3 Big Ben

SQUARE

St James's Park

STREET

Houses of Parliament

ROAD

WESTMINSTER

Lambeth North

BRIDGE

BAYLIS ROAD

VICTORIA STREET

2 Westminster Abbey

MARSHAM

MILLBANK

T h a m e s

LAMBETH

PALACE

Archbishop's Park

KENNINGTON ROAD

ROAD

Impe

Muse

Lambeth Palace

HORSEFERRY ROAD

LAMBETH BRIDGE

LAMBETH ROAD

STREET

ISLIP STREET

Millbank Tower

MILLBANK

1 Tate Britain

ATTERBURY ST

JOHN

Pimlico (250m)

VAUXHALL BRIDGE

Previous page: The Big Ben Clock Tower (1859). Strictly speaking, Big Ben is the name of the 13-tonne bell

The river's banks present two contrasting images. The north bank is lined, in general, with stately buildings connected with money, power and government, such as the Houses of Parliament, Westminster Abbey, and Somerset House, providing the focus for administrative offices and large commercial enterprises. The status quo is occasionally disturbed by new buildings – Charing Cross

railway station is a notable example – but generally the river's
north side is stable and established, retaining the political, historical and religious significance it has enjoyed for centuries.

The South Bank has a very different flavour. In Shakespeare's
time it was the place to which actors, considered a bad influence, were banished and where early theatre flour-
ished. The reborn Globe is turning the
clock back 400 years. By the
early 20th

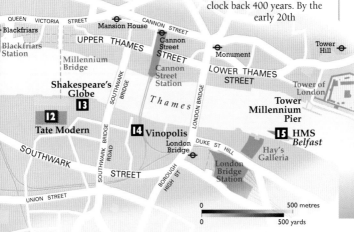

century the area was a mixture of wasteland and heavy
industry, but after World War II, the South Bank Centre, and
the Royal Festival Hall in particular, marked the start of a
makeover. Continuing the shift, as London entered the new
millennium, the old Bankside Power Station was transformed
from industrial behemoth to cultural superstar in the shape of
the Tate Modern gallery. Yet even Tate Modern has been
eclipsed in popularity and profile by the surprise success of the
British Airways London Eye. This elegant, slow-moving observation wheel has rapidly become London's hottest ticket and
is the perfect vantage point for planning your day.

Art, religion, the world's most famous clock and a scenic river walk form the heart of this day's sightseeing. Note that Westminster Abbey closes early on Saturday and is open on Sunday only for services.

Westminster and the South Bank in a Day

9:30 am

Allow 2 hours to enjoy the grandeur of **2 Westminster Abbey** (right, ➤ 94–97), Seeking out the numerous memorials to royal and literary figures among breathtaking architecture, particularly the Royal Chapels.

11:30 am

Admire the **4 Houses of Parliament** and **4 Big Ben** (➤ 98–99), cross **3 Westminster Bridge** and turn left, towards the landmark **8 British Airways London Eye** (➤ 104). Here you are spoiled for choice, with the Eye, the **6 London Aquarium** (➤ 104), **5 Dalí Universe** (➤ 103) and the **7 Saatchi Gallery** (➤ 104). Note: trips on the London Eye should be reserved in advance.

1:30 pm

Stroll along the river to the **11 Oxo Tower** (below; ➤ 105), take a lift (elevator) to the top for a wonderful view over the Thames, and have lunch in their brasserie (➤ 109).

2:30 pm

After lunch, browse in the tower's designer workshops, then make your way to **12 Tate Modern** (➤ 100–101), London's striking modern art gallery, set in the former Bankside Power Station (right). Choose a couple of galleries and take an audio tour rather than trying to see the whole collection. If you have any energy left, **13 Shakespeare's Globe** (➤ 106), a reconstruction of the original Globe Theatre, is just a short walk away. If you've timed it right, you could finish off your day by seeing a play here.

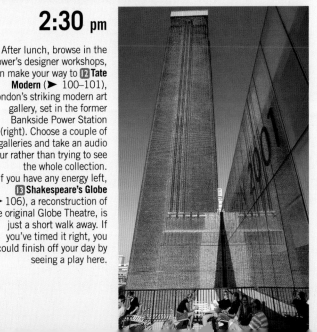

2 Westminster Abbey

Britain's greatest religious building is a church, a national shrine, the setting for coronations and a burial place for some of the most celebrated figures from almost a thousand years of British history. Most of the country's sovereigns, from William the Conqueror in 1066 to Queen Elizabeth II in 1953, have been crowned at Westminster, while in 1997 it was the setting for the funeral of Diana, Princess of Wales. The building has ancient roots, but construction of the present structure, a masterpiece of medieval architecture, began in the 13th century. Since then the building has grown and evolved, a process that continues to the present day as ever more modern memorials are erected.

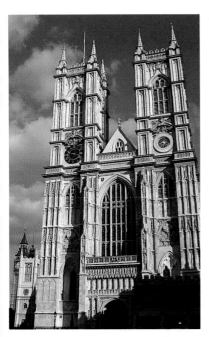

Westminster Abbey is one of London's top tourist destinations, drawing huge crowds. It's impossible to appreciate all the abbey's abundance of riches in one visit, so concentrate on the selected highlights below.

Visitors follow a set route around the abbey. From the entrance through the North Door you head first along the ambulatory, the passageway leading to the far end of the abbey. At the top of the steps, the chapel on the left contains the **tomb of Elizabeth I** (1533–1603) and her older half-sister, Mary Tudor (1516–58), daughters of the much-married Henry VIII. Although they lie close in death, there was little love lost beween them in life – Mary was a Catholic, Elizabeth a Protestant at a time when religious beliefs

Left: The nave and vaulting of Westminster Abbey

Above: The West Towers

➕ 199 F4 ✉ Broad Sanctuary, SW1 ☎ 020 7222 5152; www.westminster-abbey.org
🕐 Mon–Fri 9:30–4:45, Sat 9:30–1:45. Last admission 1 hour before closing. Sun open for worship only. College Garden: Tue–Thu 10–6, Apr–Sep; 10–4, rest of year. Chapter House, Abbey Museum and Pyx Chamber: daily 10:30–4
🍴 Coffee counter in cloisters and Broad Sanctuary
Ⓜ Westminster, St James's Park 🚌 3, 11, 12, 24, 53, 77A, 88, 159, 211
💷 Expensive

divided the country and religious persecution was rife.

Next comes the sublime **Henry VII Chapel** built in 1512, possibly to ease Henry's troubled conscience: his route to the throne was a violent one. The abbey's most gorgeous chapel, it was described by one commentator as *orbis miraculum*, or a wonder of the world. The brilliantly detailed and gilded fan vaulting of the roof is particularly fine, as are the vivid banners of the Knights of the Order of the Bath (an order of chivalry bestowed by the monarch) above the oak choir stalls. Behind the altar are the magnificent tombs and gilded effigies of Henry VII and his wife, Elizabeth, created to a personal design by Henry himself.

Breathtakingly delicate fan vaulting in the Henry VII Chapel

As you leave this area, a side chapel holds the tomb of Mary, Queen of Scots (1542–87). Mary, a rival to Elizabeth I's throne, was imprisoned for 19 years before finally being executed in 1587. Mary's son, James VI of Scotland, became James I of England when the unmarried, childless Elizabeth died. He had his mother's body exhumed and brought to the abbey 25 years after her death and erected the monuments to both Elizabeth I and Mary – but his mother's is much the grander.

Poets' Corner Notables

Alfred, Lord Tennyson
Dylan Thomas
Henry James
T S Eliot
George Eliot
William Wordsworth
Jane Austen
The Brontë sisters

WILLIAM SHAKESPEARE 1564 – 1616
BURIED AT STRATFORD-ON-AVON

NOËL COWARD
Playwright Actor
Composer

16 December 1899
26 March 1973
Buried in Jamaica

'A TALENT TO AMUSE'

As you go back down the stairs don't miss the unassuming chair facing you. This is the **Coronation Chair**, dating from 1296, and has been used at the coronation of most British monarchs. For several centuries anyone could sit on it: many who did left their mark in the form of graffiti.

Next comes **Poets' Corner**, packed with the graves and memorials of literary superstars. You'll spot Geoffrey Chaucer, author of *The Canterbury Tales*; Shakespeare, commemorated by a memorial (he is buried

The Battle of Britain window contains the badges of the 65 fighter squadrons who took part in that World War II battle

in Stratford-upon-Avon); and Charles Dickens, who was buried here against his wishes on the orders of Queen Victoria. Thomas Hardy's ashes are here but his heart was buried in Dorset, the setting for many of his novels.

From Poets' Corner, walk towards the centre of the abbey and the highly decorated altar and choir stalls. One of the loveliest views in the abbey opens up from the steps leading to the altar, looking along the length of the nave to the window above the West Door. For a restful interlude head into the 13th-century **cloisters**, a covered passageway around a small garden once used for reflection by the abbey's monks. Contemplation is also the effect created by the simple black slab memorial at the western end of the abbey – the **Tomb of the Unknown Soldier**, an eloquent testimony to the dead of war.

WESTMINSTER ABBEY: INSIDE INFO

Top tips Attend a **choral service** to see the abbey at its best. Evensong is at 5 pm on weekdays, except Wednesday, 3 pm Saturday and Sunday. Times of other services are displayed, otherwise ring for details.
• **Guided tours** led by abbey vergers leave several times daily (90 min, additional charge). Book at the information desk. There is also an **audio guide**, available in several languages, which provides good additional background (charge).

In more detail Off the cloisters, explore the beautiful 13th-century **Chapter House**, the **Pyx Chamber**, also a survivor of the original fabric, and the **Abbey Museum** with its fascinating wax effigies of royalty.

Hidden gems The **College Garden** (Open 10–6, Apr–Sep; 10–4 rest of year) is a haven of tranquillity. On Wednesdays in July and August there are brass band concerts. Access to the garden is from the cloisters, via the delightful Little Cloister.
• Look for the **statues above the West Door** celebrating modern Christian martyrs.

3 The Thames

This short but panoramic walk takes in Westminster and Waterloo bridges and some of the best sights of the river's south and north banks. It offers an opportunity to appreciate a selection of London's finest views and a chance to enjoy a different outlook on examples of the capital's historical and more modern architecture.

Start on the north bank in front of the **Houses of Parliament** (a complex officially known as the Palace of Westminster), which is the country's seat of government. Much of the structure was rebuilt in the 19th century following a fire, but Westminster Hall, part of the original palace, dates from 1097. The Victoria Tower (335 feet/102m tall) stands at one end and the tower holding Big Ben (322 feet/98m tall) at the other. Strictly speaking **Big Ben** is the name of the tower's 13-tonne bell, not the tower itself. How the name was coined is uncertain – the bell may have been named after the heavyweight boxing champion, Benjamin Caunt, or the works commissioner Sir Benjamin Hall, who supervised installation.

Walk across **Westminster Bridge** to the south bank of the river for the best views of the Houses of Parliament. Today this bridge (built in 1862) is one of over 30 across the Thames, but in 1750 the original bridge on this site was only the second crossing, built after London Bridge. As you walk across look at the water which, despite its murky appearance, supports over a hundred species of fish, including salmon – there have even been recent sightings of seals in the river.

On the bridge's south side turn left along the footpath beside the river. The huge building to your right is County Hall, once the seat of London's metropolitan council. It now houses hotels, restaurants, the **London Aquarium** (▶ 104), the **Dalí**

Universe (► 103), the **Saatchi Gallery** (► 104) and the booking office for the **British Airways London Eye** (► 104), a massive wheel from whose slow-moving capsules you get spectacular views of the city. Look across the river from here for dramatic views of modern Charing Cross station.

Continue on past the somewhat drab concrete buildings of the **South Bank Centre**, one of the city's main cultural and arts venues (► 105 and 110).

Climb the steps up on to **Waterloo Bridge** for one of the finest views of London. Looking east, the dominant landmarks are St Paul's Cathedral (► 78– 81), St Bride's Church spire, Tower 42 (formerly the NatWest Tower), Lloyd's Building (► 173) and – in the far distance – Canary Wharf. In the near distance, on the right, stands the Oxo Tower (► 105).

As you walk to the north side of the bridge, the grand building just to the right is Somerset House, the only remaining example of the 18th-century mansions that once lined the Strand. It now houses three world-class collections (► 85).

Walk down the steps on to Victoria Embankment on the river's north bank. The road is busy and noisy, but you can look back to the south bank from here and there are plenty of seats *en route* to Westminster. You also pass Cleopatra's Needle, a 59-foot (18m) high Egyptian obelisk dating from 1475 BC, given to Britain in 1819 by the Viceroy of Egypt.

Near Westminster Bridge stop at Westminster Pier to check on the times, prices and destinations of the river trips (► 102–103) available.

TAKING A BREAK

Try either **Festival Square Café** (► 108) or the National Film Theatre café, both in the South Bank Centre.

⑫ Tate Modern

One of Britain's newest art museums, housed in a strikingly converted power station right in the centre of the rejuvenated South Bank, Tate Modern was greeted with universal acclaim when it opened in May 2000. The gallery encompasses the spectrum of modern art movements from 19th-century Impressionism to the challenging work of young British artists of the late 20th and early 21st centuries.

Once inside, many visitors find the scale of the Turbine Hall, which occupies the bulk of the building, amazing: it resembles a vast, vacant cathedral, measuring 525 feet (160m) in length and 115 feet (35m) in height. This space is partly filled by works especially commissioned for the venue.

The **permanent collection** is exhibited on Levels 3 and 5. Each level is divided into two: the east end of **Level 3**, devoted to "Still Life/Object/Real Life", is the place to begin. It opens conventionally enough with Cezanne's *Still Life with Water Jug*, but soon becomes more challenging. Salvador Dalí's *Lobster Telephone* is in the room titled "Subversive Objects", while Peter Fischli and David Weisse have created a gallery of clutter – boards stacked carelessly, an empty yogurt carton, cigarettes and paint-spattered boots – that resembles work in progress. The west side of Level 3 is allotted to "Landscape/Matter/Environment", with a whole room devoted to Mark Rothko's *Seagram Murals* – massive Abstract Expressionist works in maroon and black.

The eastern half of **Level 5** is titled "Nude/Action/Body". It starts with a dynamic Rodin sculpture, *The Kiss*, and proceeds with work by Henri Matisse and Francis Bacon. To the west, "History/Memory/Society" is a highlight for many, with Picasso's *Weeping Woman* and Warhol's multiple images of Marilyn Monroe in *Marilyn Diptych*.

For many visitors, the views of London afforded from the upper floors of the gallery are as exciting as the works of art. From the East Room of **Level 7**, there is a superb panorama north across the river, over the Millennium Bridge to St Paul's Cathedral. The view from the east window looks down upon Shakespeare's Globe (➤ 106) and spreads across towards

Above: The dramatic Turbine Hall

Docklands. From the south window, you can look across to the British Airways London Eye (▶ 104).

TAKING A BREAK

The **Globe Café** (▶ 109) serves light lunch dishes. The museum's top-floor restaurant is also good.

Below: Jackson Pollock's lively *Summertime*, one of the works on display

🔲 201 E3 ✉ Bankside, SE1 ☎ 020 7887 8000; www.tate.org.uk 🕐 Daily 10–6 (also 6–10 pm Fri–Sat) 🚇 Southwark 🚉 Waterloo (East), Blackfriars, London Bridge 🚌 45, 63, 100, 344, 381, RV1 💷 Free; admission charge for special exhibitions on Level 4

TATE MODERN: INSIDE INFO

Top tips To avoid the crush, visit on weekday mornings or take advantage of the late opening on Fridays and Saturdays – by 8:30 pm the crowds tend to thin out.
• **Self-guided audio tours**, with special interest tours on architecture and for children, are available.
• **Photography** is allowed only in the Turbine Hall.
• The **Millennium Bridge**, which links St Paul's Cathedral to Tate Modern, is the best way to approach the gallery, taking visitors across the Thames and straight into its heart.

At Your Leisure

❶ Tate Britain

Until 2000, this Millbank gallery
housed the Tate's entire collection,
though limited gallery space meant
that only a fraction of the works were
on display at any one time. The
solution was simple: divide the
collection between two sites. Since
the creation of Tate Modern
(➤ 100–101), the gallery space has
been refurbished and expanded. Both
critics and general public seem
delighted with the results.

Tate Britain covers five centuries of
British art, from *A Man in a Black Cap*
by John Bettes (1545), to work by
latter-day British painters David
Hockney, Francis Bacon, Lucian
Freud, Stanley Spencer and sculptures
by Henry Moore and Jacob Epstein.

All the paintings at Tate Britain are
periodically rehung and sometimes
disappear into storage for lack of space
– though since the split this is much
less of a problem. During any visit,
however, you can count on seeing
great works by Hogarth, Reynolds,
Gainsborough, Constable and, of
course, J M W Turner. Turner is
regarded as the greatest homegrown

Ophelia by John Everett Millais, one of Tate
Britain's popular Pre-Raphaelite works

talent and has his very own wing, the
Clore Gallery. But many visitors'
favourites are still the impossibly
romantic works of the late 19th-
century Pre-Raphaelites – principally
John Everett Millais, William Holman
Hunt and, in particular, Dante Gabriel
Rossetti. Look out for Millais's *Ophelia*,
Rossetti's *Beata Beatrix* and *The Lady of
Shalott* by John William Waterhouse.

➕ 199 F2 ✉ Millbank SW1 ☎ 020
7887 8000; www.tate.org.uk ⏰ Daily
10–5:50; closed 24–26 Dec 🍴 Café,
espresso bar and restaurant Ⓟ Pimlico
🚌 2, 3, 36, 88, 77A, 159, 185, 507, C10
Ⓦ Free

❹ River Trips

A trip along the Thames is a tremendous way to see the city, away from the
Underground or traffic-clogged streets.
Piers in central London from which
you can take trips are Westminster,
Charing Cross/Embank-ment, Temple
and the Tower of London. Services east
to Greenwich (with connections out to
the Thames Barrier) pass through a

largely urban and industrial landscape, but offer excellent views of Greenwich (➤ 176–179). Services upstream to Hampton Court via Kew (➤ 162–163), Putney, Richmond and on to Kingston are more rural, the river meandering through parks and alongside some of London's more village-like residential enclaves. An evening cruise is also a lovely way to see the city, the river banks enlivened by the twinkling and gleaming of a million lights. Note that timetables vary from month to month, so be sure to go to the piers or telephone for latest details.

DuckTours

London's most novel river ride is aboard a yellow amphibious ex-World War II DUKW vehicle. It begins on dry land, behind County Hall, tours various central London landmarks, then returns to Vauxhall to splash down into the Thames and cruise the river for 30 to 35 minutes. It's expensive but fun. Reservations are essential, tel: 020 7928 3132; www.londonducktours.co.uk.

From Westminster Pier

Upriver to Kew (1.5 hours), Richmond (3 hours) and Hampton Court (4.5 hours) tel: 020 7930 2062 or 020 7930 4721.
Downriver to Tower Pier (35–45 min) and Greenwich (65–75) tel: 020 7740 0400.

From Embankment Pier

Downriver to Greenwich (1 hour) and Circular Cruise (50 min) non-stop to Houses of Parliament/Tower Bridge tel: 020 7987 1185.

From Tower Pier

Upriver to Westminster (30 min) tel: 020 7515 1415 and Embankment (25 min) tel: 020 7987 1185.
Downriver to Greenwich (30–40 min) tel: 020 7987 1185.
Evening cruises On a dinner and cabaret cruise (3 hours) you can sightsee while wining, dining and dancing aboard the London Showboat. The cruise operates three to four times weekly, tel: 020 7237 5134.

5 Dalí Universe

As you wander into this surreal space and read on the walls such epigrams as "To be a real Dalinian one must first be a real masochist" and "There is less madness to my method than there is method to my madness", you begin to get some idea of what is in store. The most notable of the 500-plus exhibits are the sculptures – the largest collection of such in the world. Many of these are eye-popping, such as the disturbingly dislocated *Space Venus* (a copy of which stands outside) and will entertain seasoned Dalí watchers and first-timers alike. Look out for the Mae West red lips sofa and beautiful glass sculptures of Dalí's trademark soft watches (though note that Dalí's most famous paintings are elsewhere).

🕂 200 B1 ✉ County Hall, Riverside Buildings, SE1 ☎ 0870 744 7485; www. daliuniverse.com 🕐 Daily 10–5:30 (last admission) 🍴 Café Ⓔ Westminster, Waterloo 🚌 1, 4, 26, 59, 68, 76, 77,168, 171, 172, 176, 188, 211, 243, 341, 381, 501, 507, 521, X68 💷 Expensive

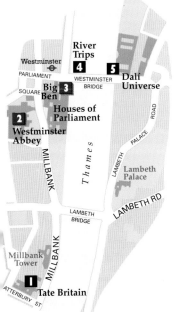

Marine marvels at the London Aquarium

6 London Aquarium

Even if the sight of fishes behind glass usually leaves you cold, you are likely to be captivated by this modern aquarium. Its centrepiece is a huge glass tank, three storeys high, in which all manner of sea life swims serenely past as visitors spiral down wide walkways and gaze in from all levels. There is something mesmeric about the gentle glide of the sharks and rays, and the bottom-hugging immobility of the flat fish such as flounder and sole. Smaller surrounding tanks are devoted to different watery environments, and there's an open tank full of rays for visitors to stroke.

✚ 200 B1 ✉ County Hall, Westminster Bridge Road, SE1 ☎ 020 7967 8000; www.londonaquarium.co.uk ⊙ Daily 10–6 🍴 Café 🚇 Westminster, Waterloo 🚌 12, 53, 76, 109, 171A, 211, P11 💷 Expensive

7 Saatchi Gallery

Advertising mogul Charles Saatchi's art gallery, opened in April 2003, aims to showcase contemporary art by unseen young artists and work by artists of international repute who have had little or no exposure in the UK. Oak panelling lines most of the galleries, recalling the building's former use as

government offices. Among Saatchi's notorious acquisitions shown here are Tracy Emin's *My Bed* and Damien Hirst's *Away From The Flock*.

✚ 200 B1 ✉ County Hall, Southbank, SE1 ☎ 020 7823 2363; www.saatchi-gallery.co.uk ⊙ Daily 10–10 🚇 Waterloo 💷 Expensive

8 British Airways London Eye

The London Eye is the country's most successful Millennium project. At 443 feet (135m) in diameter, it is the biggest wheel of its kind in the world, and as the 32 glass capsules are fixed on the outside (rather than hung from it), you can enjoy totally unobstructed views over the city. On a clear day you can see as far as 25 miles (40km). The capsules give almost total all-round visibility, so everyone gets the best view.

The Eye is in constant motion, just a couple of centimetres per second, and takes 30 minutes for a full revolution. At busy times, it is essential to make a reservation by telephone or in person. Even then, you may wait 30 minutes or so before boarding.

✚ 200 B2 ✉ County Hall Riverside Buildings ☎ Ticket hotline 0870 500 0600 (small booking charge); www.ba-londoneye.com ⊙ Daily 9:30 am–10 pm, Jul–Aug; 9:30–9, May, Jun, Sep; 9:30–8, rest of year. Closed Jan 🍴 Cafés outside and in booking area 🚇 Westminster or Waterloo 🚌 1, 4, 26, 59, 68, 76, 77,168, 171, 172, 176, 188, 211, 243, 341, 381, 501, 507, 521, X68 💷 Very expensive

9 Imperial War Museum

This fascinating but sobering museum is much more than a display of military might or a glorification of war – despite the name, the monstrous guns

Tallest in London

- Canary Wharf Tower 797 feet (243m)
- Tower 42 604 feet (184m)
- Swiss Re Tower 591 feet (180m)
- Telecom Tower 577 feet (176m)
- BA London Eye 443 feet (135m)
- Nelson's Column 174 feet (53m)

in the forecourt and the militaristic slant of the vehicles on show in the main hall. The museum's real emphasis and strengths are the way in which it focuses on the effects of war in the 20th century on the lives of soldiers and civilians alike. This is achieved through a comprehensive collection of artefacts, documents, photographs, works of art, and sound and film archive footage. Some of the most moving testimonies come from oral descriptions recorded by ordinary people whose lives were deeply affected by their wartime experiences. For those who have never experienced war at first hand, this is the place to deepen your understanding.

🔶 Off map 200 C1 ✉ Lambeth Road, SE1 ☎ 020 7416 5320; www.iwm.org.uk 🕐 Daily 10–6; closed 24–26 Dec 🍴 Café 🚇 Lambeth North, Elephant and Castle, Waterloo 🚌 1, 12, 45, 53, 63, 68, 168, 171, 172, 176, 188, 344, C10 🎟 Free

🔟 South Bank Centre

The vibrant South Bank arts complex is crammed with theatres, concert halls, cinemas, bars, a

Fighter planes and rockets in the Imperial War Museum's main hall

gallery and restaurants. Though architecturally austere, on a warm summer's day it can still be a pleasant spot in which to relax. There is a genuine buzz, thanks to the crowds of people drawn to the complex's restaurants and cafés, and the (often free) concerts and exhibitions held in the major lobbies. An on-going programme of redevelopment is set to give the complex a complete makeover. For more information on booking tickets ➤ 110.

🔶 200 C2 ☎ 0870 380 4300; ww.sbc.org.uk 🚇 Waterloo 🚌 Waterloo Bridge 1, 4, 26, 59, 68, 76, 77, 168, 171, 172, 176, 188 211, 243, 341, 381, 501, 507, 521, X68

🔟 Oxo Tower

This landmark building houses a dynamic mixture of private and public housing, restaurants and bars (➤ 109), and designer workshops. The tower's windows are carefully placed to spell out the word "OXO" (a brand of stock cube), a clever ploy by the architect to evade regulations

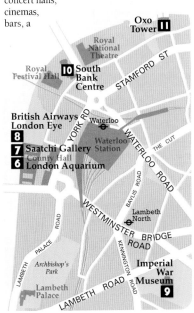

against riverside advertising. It's worth a visit for the superb views from the observation area alone.

🚩 201 D3 ✉ Barge House Street, SE1
☎ 020 7401 2255; www.oxotower.co.uk
🕐 Observation area, Level 8: daily 11–10; studios and shops Tue–Sun 11–6
🚇 Blackfriars, Waterloo 🚌 45, 63, 100, 381 🎫 Free all areas

The project was the brainchild of Sam Wanamaker, the American film actor and director, who died before its completion. His legacy is an extraordinary achievement, not least because the theatre itself is a wonderfully intimate and atmospheric space. It is built of unseasoned oak held together with 9,500 oak pegs, topped by the first thatched roof completed in the city since the Great Fire of London in 1666. It is also partly open to the elements, as was

QUEEN VICTORIA STREET ⊕ Mansion House CANNON STREET
UPPER THAMES STREET Cannon Street ⊕ Monument
Millennium Bridge Cannon Street Station LOWER THAMES STREET
Shakespeare's Globe **13** SOUTHWARK BRIDGE *Thames* Tower of London
12 LONDON BRIDGE Tower Millennium Pier
Tate Modern **14** Vinopolis **15** HMS *Belfast*
London Bridge ⊕ DUKE ST HILL Hay's Galleria

13 Shakespeare's Globe

How about a visit to Shakespeare's theatre? Well, almost: this is a reconstruction of the Globe Theatre (whose original site lay some 330 yards/300m away) in which Shakespeare was an actor and shareholder, and in which many of his plays were first performed.

The Globe is a faithful re-creation of Shakespeare's original Elizabethan theatre

Shakespeare's original Globe, with standing room in front of the stage where theatre-goers can heckle the actors in true Elizabethan fashion.

A visit to the exhibition and a tour of the theatre is highly worthwhile and will certainly whet your appetite for a performance. The tours cover the history of the project, future plans

and costumes from past productions.

➕ 201 E3 ✉ New Globe Walk, Bankside, SE1 ☎ 020 7902 1400; box office 020 7401 9919; www.shakespeares-globe.org 🕐 Exhibition and tours: daily 9–4 (last tour noon), May–Sep; 10–5, rest of year 🍴 Coffee bar, café and restaurant 🚇 Mansion House, London Bridge, Cannon Street 🚌 Blackfriars Bridge 45, 63, 100; Southwark Street 344, 381 💷 Expensive

🔢 Vinopolis

If your idea of a good museum is the sort of place where you can saunter about with a glass of fine wine in your hand then you will enjoy Vinopolis. Set in historic vaults, which were once at the centre of Europe's wine trade, this award-winning attraction takes visitors on an encyclopaedic trawl through the world of wine, visiting every major wine-producing country and region, assisted by tutored tastings, touch-screen technology and audio-guides. There's a great wine, food and accessories shop, plus an excellent restaurant and wine bar.

➕ 201 F3 ✉ 1 Bank End, Bankside SE1 ☎ 0870 4444 777; www.vinopolis.co.uk 🕐 Wed–Mon noon–6 (also 6–9 Mon, Fri and Sat) 🍴 Restaurant, wine bar 🚇 London Bridge 🚌 17, 21, 35, 40, 43, 48, 133, 149, 343, 501, 521, P3, RV1 💷 Very expensive (includes wine tasting)

🔢 HMS *Belfast*

This World War II vessel, the biggest cruiser ever built by the Royal Navy, took part in the Normandy landings, and remained in service until 1965. Preserved in the state it enjoyed during active service, the ship is now moored between Tower Bridge and London Bridge on the south side of the Thames. It houses displays connected with recent Royal Navy history, but it is the ship itself that is the true attraction. You can explore all the way from the bridge to

HMS *Belfast*, high seas warrior until 1965

engine and boiler rooms nine decks below, taking in the cramped quarters of the officers and crew, the galleys, punishment cells and sick bays, as well as the gun turrets, magazines and shell rooms.

➕ 202 B2 ✉ Moored off Morgans Lane, Tooley Street, SE1 ☎ 020 7940 6300; www.org.uk/belfast 🕐 Daily 10–6, Mar–Oct (last admission 5:15); 10–5, rest of year (last admission 4:15). Closed 24–26 Dec 🍴 Many near by in Hay's Galleria (▶ 110) 🚇 London Bridge, Tower Hill, Monument 🚌 42, 47, 78, 188, 381 💷 Expensive; free for children 15 or under

For Kids

- London Aquarium (▶ 104)
- Boat trip downriver or on the Duck Tour (▶ 102–103)
- BA London Eye (▶ 104)
- HMS *Belfast* (▶ 107)

Where to...
Eat and Drink

Prices
Expect to pay per person for a meal excluding drinks and service
£ up to £25   ££ £25–£50   £££ more than £50

Bengal Clipper £

A former spice warehouse at Butler's Wharf makes a particularly fitting setting for this respected Indian restaurant. The spacious dining room is dominated by a central grand piano, the surroundings have a strong sense of style and comfort, and the service is elegant. The short menu specialises in mainly Bengali and Goan dishes.

✚ 202 F2 ⊠ Butler's Wharf, SE1
☎ 020 7357 9001;
www.bengalrestaurants.com
◉ Lunch: daily noon–2:30 (also Sun noon–4). Dinner: Mon–Sat 6–11:30, Sun 6–11 ⓔ London Bridge, Tower Hill

Cantina del Ponte £–££

This simple Italian-style eatery, set on the wharf by Tower Bridge, has fabulous views back over the City. It is the least expensive of the Conran Gastrodome restaurants and the mainly Italian-inspired menu brings a simple choice of grilled or roasted meats and fish. In summer, ask for a table on the terrace.

✚ 202 F2 ⊠ Butler's Wharf Building, 36c Shad Thames, SE1 ☎ 020 7403 5403; www.conran.com ◉ Lunch: daily noon–2:45 (also Sat–Sun 12:45–3). Dinner Mon–Sat 6–11:45, Sun 6–9:45 ⓔ London Bridge, Tower Hill

The Circle Bar Restaurant £

The Circle is one of a collection of fashionable eateries to be found at Butler's Wharf. The unusual layout features a restaurant set on a balconied mezzanine, which in turn overlooks the popular bar (where informal snacks are available). There's a definite buzz, and the kitchen copes well with the mix of styles dictated by the globally influenced menu.

✚ 202 F2 ⊠ The Circle, 13–15 Queen Elizabeth Street, SE1 ☎ 020 7407 1122 ◉ noon–11:30 ⓔ London Bridge, Tower Hill

Festival Square Café £

This bright, cheerful, contemporary café-restaurant is popular with South Bank theatre-goers and local business people, particularly in summer when there is open-air seating for 200. There's a short modern menu of full meals, well-priced tapas-style bar food and a good-value lunch and dinner (the latter available only from 7:30 pm).

✚ 200 B2 ⊠ Royal Festival Hall (ground floor) ☎ 020 7928 2228; www.digbytrout.co.uk
◉ Mon–Fri 8:30 am–11 pm, Sat 10:30 am–11 pm, Sun 10:30–10 ⓔ Waterloo

Alternatively, you can just pop in for a coffee.

Fina Estampa £

This small, intimate Peruvian restaurant is set not far from London Bridge. The cooking is authentic and good value, the surroundings kitsch, but as peaceful as you can get with traffic rushing by. Shellfish is excellent, as is the ceviche (marinated raw fish), and it should all be washed down with a pisco sour (Peruvian brandy with lime juice).

Otherwise the rest of the cooking is bulked out with beans and potatoes.

✚ 202 D2 ⊠ 150–2 Tooley Street, SE1 ☎ 020 7403 1342 ◉ Lunch: Mon–Fri noon–10:30; Sat 6–10:30 ⓔ London Bridge

Globe Café £

There are stunning river views from the Georgian building that forms part of the Shakespeare's Globe theatre complex on the South Bank. This airy, bright café serves light lunch and supper dishes such as pasta and salads, as well as cakes and sandwiches. The grill/restaurant on the first floor has the same river views, and offers an a la carte menu as well as good-value pre- and post-theatre menus.

✚ 201 F3 ☒ New Globe Walk, Bankside, SE1 ☎ 020 7902 1576 ⊘ Café: Daily 10 am–11 pm, May–Sep; 10–6, rest of year ☻ Cannon Street, London Bridge, Mansion House

Livebait £

The menu at this informal and slightly cramped seafood restaurant incorporates traditional dishes such as rock and native oysters, cock crabs from Dorset, and langoustines with mayonnaise. Added to this are a selection of interesting dishes

that reflect Asian, oriental and Mediterranean influences (often on the same plate). Close to the Old Vic and South Bank Centre.

✚ 201 D2 ☒ 43 The Cut, SE1 ☎ 020 7928 7211; www.santeonline.co.uk/ livebait ⊘ Mon–Sat noon–11, Sun 12:30–9 ☻ Waterloo

Oxo Tower ££–£££

The Oxo Tower may be a Thames-side landmark but it can be hard to find the entrance. However, the 8th floor restaurant brings ample reward in stunning river vistas taking in St Paul's and the Houses of Parliament. Window tables are not essential, as the view dominates the entire ultra-chic space. Dishes are drawn from a global melting pot of influences, but in the evening there are more classic interpretations of European cooking.

✚ 201 D3 ☒ 8th Floor, OXO Tower Wharf, Barge House Street, SE1 ☎ 020 7803 3888; www.oxotower.co.uk ⊘ Lunch: daily noon–3. Dinner: Mon–Sat 6–11:30, Sun 6:30–10:30 ☻ Blackfriars

RSJ ££

The name RSJ refers to the rolled steel joist that crosses the ceiling of this long-established family-owned restaurant. Among its numerous charms are a comfortably warm but contemporary interior, good, modern Anglo-French cooking strong on seasonal ingredients, great vegetarian dishes, and a much applauded wine list. The special lunch is excellent value should you be heading for a matinée at the Royal National Theatre. Highly recommended.

✚ 200 C2 ☒ 33 Coin Street, SE1 ☎ 020 7928 4554; www.rsj.uk.com ⊘ Lunch: Mon–Fri noon–2. Dinner: Mon–Sat 5:30–11 ☻ Waterloo

Tas Restaurant £

In a street full of places to eat, Tas offers something different with its Turkish food and choice of meze. The restaurant is large and brightly lit, with pale wooden tables and flooring and an open kitchen at the back; the chatter and hubbub create a definite buzz. Main courses are

served in generous portions and represent excellent value for money.

✚ 201 D2 ☒ 33 The Cut SE1 ☎ 020 7928 1444; www.tasrestaurant.com ⊘ Mon–Sat noon–11:30, Sun noon–10:30 ☻ Waterloo

BARS

Gordon's Wine Bar £

Dating from 1890 and claiming to be the oldest established wine bar in town, this dark cobwebby place is a gem. Descend the stone steps to rub shoulders with commuters, wine lovers and inquisitive visitors who come not only to drink in the atmosphere but to sample an excellent range of wines, plus traditional ports and madeiras. A healthy buffet salad bar, hot meals and a traditional roast on Sunday are served.

✚ 200 3B ☒ 47 Villiers Street, WC2 ☎ 020 7930 1408; www.gordonswinebar.com ⊘ Mon–Sat 11–11, Sun noon–10 ☻ Embankment

Where to...
Shop

Borough Market (open Mon–Fri 6–noon, Sat 9–4. Tube: London Bridge), at the junction of Borough High Street and Southwark Street, is the capital's best for fine food shopping and attracts not only London's more discerning shoppers but celebrity chefs too. It's worth a visit also to glimpse one of the few truly Dickensian areas left in London.

Hay's Galleria, opening on to the River Walk by the Thames (Tube: London Bridge), was one of the first warehouse developments. An impressive Victorian-style iron-and-glass roof covers a huge atrium that is surrounded by a mixture of offices, shops and cafés. The Galleria is noted for some quirky shops and cafés during the week the shops and eateries tend to cater for the needs of office workers. Though not worth a detour in itself, Hay's Galleria provides a pleasant watering hole if you are looking for a respite from some of the nearby attractions.

Gabriel's Wharf (Upper Ground, SE1. Tube: Waterloo), by Waterloo Bridge, close to the South Bank Centre, is a great place to buy unusual gifts. The lively complex contains design and craft workshops, where silversmiths and ceramicists sell their work, as well as several cafés. In summer a number of open-air events create a lively atmosphere.

The **Riverside Walk Market**, which sells second-hand books, is set up on the wide, paved space by the Thames under Waterloo Bridge every weekend between 10 am and 5 pm, and irregularly during the week. The stalls stock mostly old paperbacks, but there are a few gems, including children's books, plays, poetry, science fiction and old map prints, to be found if you persevere.

Where to...
Be Entertained

FILM AND THEATRE

The **South Bank Centre** (tel: 020 7960 4242. Tube: Waterloo) is London's major performing arts complex: the **Royal Festival Hall** (closed for renovation until 2007), the **Queen Elizabeth Hall** and the **Purcell Room** are venues for music and dance; **The Royal National Theatre** comprises the Lyttelton, Olivier and Cottesloe theatres, and the **National Film Theatre** (tel: 020 7928 3232) shows both subtitled foreign films and mainstream releases. A major restoration project to improve the complex is underway.

The retrospectives and exhibitions of contemporary art, painting, sculpture and photography at the **Hayward Gallery** (Belvedere Road, SE1, tel: 020 7960 5266. Tube: Waterloo) are a must for art lovers.

Close by, the **British Film Institute London IMAX Cinema** (1 Charlie Chaplin Walk, SE1, tel: 020 7902 1234. Tube: Waterloo) and screens 2D and 3D films on the largest screen in Europe.

CLUBS

Try the cutting-edge **Ministry of Sound** (103 Gaunt Street, SE1, tel: 020 7378 6528. Tube: Elephant and Castle). As with many London clubs, MoS plays different music on different nights (with dress codes in operation), so check listings magazines (▶ 43) or visit the website (www.ministryofsound.com). An evening here won't be cheap.

Knightsbridge, Kensington and Chelsea

Getting Your Bearings

Ladbroke Grove (800m)

9 Portobello Road Market

PORTOBELLO ROAD

KENSINGTON PARK ROAD

PEMBRIDGE ROAD

Bayswater

QUEENSWAY

INVERNESS TERR

LEINSTER TERR

Queensway

BAYSWATER ROAD

Notting Hill Gate

NOTTING HILL GATE

PALACE GDNS TERRACE

KENSINGTON CHURCH STREET

THE BROAD WALK

8 Kensing Garde

Round Pond

Kensington Palace 7

KENSINGTON ROAD

KENSINGTON HIGH ST

High Street Kensington

PALACE GATE

GLOUCESTER RD

These premier residential districts were once leafy villages, favoured by the wealthy for their healthy distance from the dirt and pollution of early London. Today they still retain an ambience of exclusivity: their houses are grand, the streets still leafy, and the area has attracted many consulates and embassies to its genteel environs.

Kensington first gained its fashionable reputation in the late 17th century when royalty moved to Kensington Palace. The palace remains a royal home – though parts are open to the public – and the gardens are among London's prettiest. Kensington Gardens occupies the western swathe of Hyde Park, which extends all the way to Marble Arch, affording a magnificent green space at the very heart of the city. In the middle is the Serpentine, an artificial lake.

Much of Kensington is scattered with monuments to Queen Victoria's husband, Prince Albert, who died prematurely in 1861. The Albert Memorial on the edge of Kensington Gardens is the principal example, but more subtle reminders of the royal consort survive elsewhere. It was the Prince's idea that profits from the Great Exhibition (held in Hyde Park in 1851) should be used to establish an education centre in the area. The many colleges and institutions of South Kensington were the result, among them three of the capital's foremost museums: the Victoria and Albert Museum, the Science Museum and the Natural History Museum.

Knightsbridge is Kensington's neighbour to the east and, if anything, is even more exclusive as a residential address. It also has a smart commercial aspect, including the department store Harrods. More affluent residents use the shop as a local store, but most Londoners and tourists are content with a voyeuristic look at the richness and variety of its stock, its lavish interiors and the tempting food halls.

Previous page: The decorative frieze on the Royal Albert Hall depicts the Triumph of Arts and Letters

Marble
Arch

Marble
Arch

BAYSWATER   ROAD

Lancaster
Gate

Speakers'
Corner

PARK LANE

Italian
Gardens

8
Hyde Park

PARK LANE

The Long Water

Serpentine
Bridge

The *Serpentine*

Serpentine
Gallery

Diana, Princess of Wales
Memorial Fountain

Hyde Park
Corner

Albert
Memorial
6

Knightsbridge
Barracks

K N I G H T S B R I D G E

KENSINGTON
ROAD

Knightsbridge

NGTON GORE

BROMPTON   ROAD

SLOANE

Royal
Albert Hall

yal College
of Music

EXHIBITION ROAD

Harrods
2

perial College

Science
Museum **4**

Victoria &
Albert Museum
3

BEAUCHAMP
PLACE

PONT   STREET

5 **Natural**
History Museum

CROMWELL
ROAD

THURLOE
PLACE

BROMPTON
RD

STREET

South
Kensington

SLOANE
SQUARE

Sloane
Square

LWR SLOANE
STREET

KING'S   ROAD

CHELSEA BRIDGE RD

ROYAL HOSPITAL ROAD

Royal
Hospital

0		500 metres
0		500 yards

National
Army
Museum

Chelsea
Physic
Garden **1**

CHELSEA

EMBANKMENT

Thames

Ensure a relaxed start to your day by browsing or luxury shopping in Harrods before heading to South Kensington's three principal museums and a royal palace set in beautiful gardens.

Knightsbridge, Kensington and Chelsea in a Day

10:00 am

2 Harrods (➤ 116) is essential viewing even if you don't want to spend any money. Don't miss the food halls, the pet department, the exotic Egyptian Hall and the splendid Egyptian escalators. Have a coffee in one of the many in-store cafés.

11:30 am

Wander along **Brompton Road**, lined with exclusive shops, to the Victoria and Albert Museum. Alternatively, if you don't fancy the half-mile (800m) walk, catch a number 14, 74 or C1 bus, any of which will drop you near the museum. The other museums are across the road.

The **3 Victoria and Albert Museum** (➤ 117–120), the national museum of art and design, is filled with all manner of beautiful objects; the **5 Natural History Museum** (entrance hall, below, ➤ 124–126) covers the earth's flora, fauna and geology; and the **4 Science Museum** (➤ 121–123) investigates every imaginable aspect of science. The best approach is to choose one museum and give it a couple of hours – don't try to tackle too much in one go.

1:30 pm

Have a leisurely lunch in the area at one of the museum cafés or in a patisserie or pub in nearby Brompton Road.

2:45 pm

Walk north up Exhibition Road, turn left into Kensington Gore to the Royal Albert Hall and admire the **6 Albert Memorial** opposite (➤ 129). If the weather is fine head into Kensington Gardens and across to the Round Pond and Kensington Palace. Otherwise, buses number 9, 10 or 52 run towards Kensington High Street along Kensington Gore; get off at the Broad Walk (it's just a couple of stops along) and walk straight into the gardens near the palace. (Note that in winter the last admission to Kensington Palace is at 4 pm.)

3:30 pm

Look around **7 Kensington Palace** (➤ 127–128), which is less grand than Buckingham Palace, but the sort of place where you can imagine people actually living. The palace's royal dress collection is especially good.

5:00 pm

Have a break in the **Orangery** (➤ 133) and then enjoy an evening walk through **8 Kensington Gardens** and into **8 Hyde Park** (above, ➤ 130–131): you might even take a rowing boat out on the Serpentine as a peaceful finale to the day.

2 Harrods

Harrods is a London institution. It began life when Henry
Charles Harrod, a grocer and tea merchant, opened a small
shop in 1849. Today it contains more than 300 departments
spread across seven floors, still striving to fulfil its motto
Omnia Omnibus Ubique – all things, for all people, everywhere.

Harrods works hard to maintain its reputation as London's
premier department store. Liveried commissionaires (known as
Green Men) patrol the doors and if you are deemed to be
dressed inappropriately you'll be refused entry. Rucksacks,
leggings, shorts or revealing clothing are to be avoided.

The store's most popular departments are the cavernous
ground-floor **food halls**, resplendent with decorative tiles and
vaulted ceilings, where cornucopian displays of fish, fruit and
myriad other foodstuffs tempt shoppers. Handsomely packaged
teas and coffees, and jars bearing the distinctive Harrods logo
are available: good for gifts or souvenirs, and an inexpensive
way to acquire the trademark carrier bag!

Also worth a special look are the **Egyptian Hall**, complete
with sphinxes (also on the ground floor) and the **Egyptian
Escalator** that carries you to the store's upper floors. One
perennial favourite is the **pet department** (on the second
floor), whose most publicised sale was a baby elephant in 1967;
the shop keeps smaller livestock these days.

During your visit, keep an ear open for the distinctive sound of
The Harrods' bagpipers
who perform occasionally,
usually in the late morn-
ing on the ground floor
(telephone for details).

> Harrods' food
> halls are the
> most famous of
> the store's 300
> or more
> departments

The Harrods experi-
ence isn't complete
unless you come back
after dark when the vast
exterior is brilliantly
illuminated with thou-
sands of lights.

TAKING A BREAK
Stop in the ground-floor
food halls at the **Harrods
Famous Deli** for deli-
cious salt beef bagels or
smoked salmon on rye.

✚ 195 F2 ✉ 87–135 Brompton Road, SW1 ☎ 020 7730 1234;
www.harrods.com 🕐 Mon–Sat 10–7 🍽 19 bars and restaurants including a
deli, pizzeria, sushi bar and a pub (serving Harrods' own beer)
🚇 Knightsbridge 🚌 C1, 14, 74

3 Victoria and Albert Museum

The Victoria and Albert Museum (also known as the V&A), the national museum of art and design, was founded in 1852 with the aim of making art accessible, educating working people, and inspiring designers and manufacturers. One of Europe's great museums, its 6 miles (10km) of galleries are crammed with exquisite exhibits from across the world and across the centuries. This is the sort of place where you want to take just about everything home: some Meissen, perhaps, a few Persian carpets, an Indian throne, or the Heneage Jewel once owned by Queen Elizabeth I. The range of objects is staggering – sculpture, ceramics, glass, furniture, metalwork, textiles, paintings, photography, prints, drawings, jewellery, costume and musical instruments. In addition to the wealth of beautiful works of art, the V&A also has the most peaceful atmosphere and most interesting shop of all the major London museums.

Casts and copies from the Italian Renaissance – just a fraction of the many beautiful works in the Victoria and Albert Museum

---

🛉 195 E1 ✉ Cromwell Road, SW7 ☎ 020 7942 2000; www.vam.ac.uk
🕐 Daily 10–5:45; Wed and last Fri of month 10–10 (Henry Cole Wing 10–5:30); closed 24–26 Dec 🚇 South Kensington
🚌 C1, 14, 74 💶 Free

One of many highlights in the **Medieval Treasury** is the Limoges enamel Becket Casket, dating from 1180. It is covered with images depicting the death of St Thomas à Becket at the hands of four knights loyal to King Henry II, whom Becket had angered by refusing to let Church authority be compromised by the Crown. The casket reputedly contained a bloodstained scrap of fabric from the clothes St Thomas was wearing at his death. Look out also for the early church vestments, especially the Butler-Bowden Cope, embellished with fine embroidery.

The **Nehru Gallery of Indian Art** features a fine display of textiles and paintings, together with a variety of other interesting artefacts such as a white jade wine cup and thumb ring belonging to Shah Jehan (a 17th-century Mogul emperor of

Suggested Route
- Medieval Treasury
- Nehru Gallery of Indian Art
- Raphael Cartoons
- Dress Collection
- Morris, Gamble and Poynter Rooms
- Canon Photography Gallery
- Cast Rooms
- Silver Gallery
- Glass Gallery

India and the builder of the Taj Mahal). One of the museum's most idiosyncratic items is also here – Tipu's Tiger (*c*1790), a life-size wooden automaton from Mysore depicting a tiger eating a man. A musical box inside the tiger's body can reproduce the growls of the tiger and screams of the victim.

Tipu's Tiger, one of the museum's most popular exhibits, shows a tiger mauling a British soldier

The V&A's **Raphael Cartoons** were commissioned by Pope Leo X in 1515 as designs for tapestries to hang in the Sistine Chapel in the Vatican. The word cartoon properly refers to a full-size preparatory drawing for works in other media. Important works of art, they depict scenes from the lives of St Peter and St Paul.

The **Dress Collection** traces the development of men's, women's and children's clothing through the ages. One of the museum's most popular sections, it gives you a chance to smirk at the fashions of your forebears, admire the often sumptuous dresses of centuries past, or marvel at historical oddities such as the 5-foot (1.5m) wide mantua, a formal dress worn by 18th-century women for ceremonial occasions. Clothes from designers such as Dior, Issey Miyake, Versace, and Chanel represent modern fashion.

A thousand years of fashion – the V&A's collection of historic dress is a highlight of any visit

The **Morris, Gamble and Poynter Rooms** are named after and decorated in the styles of three leading 19th-century artists and designers; the hugely influential William Morris (1834–96), who designed furniture and textiles, among much else; James Gamble (1835–1919), who worked as part of the museum's design team and produced stained glass and ceramics for his room, and artist Edward Poynter (1836–1919). They retain their original function as public refreshment rooms, the V&A having been the first museum in the world to provide its patrons with such facilities. Their painted tiles, friezes, columns, quotations and glass windows provide plenty to admire as you sip your coffee. Look in particular for some of the quotations that form part of the decorative scheme.

Left: The Italian Rooms display remarkable examples of Renaissance art and craftsmanship

A selection of the museum's 300,000 photographic works is displayed in the **Canon Photography Gallery**, alongside two

changing displays. This is one of the few spaces devoted to photography in a major London museum.

The **Cast Rooms** contain some of the museum's largest exhibits. In the 19th century art students were less able to travel to study masterpieces at first hand and to aid them reproductions (often casts) were made of famous sculptures. The rooms are packed with statues, windows, pulpits and altars: size was clearly of no concern – parts of Trajan's Column in Rome and the enormous Portico de la Gloria from Santiago de Compostela in Spain are both reproduced.

The Victoria and Albert Museum moved to its present home in 1857. Until 1899 it was known as the South Kensington Museum

The **Silver Gallery** traces the history of silver from the 14th century, with examples of every size, shape and provenance. Exhibits range from the dramatic 18th-century Macclesfield Wine Service, testimony to an era of grand living and extravagant entertaining, to the silver snuff box that King Charles II gave to Nell Gwynn, the most beautiful of his many mistresses. In the How Do We Know exhibit, you learn how to identify a forgery, and in the discovery area visitors are allowed to handle some of the pieces in the collection.

The sparkling **Glass Gallery** tells the story of glass from 2500 BC to the present day. Make a special point of seeing *The Luck of Edenhall*, a 13th-century Syrian vessel probably brought home by a crusader, but said by legend to have been created by fairies. A fabulous example of modern glass design is provided by the balustrade up to the mezzanine floor, the work of the American glass artist Danny Lane.

TAKING A BREAK

Stop at **Emporio Armani Caffè** (191 Brompton Road, SW3, tel: 020 7823 8818, closed Sun), an elegant first-floor café where Armani-clad waiters serve delicious Italian food.

VICTORIA AND ALBERT MUSEUM: INSIDE INFO

Top tips Late view takes place on Wednesday evenings and the last Friday of the month, with certain galleries remaining open until 10 pm. A lecture is given each Wednesday (charge) and themed events are staged on Fridays. Admission to the galleries is free though some events may carry a separate charge.

Hidden gems Take time to see the office of Pittsburgh department store proprietor Edgar J Kaufmann, designed by American architect Frank Lloyd Wright (1869–1959). It is the only example of Wright's work in Europe.
• The **John Constable Collection** is the world's largest collection of works by this leading 19th-century British landscape artist.

4 Science Museum

Technophobes needn't be afraid of this museum: the science here is presented in a simple and user-friendly way, with plenty of child-pleasing hands-on displays and clever devices to make sense of complex and everyday items alike. The museum embraces all branches of pure and applied science from their beginnings to modern times, covering the ground with enormous visual panache and a real desire to communicate the excitement and vibrancy of science.

Great working engines from the Industrial Revolution are popular exhibits at the Science Museum

Be warned before you start, you can easily spend the whole day here and still not see everything. With the addition of the stunning new Wellcome Wing, and its attendant IMAX cinema and space simulator ride, the Science Museum, always one of London's biggest and best museums, has taken on an even larger dimension. It is best to concentrate on just a couple of themed galleries interspersing these with fun areas such as the cinema and rides. If you have children, let them off the leash in the museum's many acclaimed hands-on areas.

The best way to start your visit is by strolling through **Making the Modern World**, on the ground floor. This dramatic gallery displays many icons and "firsts" of the modern age; from Stephenson's record-breaking 1829 locomotive, the *Rocket*, to the scorched and battered Apollo 10 Command Module that orbited the moon in May 1969 as a precursor to the lunar landings (for a full history of space flight head to the adjacent Space gallery). Many peoples' favourites, however, are the huge, hypnotically rotating mill engines that powered the Industrial Revolution and are still steamed for museum visitors.

195 E1　✉ Exhibition Road, SW7
☎ 0870 870 4868; www.sciencemuseum.org.uk
🕐 Daily 10–6; closed 24–26 Dec
🍴 Restaurant and cafés　Ⓢ South Kensington
🚌 9, 10, 14, 49, 52, 70, 74, 345, 360, 414, C1　♿ Free

To enter the deep-neon-blue world of the **Wellcome Wing**, its three upper floors suspended almost magically in mid air, is truly to walk into the future. Many of the exhibits in this part of the museum deal with cutting-edge technology, and just-breaking scientific stories are monitored here in real time. If the latest advances in medicine and nuclear physics sounds a bit too much like hard work, however, take a ride across the galaxy on a virtual voyage simulator, or for an even more exciting show, head to the top floor where the IMAX cinema will astound you with images as tall as five double-decker buses, and suck you right into the screen. Films portray themes such as the universe and Earth as you have never seen them before, but for eye-popping state-of-the-art cinematic special effects take the kids to *Cyberworld 3D*.

Above: A replica of the Apollo lunar module in the Making the Modern World gallery

Below: Historic planes on show in the Flight gallery

There are so many other diverse galleries to explore – Food, Gas, Computers, Time, Chemical Industry, Marine Engineering, Photography, Health, Geophysics and Oceanography, to name just a few – that it is difficult to know where to head for next. Try to make time, however, for **Flight**, a fascinating display chronicling the history of manned flight from Montgolfier's balloons to supersonic engines. Historic aircraft duck and dive, slung from every available piece of ceiling, and high-level walkways get you right up into the air alongside these beautiful gleaming machines.

TAKING A BREAK

Despite its name, the **Deep Blue Café** is a high-quality waiter-service restaurant serving suitably up-to-the-minute meals in an open-plan setting from which you can gape at the £40 million Wellcome Wing. The Museum Café on the ground floor sits right next to a splendid mill engine behemoth of the Industrial Revolution.

Detailed models and innumerable hands-on displays around the museum help to bring science to life

For Kids

The museum is committed to involving children and the four specialist galleries for them are all staffed by informative "Explainers".

- **The Garden** (basement): aimed at 3 to 6 year olds.
- **Flight Lab** (third floor): explains the mysteries of flight.
- **Launch Pad** (basement): a range of scientific principles explained in a fun, hands-on environment.

At weekends and holidays access to these areas may be restricted and timed ticketing may operate. If this is the case tickets are allocated at the entrance to each gallery. Pick up a Children's Trail guide from the bookshop.

SCIENCE MUSEUM: INSIDE INFO

Top tips The **Launch Pad** (► For Kids panel, above) is particularly popular. To avoid the worst of the crowds, visit it either early or late in the day.

In more detail The **Science and Art of Medicine** (fifth floor) provides a fascinating and detailed history of medicine. It also looks at how different cultures interpret and treat illnesses. The range of items on display is remarkable, and includes old medical instruments, skulls, costumes, anatomical models and even shrunken heads.

- The **Secret Life of the Home** (in the basement) houses a fun collection illustrating how the everyday household items we take for granted have evolved and operate. There's also a set of household objects that never caught on – visitors are invited to guess their function.

⑤ Natural History Museum

The Natural History Museum has a staggering 69 million specimens, many (but not all) of which are on display. They cover lifeforms and the Earth's building blocks from the most distant past to the modern day. Everything in, under or on the Earth is here, the flora and fauna – from dinosaurs and whales to butterflies, humming birds and human beings – in the Life

Galleries, and the geological material in the Earth Galleries. Displays in both sets of galleries are entertaining and interactive – be warned, you could easily spend a whole day here.

Before you go in, take a look at the museum building, designed in the late 19th century in the style of a cathedral. Measuring some 220 yards (200m), it was the first building in Britain to be entirely faced in terracotta.

The suggested route below will take about two hours; or pick up the free museum plan, which has a useful break-down of the museum's highlights.

The Natural History Museum is home to more than 69 million objects

Life Galleries
The Wonders of the Natural History Museum (Gallery 10). This remarkable gallery is the entrance hall to the Life Galleries and contains a variety of breathtaking exhibits. The 85-foot (26m) long cast of the fossilised skeleton of a Diplodocus dinosaur holds centre stage, but the alcoves around the hall display remarkable items such as the fossilised egg of the Madagascan elephant bird (which is as big as a football). Follow the stairs to the third floor to see the section of a giant sequoia tree from San Francisco (giant

➕ 195 D1   ✉ Cromwell Road, SW7   ☎ 020 7942 5000; Sat–Sun: 020 7942 5011; www.nhm.ac.uk
🕐 Mon–Sat 10–5:50, Sun 11–5:50 (last admission 5:30); closed 24–26 Dec
🍴 Cafés, restaurant, snack bar and fast-food restaurant
🚇 South Kensington   🚌 Near by 14, 49, 70, 74, 345, C1
♿ Free

Dinosaur skeletons are among the largest and most popular of the museum's exhibits. Of the 350,000 items that come to the museum every year, 250,000 are insect specimens

sequoias are the largest living things on the planet) and notice how the dates of major historical events have been marked on the tree's growth rings.

Dinosaurs (Gallery 21). The dramatic and popular displays here examine many aspects of most species of dinosaur, including some of the many theories as to why they became extinct. A raised walkway enables visitors to get close to the exhibits, and the exhibition includes a robotics display of dinosaurs in action.

Special raised walkways bring you face to face with the likes of Tyrannosaurus Rex in the Dinosaur Gallery

Mammals (Galleries 23–24). Some of the material in these galleries consists of stuffed animals behind glass, and has been part of the museum for years. This said, the straightforward displays are almost a relief after the overwhelming variety of exhibits in other galleries: the model of the blue whale (92 feet/28m long), in particular, is a perennial favourite.

Ecology (Gallery 32). This is one of the most visually impressive areas in the museum, with a striking mirrored video display of the Water Cycle, and a walk-in leaf to illustrate just how vital plants are to the life of the planet. It does a good job of explaining often complex ecological issues and the need for responsibility with regard to the environment.

The dramatic entrance to the Earth Galleries

Creepy Crawlies (Gallery 33). In this gallery devoted to bugs and beasties, you'll learn more than you ever wanted to know about insects, spiders, crustaceans and centipedes. It will leave you wondering just what lurks in your home; not for the squeamish.

Earth Galleries

Visions of Earth (Gallery 60). An escalator carries visitors away from the Earth Galleries' impressive entrance hall through a huge hollow earth sculpture into the upper galleries. It's a stunning introduction to this part of the museum, but before you go up examine the displays behind the tiny portholes in the walls: many of the specimens on show here are beautifully shaped and have almost impossibly brilliant colours. Look out, in particular, for the piece of moon rock and the ancient fossils that were once believed to have been the devil's toenail and the weapons of Zeus.

The Power Within (Gallery 61). This highly visual gallery seeks to explain volcanoes and earthquakes; its memorable centrepiece is a mock-up of a supermarket which simulates the 1995 Kobe earthquake in Japan that killed 6,000 people.

Earth's Treasury (Gallery 64). Such is the beauty and variety of the items on show, it takes a while to realise that what is on display is simply specimens of gems, rocks and minerals. Exhibits range from priceless diamonds, emeralds and sapphires to grains of sand: you'll never look at a humble rock in quite the same way again.

TAKING A BREAK

A fossil exhibit

Stop for lunch at either **Emporio Armani Caffè** (➤ 120), on the Brompton Road, or in one of the museum's cafés.

NATURAL HISTORY MUSEUM: INSIDE INFO

Top tips The main museum entrance on Cromwell Road leads into the Life Galleries: during busy periods use the entrance in Exhibition Road which takes you to the Earth Galleries. The two are joined by Gallery 50.

• The museum is **quietest** early or late on weekdays, but all periods during school holidays are busy.

• **Investigate** (Gallery B2) is a special children's discovery area.

7 Kensington Palace

Kensington Palace has been the home of various members of royalty for many centuries, and came to recent public notice when the late Diana, Princess of Wales moved here. This is an attractive and historic palace, well worth a visit for its setting, art treasures, State Rooms, fine furnishings and Royal Ceremonial Dress Collection.

Flowers are still left at the gates of the palace in memory of Diana, Princess of Wales

The mansion began life as a country house in 1605, but was converted into a palace by Sir Christopher Wren for King William III and Queen Mary II following their accession to the throne in 1689 and their decision to move from damp, riverside Whitehall. Later resident monarchs included Queen Anne, George I and George II, while Queen Victoria was born, baptised and grew up in the palace. It was also here that she was woken one morning in June 1837 to be told that her uncle (William IV) had died and that she was Queen. Today, several members of the royal family have private apartments in the palace.

The south front of Kensington Palace was designed in 1695 by Nicholas Hawksmoor

Visits to the palace begin downstairs with the **Royal Ceremonial Dress Collection** and then move upstairs to the **State Apartments**. In the former, you can see the sumptuous clothes that would have been worn by those being presented at

➕ 194 B3 ✉ The Broad Walk, Kensington Gardens, W8
☎ 020 7937 9561; www.kensington-palace.org.uk
🕐 Daily 10–5 (last entry) Mar–Oct; daily 10–4 (last entry) rest of year
🍴 Restaurant in the Orangery

(► 133) serving light meals and snacks, afternoon tea
🚇 High Street Kensington, Queensway, Notting Hill
🚌 9, 10, 12, 27, 28, 33, 49, 52, 52A, 70, 94, 328, C1
💰 Very expensive

court at the turn of the 19th century. For many visitors, the most interesting part of the exhibition are the dresses belonging to the late Diana, Princess of Wales.

Upstairs, the apartments of King William III and (less grand) rooms of his wife, Queen Mary II, have been restored to their 18th-century appearance. Their most impressive corner is the Cupola Room, decorated in the style of ancient Rome with an excess of gilded statues and classical painting: it was here that Queen Victoria's baptism took place in 1819. The room's centrepiece is an 18th-century clock called *The Temple of the Four Grand Monarchies of the World*, whose intricate decoration far outshines the tiny clockface itself.

Top: The King's Gallery displays the palace's finest paintings

Above: The King's Stair-case, with portraits of royal courtiers

The palace has seen its share of tragedy. Mary II succumbed to smallpox here at the age of 32 in 1694, and when Queen Anne's beloved husband, Prince George, died in 1708, she did not return to the palace for many months. Like Mary, she also died here six years later, at 49 years of age, a sad figure who, despite 18 pregnancies, saw none of her children live beyond the age of 11. King George II ended his days here too – while on the lavatory.

TAKING A BREAK

Enjoy a classic English afternoon tea in pleasant surroundings in the **Orangery** (➤ 133).

KENSINGTON PALACE: INSIDE INFO

Top tips **Access to the palace** is from the back of the building, from The Broad Walk in Kensington Gardens.
• There is no official monument here to Diana, Princess of Wales, but in Kensington Gardens is a Memorial Playground and in Hyde Park is a fountain (➤ 130–131).
• Be sure to visit the **Orangery** (➤ 133), built for Queen Anne and now a restaurant, and don't miss the pretty **Sunken Garden**.

At Your Leisure

◻ Chelsea Physic Garden

This small garden is a quiet corner of pretty, rural tranquillity in the heart of the city, with more than 5,000 species of plants growing in attractive profusion. Established in 1673, it was founded by the Royal Society of Apothecaries to study medicinal plants, making it the oldest botanical garden in England after Oxford's. It also retains the country's oldest rockery (1773) and the first cedars in England were planted here in 1683. After green-seeded cotton plants from the West Indies were nurtured in the garden, seed was sent to Georgia in the American colonies in 1732 and contributed to what would later develop into the huge cotton plantations of the South.

🔲 198 A1 ✉ Swan Walk, 66 Royal Hospital Road, SW3 ☎ 020 7352 5646; www.chelseaphysicgarden.co.uk 🕐 Wed noon–5, Sun 2–6, Apr–Oct 🚇 Sloane Square 🚌 239 💷 Moderate

◳ Albert Memorial

This gleaming memorial, is the most florid and exuberant of all London's monumental statues. It was completed in 1872 by Sir George Gilbert Scott, winner of a competition to design a national memorial to Prince Albert of Saxe-Coburg-Gotha (1819–61), Queen Victoria's husband, though it was not unveiled until four years later. Victoria and Albert married in 1840, but Albert died of typhoid aged just 41 years, a blow from which Victoria never quite recovered.

For Kids

- Science Museum (► 121–123)
- Natural History Museum (► 124–126)
- Boating on the Serpentine or feeding the ducks in Kensington Gardens and Hyde Park (► 130–131)
- Harrods' toy department (► 116)

What Albert – who didn't want a memorial – would have made of the neo-Gothic pile is hard to imagine: his spectacularly gilded statue is some three times life size, and the edifice as a whole rises 180 feet (55m), its apex crowned by the figures of Faith, Hope and Charity. The figures around the edges portray subjects such as astronomy, poetry and sculpture, plus enterprises close to Albert's heart such as agriculture, manufacturing and commerce. The 169 sculptures around the statue's base portray figures from history – there's not one woman among them – while those set slightly apart are allegories of the four continents: Europe, Africa, America and Asia.

🔲 195 D2 ✉ South Carriage Drive, Kensington Gardens, SW7 ☎ 020 7495 0916 for guided tours 🚇 High Street Kensington, Knightsbridge 🚌 9, 10, 52

The Albert Memorial, restored to its original gilded glory

Above: Boats on the Serpentine in the rural haven of Hyde Park. Below: Sculpture by Henry Moore in Hyde Park

BAYSWATER ROAD

BAYSWATER ROAD

Italian Gardens

8
Hyde Park

The Long Water

8
Kensington Gardens

Round Pond

Serpentine Bridge

Serpentine Gallery

The Serpentine

Diana, Princess of Wales Memorial Fountain

Albert Memorial
6

Knightsbridge Barracks

KENSINGTON GORE

KENSINGTON RD

8 Hyde Park and Kensington Gardens

Most of the large swathe of green southwest of Marble Arch is Hyde Park, but Kensington Gardens, formerly the grounds of Kensington Palace (▶ 127–128), occupies an area to the west of the Serpentine lake.

Originally a hunting ground for Henry VIII, **Hyde Park** was opened to the public in the early 17th century, and today provides a magnificent and peaceful area in which to escape the city. **Speakers' Corner**, at its north-eastern edge near Marble Arch, is the place to air your views – anyone is entitled to stand up here and (within certain parameters) speak their mind: Sunday afternoons draw the most orators. Further west stretches the **Serpentine**, an artificial lake created in 1730 by Caroline, queen to George II, for boating and bathing. It's now a good a place to while away an hour on the water – rowing boats and pedaloes are available for a fee on the

Above: Hyde Park's Speakers' Corner

northern bank. You can also swim at certain times in a designated area off the south shore. Close by is the **Diana, Princess of Wales Memorial Fountain**, an 88-yard (80m) oval ring of Cornish granite in which water flows at different speeds. The **Serpentine Gallery** shows a changing programme of often controversial modern art throughout the year. Other art in the park includes a variety of statues, most famously that of Peter Pan (1912), which was paid for by the story's author, J M Barrie, who lived near by. It's just off a walkway on the Serpentine's west bank, near the lake's northern limit.

Hyde Park
➕ 195 E3 🕐 Daily 5 am–midnight
🚇 Hyde Park Corner, Knightsbridge, Lancaster Gate, Marble Arch

Kensington Gardens
➕ 194 C3 🕐 Daily 5 am–midnight
🚇 High Street Kensington, Bayswater, Queensway, Lancaster Gate

Serpentine Gallery
➕ 195 D3 ☎ 020 7402 6075
🕐 Daily 10–6 during exhibitions
💷 Free

🄨 Portobello Road Market

Portobello is London's largest market, the long street and its environs hosting a wide variety of food, modern clothing, crafts and junk markets, as well as the specialist small shops and antiques shops (and stalls) that first made it famous. On Saturdays it is the scene of what is reputedly the world's largest antiques market, with more than 1,500 traders, the majority of whom are located at the street's southern end after the intersection with Westbourne Grove. Fruit stalls dominate beyond Elgin Crescent, while junk, second-hand clothes and more off-beat shops and stalls take over beyond the "Westway" elevated section of road.

The range and quality of antiques and other goods is enormous. At the top end prices are as high as any in London, but bargains and one-offs can still be found; it's great fun to browse and people-watch even if you don't want to spend anything.

Note that on fine summer days the market is often extremely crowded (beware of pickpockets).

➕ 194 A4 🕐 General: Mon–Wed 8–7, Thu 8–1, Fri 8–6, Sat 8–7. Antiques: Sat; Clothes/bric-à-brac: Fri, Sat, Sun
🚇 Notting Hill Gate, Ladbroke Grove
🚌 7, 12, 23, 27, 28, 31, 70, 328

A colourful corner of Portobello Road

Where to...
Eat and Drink

Prices
Expect to pay per person for a meal excluding drinks and service

£ up to £25   ££ £25–£50   £££ more than £50

The Ark ££

The clever use of mirrors has given extra depth to the narrow room at this revamped Kensington favourite. The menu includes a mixture of classic, modern and regional Italian dishes. Expect good *al dente* pasta and rustic meat dishes served with polenta. An attractively priced lunch menu has proved immensely popular, and in the evening the menu expands and gains some specials.

➕ 194 B3 ✉ 122 Palace Gardens Terrace, W8 ☎ 020 7229 4024; www.thearkrestaurant.co.uk ⏰ Daily noon–3; 6:30–11 (closed Mon lunch and Sun dinner) Ⓤ Notting Hill Gate

Bibendum ££

Sir Terence Conran opened his flagship restaurant in the acclaimed Michelin building in 1987. It is relaxed and highly professional, and the magnificent dining room is a great setting. The wide range of classic European dishes on the menu are given a modern twist and the depth of the wine list is a real talking point.

➕ Off map 195 E1 ✉ Michelin House, 81 Fulham Road, SW3 ☎ 020 7581 5817; www.conran.com ⏰ Lunch: Mon–Fri noon–2:30, Sat–Sun 12:30–3. Dinner: Mon–Sat 7–11:30, Sun 7–10:30 Ⓤ South Kensington

Bluebird ££

A flower shop, café, high-profile bar, kitchen shop and classy supermarket are all part of the experience at Terence Conran's Bluebird/ Gastrodome. There is a great buzz from the smart restaurant. The menu is simply conceived, with dishes from the crustacea bar, rotisserie, and the large wood-fired brick oven where a wide variety of meats, fish, poultry and vegetables are cooked over different types of wood.

➕ Off map 198 A2 ✉ 350 Kings Road, SW3 ☎ 020 7559 1000; www.conran.com ⏰ Mon–Fri 12:30–3, 6–11, Sat noon–3:30, 6–11, Sun noon–3:30, 6–10 Ⓤ Sloane Square

Cambio de Tercio ££

Acclaimed as one of the best Spanish restaurants outside the Iberian Peninsula, this friendly restaurant serves up exquisite Modern Spanish cooking. Dishes veer from the innovative – Cuba libre of foie (duck liver mousse, coca-cola and rum gelée) lemon snow – to the classic, such as beef *solomillo* (fillet), oxtail or grilled tuna, albeit with a modern twist. Desserts are superb; leave room for the creamy thyme-lemon ice cream. If you want a less expensive or lighter but equally authentic Spanish meal, just cross the road to their tapas bar offshoot, Tendido Cero.

➕ Off map 195 1C ✉ 163 Old Brompton Road, SW3 ☎ 020 7244 8970; www.cambiodetercio.co.uk ⏰ Daily 12:30–2:30, 7:30–11:30 (Sun 11). Tendido de Cero daily noon–11) Ⓤ Gloucester Road, South Kensington

Fifth Floor at Harvey Nichols ££

The Fifth Floor restaurant, on the top floor of the designer-label Harvey Nichols department store (▶ 134), forms part of a food lover's paradise that takes in a food hall, café and bar, even *kaiten zushi* (a conveyor-belt sushi bar). The dining room is chic, the food slick, using British produce in an innovative way. Both the restaurant and bar can become crowded at peak times. Reservations are essential.

🕂 198 A4 ⊠ **Harvey Nichols, Knightsbridge, SW1** ☎ 020 7235 5250; www.harveynichols.com
🕘 Lunch: Mon–Fri noon–3, Sat–Sun noon–3.30. Dinner: Mon–Sat 6–11:30
🚇 Knightsbridge

Gordon Ramsay Restaurant £££

One of the country's most acclaimed chefs, Gordon Ramsay learned his skills in the best kitchens in France, and in London where he worked under Marco Pierre White and Albert Roux. Now installed at the former La Tante Claire (discreetly restyled), Gordon Ramsay enthrals customers with a rich, yet light style of haute cuisine. The best value – and the best way to sample the Ramsay style – is the set three-course lunch. Reserving well in advance is essential.

🕂 198 A1 ⊠ **68–9 Royal Hospital Road, SW3** ☎ 020 7352 4441; www.gordonramsay.com 🕘 Mon–Fri noon–2.50, 6:30–11 🚇 Sloane Square

The Orangery £

The elegant, white, light Orangery provides a pleasant, informal setting for English afternoon tea. Three set teas are offered, the grandest including champagne, or you could just plump for a selection of delicious cakes and a pot of tea. Light lunches are available between noon and 3 pm.

🕂 194 B3 ⊠ **Kensington Palace, Kensington Gardens, W8** ☎ 020 7376 0239 🕘 Daily 10–6, Mar–Oct; 10–5, rest of year 🚇 High Street Kensington

Racine ££

Only in France does it get any more French than in this popular Knightsbridge brasserie just opposite the South Kensington museums. There's an authentic bustle and a rather masculine décor of dark wood and deep brown leather. This is just the place for hearty bourgeois fare such as rabbit in mustard sauce, steak and frites, or perhaps langoustines, and for

dessert, pot au chocolat. Even the simple dishes have big flavours.

🕂 195 1E ⊠ **239 Brompton Road, SW3** ☎ 020 7584 4477 🕘 Mon–Fri noon–3, 6–10:30; Sat noon–3.30, 6–10, Sun noon–3:30 🚇 South Kensington

Zafferano £££

In an understated room, the plain walls, terracotta floor, comfortable chairs and closely set tables all contribute to an air of classy informality. Star chef Giorgio Locatelli established Zafferano as London's leading Italian restaurant and, although he has now gone, the cooking is still excellent. Italian food is presented with an understanding and flair that many more pretentious establishments have difficulty matching. Uncluttered and simply conceived dishes based on the finest ingredients, exact technique and clear flavours are the driving force behind both the lunch and dinner menus. Expect classics with a twist such as osso bucco pasta parcels

with saffron sauce. If you're looking for a romantic setting, book a table in the first room.

🕂 198 B3 ⊠ **15 Lowndes Street, SW1** ☎ 020 7235 5800; fax: 020 7235 1971 🕘 Lunch: daily noon–2:30. Dinner: Mon–Sat 7–11, Sun 7–10:30 🚇 Knightsbridge

Boisdale of Belgravia ££

An astonishing range of 170 single malt whiskies is available at London's premier whisky bar. Furnishings offer the odd spot of tartan to emphasise the Scottish theme. Despite the presence of a cigar bar, this is not in any way a male preserve. Indeed, it's a pleasant place, with an attractive courtyard, a cosy, dark, atmospheric bar, and an adjoining restaurant that specialises in Scottish dishes. Live jazz is performed nightly.

🕂 198 C3 ⊠ **15 Eccleston Street, SW1** ☎ 020 7730 6922 🕘 Mon–Fri noon–1 am, Sat 7 pm–1 am 🚇 Victoria

Where to...
Shop

The streets of Knightsbridge, Kensington and Chelsea provide some of London's most blue-blooded shopping, with the sophisticated coexisting alongside the traditional. Many shops don't open until 10 am, generally closing at 6 pm (some later). On a Sunday this becomes noon to 5 pm in most instances. Late-night shopping in this neighbourhood is Wednesday (Kensington High Street, Thursday) with shops generally adding an extra hour on to their usual closing times.

KNIGHTSBRIDGE

Harvey Nichols (109–25 Knightsbridge, SW1, tel: 020 7235 5000; www.harveynichols.com. Tube: Knightsbridge). Fashion addicts can indulge themselves on three floors of designer womenswear, two floors of menswear and a ground floor given over to up-to-the-minute accessories such as Wolford hosiery, Dolce e Gabbana sunglasses and all manner of scarves, perfumes and cosmetics. Minimalist surroundings house an industrial steel-and-glass fifth-floor food emporium consisting of an opulent food hall, a sushi bar, a café, a bar and a restaurant.

Harrods, probably London's best-known department store, is a must on most tourist itineraries (▶116). The store is renowned for food but is also known for fashion.

SLOANE STREET

Sloane Street, bounded at its northern end by Knightsbridge Underground station and on its southern end by Sloane Square, is a serious showcase for international designers. Italy is represented by the romantic designs of **Alberta Ferretti** (205–6 Sloane Street, SW1, tel: 020 7235 2349. Tube: Knightsbridge) – gauzes and shimmering silks in a chandeliered setting; by that master of understated neutrality, **Armani** (37 Sloane Street, SW1, tel: 020 7235 6232. Tube: Knightsbridge); and by the funky uniformity of **Prada** (43–5 Sloane Street, SW1, tel: 020 7235 0008. Tube: Knightsbridge). Just around the corner, **Agent Provocateur** (16 Pont Street, SW1, tel: 020 7235 0229. Tube: Knightsbridge) sells top-quality saucy lingerie.

If all the choice of high fashion sends you into a wardrobe (or wallet) crisis, slip into the old-established stationery sanctuary of **Smythson's** (135 Sloane Street, SW1, tel: 020 7730 5520. Tube: Sloane Square) to scoop up leather-bound diaries and notebooks, bags and wallets, plus perfect engraved paper and envelopes at reasonable prices, given its exclusive location.

KENSINGTON HIGH STREET AND KENSINGTON CHURCH STREET

Kensington High Street might be less slick, but it is very long and has lots of useful shops clustered around the High Street Kensington Underground station, including a major branch of Marks & Spencer and the department store Barkers.

Running north, opposite Barkers, is Kensington Church Street (Tube: Kensington High Street), an antique lover's dream, with a fabulous concentration of dealers. Works by important 19th- and early 20th-century designers such as William Morris and Pugin are for sale at **Haslam & Whiteway** (105 Kensington Church Street, W8, tel: 020 7229 1145). Early English ceramics including Staffordshire figures and early Wedgwood pieces are available at **Jonathan Horne** (66c Kensington Church Street, W8, tel: 020 7221 5658), and Cornish ware, Midwinter and Poole potteries are the speciality at **Richard Dennis**

(144 Kensington Church Street, W8, tel: 020 7727 2061, open by appointment only). Both dealers can organise shipping, as can **John Jesse** (160 Kensington Church Street, W8, tel: 020 7229 0312), who stocks 20th-century design including art nouveau prints. Wherever you buy, don't forget to thoroughly inspect the goods, haggle (it is expected) and request a receipt with an accurate description of the item.

SOUTH KENSINGTON

Individual shops at the **Natural History Museum** (▶ 124–126), the **Science Museum** (▶ 121–123) and the **Victoria and Albert Museum** (▶ 117–120) stock all the educational lines that you might expect: pocket-money toys, dinosaurs and pretty minerals at the Natural History Museum; rockets and robots at the Science Museum. The museum shops, however, are also a good hunting ground for top-quality gifts for discerning grown-ups. The **Victoria and Albert Museum shop** is a real Aladdin's cave. A Crafts Council section sells contemporary works by British artists – one-off gifts and future collectables – while the main, attractively laid-out section is filled with clever reproductions of 18th-century ceramics, antique dolls and teddy bears, a vast selection of William Morris memorabilia and lavish coffee-table art books. At the Science Museum, adults will find an unusual range of gadgetry and scientific instruments.

KING'S ROAD

The young and young at heart flock to this Chelsea thoroughfare for its boutiques and other interesting shops. A promenade can start at Sloane Square (Tube: Sloane Square) and take in the entire length of the long road, or just a fraction; either way there is a crop of coffee bars, from the chains such as Costa Coffee, Coffee Republic and Starbucks to independent cafés, at which to fuel your progress.

Peter Jones department store (Sloane Square, SW1, tel: 020 7730 3434) is in Sloane Square itself. Whistles, Kookai, Warehouse, Oasis and Next begin a roll-call of mid-price fashion names as you begin to wander down the King's Road. Further along, the vintage clothes shop **Steinberg & Tolkien** (193 King's Road, SW3, tel: 020 7376 3660) has a dazzling array of garments from past decades, including original Pucci shirts, 1970s kaftans and cases of old jewellery and wacky accessories. Teenagers love dressing up at **Ad Hoc** (153 King's Road, SW3, tel 020 7376 8829) full of hats, costume jewellery, wigs, fancy hosiery and all sorts of highly unsuitable garments! Downwind of **Lush** (123 King's Road, SW3, tel: 020 7376 8348), you can smell in advance the fragrant natural cosmetics before you see them: soaps sliced from huge blocks to order; fizzing bath bombs and gooey hand-mixed face packs, plus fun packaging and labelling.

A branch of **Heal's** (234 King's Road, SW3, tel: 020 7349 8411) has nice things for the home, from furniture to photo frames, as does the fashionable **Designers' Guild** (267–71 & 275–7 King's Road, SW3, tel: 020 7351 5775) towards the Worlds End of the King's Road (Tube: West Brompton or Earls Court). Food fans might enjoy trekking this far along to discover the **Bluebird Gastrodome** (▶ 132) with its café, bar, restaurant and food and flower market. Check out the bakery's lovely fresh breads such as rosemary or spinach, the delicatessen counters and unusual dry goods. Opposite, the sweet-toothed can indulge at **Rococo** chocolates (321 King's Road, SW3, tel: 020 7352 5857) with its bars of dark and milk artisan chocolate flavoured with ingredients like Earl Grey tea, chilli pepper, nutmeg, cardamom and wild mint leaves.

Where to...
Be Entertained

This is a cosmopolitan, well-heeled part of the city, with plenty of entertainment choices. Although it's an expensive area, there are many reasonably priced venues.

CINEMA

Commercial choice is divided between the **two multi-screen UGC cinemas**, showing recent releases (279 King's Road, SW3 and 142 Fulham Road, SW10, both tel: 0871 200 2000. Tube: Earl's Court). **The Chelsea Cinema** (206 King's Road, SW3, tel: 020 7351 3742. Tube: Earl's Court) shows similar films, with the bonus of the most comfortable cinema seats in town. It also has a small bar. At the **Gate Cinema** (Notting Hill Gate, W11,

tel: 020 7727 4043. Tube: Notting Hill Gate) both trendy art-house films and mainstream blockbusters are screened.

CLASSICAL MUSIC

The **Proms**, as the Henry Wood Promenade Concerts are known, is one of the world's greatest music festivals. Concerts are held nightly at the **Royal Albert Hall** (Kensington Gore, tel: 020 7589 8212. Tube: South Kensington) for a seven-week period every summer, beginning the third Friday in July. Visiting international orchestras, soloists and conductors join the BBC Symphony Orchestra to perform a wide-ranging selection of music. If you are prepared to wait, you can buy inexpensive standing

only tickets. Those with less stamina (but deeper pockets) can choose from a range of more expensive seats.

NIGHTLIFE

Night-clubs are not found in abundance in this part of the city. Try **Bar Cuba** (11 Kensington High Street, W8, tel: 020 7938 4137. Tube: Kensington High Street), a chic place with a smart clientele. It offers a broad spectrum of Latin music, with occasional live bands.

If you like jazz, try the **606 Club** (90 Lots Road, SW10, tel: 020 7352 5953. Tube: Earl's Court), where groups such as the bluesy modern jazz Julian Siegel Quartet play. It is open to non-members. At the sophisticated **Pizza on the Park** (11–13 Knightsbridge, SW1, tel: 020 7235 5273. Tube: Hyde Park Corner), you can listen to live music. Jazz greats such as veteran George Melly have performed in the basement room.

THEATRE

Whether shocking, disturbing or just plain brilliant, the **Royal Court** (Sloane Square, SW1, tel: 020 7565 5000. Tube: Sloane Square), home of the English Stage Company, has nurtured some of Britain's best modern playwrights, and is the place to see modern theatre at its very best. A multi-million pound refurbishment has uplifted the experience for theatregoers, replacing cramped conditions in the two theatres with state-of-the-art facilities.

The **Holland Park Theatre** (Holland Park W8, tel: 020 7602 7856. Tube: Holland Park) is a popular open-air venue that operates only in the summer months. With the ruins of the 17th-century Holland House as a backdrop, and occasional accompaniment from the peacocks wandering freely through the park, the theatre plays host to the Royal Ballet as well as offering a well-regarded opera season.

Covent Garden, Bloomsbury and Soho

Getting Your Bearings

Exploration of these districts underlines London's amazing variety: within the space of a few streets an area's character can change from classy to run down, from retail to residential, and from busy and exciting to genteel and refined.

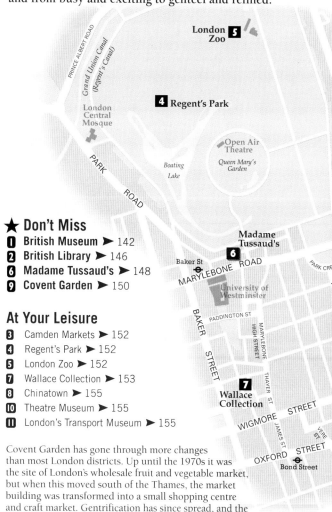

★ Don't Miss

At Your Leisure

Covent Garden has gone through more changes than most London districts. Up until the 1970s it was the site of London's wholesale fruit and vegetable market, but when this moved south of the Thames, the market building was transformed into a small shopping centre and craft market. Gentrification has since spread, and the market and surrounding area have become a vibrant shopping and entertainment district full of shops, market stalls, fun museums, bars, cafés and restaurants.

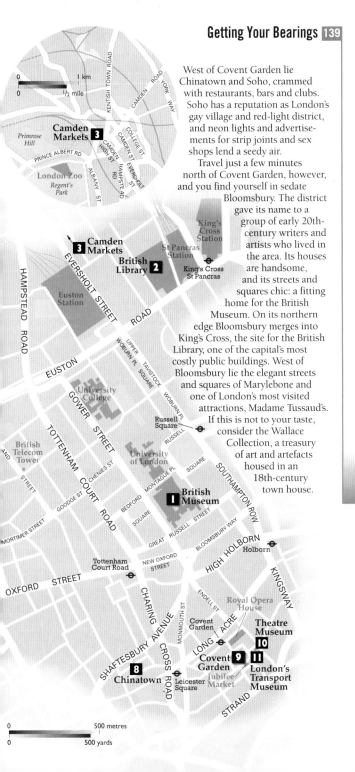

West of Covent Garden lie Chinatown and Soho, crammed with restaurants, bars and clubs. Soho has a reputation as London's gay village and red-light district, and neon lights and advertisements for strip joints and sex shops lend a seedy air.

Travel just a few minutes north of Covent Garden, however, and you find yourself in sedate Bloomsbury. The district gave its name to a group of early 20th-century writers and artists who lived in the area. Its houses are handsome, and its streets and squares chic: a fitting home for the British Museum. On its northern edge Bloomsbury merges into King's Cross, the site for the British Library, one of the capital's most costly public buildings. West of Bloomsbury lie the elegant streets and squares of Marylebone and one of London's most visited attractions, Madame Tussaud's. If this is not to your taste, consider the Wallace Collection, a treasury of art and artefacts housed in an 18th-century town house.

A variety of tempting cultural experiences awaits in a day that takes in the ancient treasures of the British Museum, the priceless books and manuscripts of the British Library, and the waxwork models of the rich, famous and notorious in Madame Tussaud's.

Covent Garden, Bloomsbury and Soho in a Day

9:00 am

Arrive at the ❶ **British Museum** (➤ 142–145) for when the Great Court opens at 9 am. Spend some time admiring this splendid new concourse, before exploring the museum itself, full of beautiful pieces from bygone civilisations (Elgin Marbles, left).

12:00 noon

Take lunch in one of the many cafés and pubs near the museum or bring along a picnic to eat in leafy Russell Square.

1:00 pm

From Russell Square catch a No 91 bus or take a 30-minute walk through Bloomsbury to the **2 British Library** (➤ 146–147). Look at the outside of the building from the spacious piazza (below left) then admire some of the world's loveliest old books and manuscripts. Stop for a coffee in the café here.

2:30 pm

The No 30 bus takes you along Euston Road to Marylebone Road and **6 Madame Tussaud's** (➤ 148–149). The wax-works are popular year-round and you will probably have a long wait to get in, so try to buy your ticket in advance.

4:30 pm

Take the Underground from Baker Street to **9 Covent Garden** (above, ➤ 150–151). The market, shops, street entertainers and the area's great choice of restaurants, pubs and bars make this a lively place to spend the early evening. It's a short walk from here to many West End theatres (➤ 160).

◼British Museum

The British Museum houses one of the world's foremost collections, containing a wealth of antiquities illuminating the history of civilizations and cultures from across the globe. Founded in 1753 around the private collection of Sir Hans Sloane, it now possesses more than 6 million artefacts arranged in a magnificent building with several miles of galleries. The exhibits on display include ancient sculpture, sublime paintings, exquisite jewellery and a host of other treasures.

The colonnaded main building of the British Museum was built in 1844 to replace the earlier Montagu House, which had become too small to house the museum's growing collection

The British Museum is vast, with more than enough beautiful exhibits to sustain several lengthy visits, so for those with only a short amount of time, the key to surviving and enjoying the museum is not to try to see it all in one visit. Be ruthlessly selective and try not to get too distracted *en route*.

Start by visiting the **(Queen Elizabeth II) Great Court.** This spectacular new concourse area, created by glassing over the museum's central courtyard, is part of an on-going programme of redevelopment. At its heart lies the beautiful 19th-century Reading Room,

✚ 197 F3 ✉ Great Russell Street, WC1 ☎ 020 7323 8000; www.thebritish-museum.ac.uk 🕐 Main galleries: daily 10–5:30, Thu–Fri some galleries open late until 8:30. Great Court: Mon–Wed 9–9, Thu–Sat 9 am–11 pm, Sun 9–6; closed 1 Jan, Good Fri, 24–26 Dec 🍴 Cafés and restaurants 🚇 Holborn, Tottenham Court Road, Russell Square 🚌 Tottenham Court Road, northbound, and Gower Street, southbound 10, 24, 29, 73, 134; Southampton Row 68, 91, 188; New Oxford Street 7, 8, 9, 22b, 25, 38, 55,188 ✋ Free

Right: The Egyptian Sculpture Gallery is home to statues, sarcophagi and the Rosetta Stone, one of the most important artefacts in the British Museum

Below: The Great Court, the largest covered square in Europe

which formerly housed the British Library (► 146–147) but is now open to the general public. Marx, Lenin, George Bernard Shaw and hundreds of other luminaries studied here. The Great Court serves as the museum's central information area: pick up a museum plan before starting your exploration of the galleries.

The **Eygptian galleries,** which house one of the best collections of Egyptian antiquities outside Egypt, are among the museum's highlights. Funerary art and artefacts dominate, with exquisitely decorated coffins, mummies, sarcophagi, jewellery, models and scrolls. The gilded inner coffin of Henutmehyt (c1290 BC) is particularly impressive. Also look for the case containing "Ginger", the 5,000-year-old mummified body of an Egyptian man, whose leathery remains always draw a crowd. He still has a few tufts of red hair, but is missing his left index finger (it was "collected" by an early visitor to the museum).

The most important exhibit in these galleries, and perhaps the entire museum, is the **Rosetta Stone** (196 BC). Its significance lies in the three languages of its inscriptions: Greek at the bottom, Egyptian hieroglyphs at the top, a cursive form of the Egyptian between the two. Discovered accidentally in 1799, the stone enabled Egyptian hieroglyphs to be deciphered for the first time, allowing much of Egyptian civilisation to be

Suggested Route
Follow this route to cover some of the museum's highlights with minimum fuss.

Ground floor:
Room 4 Egyptian Sculpture Gallery
Rooms 6–10 Assyrian Galleries
Room 18 The Sculptures of the Parthenon

First floor:
Room 41 Early Medieval (Sutton Hoo)
Room 49 Weston Gallery of Roman Britain (Mildenhall Treasure)
Rooms 61–66 Egyptian Galleries

understood. Less important, but more more visually arresting, is the huge granite **head of Rameses II**, which towers over the gallery: it was carved for the ruler's memorial temple in Thebes in the 13th century BC.

The museum's most controversial sculptures are the **Elgin Marbles**, named after Lord Elgin, a British diplomat who brought them to England in 1816. Most are taken from a 5th-century BC frieze removed from the Parthenon, the most important temple in ancient Athens, and probably depict a festival in honour of Athena, the city's patron goddess. Modern Greece believes the Marbles should be returned, claiming it is wrong that a foreign museum should possess such important national cultural relics.

The Assyrians, who lived in what is now northern Iraq, are represented in the museum by, among other things, the entrance of **Khorsabad, Palace of Sargon** (721–705 BC), a glorious example of the massive carvings of winged bulls with human heads that guarded their palaces. Equally beguiling are the reliefs of King Ashurbanipal, the last great Assyrian king; they depict a lion hunt, and once adorned his palace in Ninevah.

British artefacts are also celebrated. The 7th-century Anglo-Saxon **Sutton Hoo Ship Burial exhibits** – weapons and

An imposing reconstruction of the Nereid monument from Xanthos in the southwest of present-day Turkey

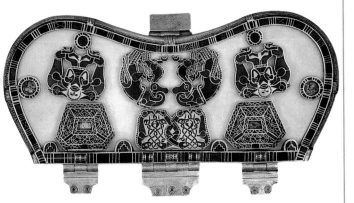

Above: A purse lid, one of the Sutton Hoo Ship Burial exhibits, displays fine Anglo-Saxon craftsmanship

helmets in particular – provide a valuable insight into the Dark Ages, a period of British and European history about which relatively little is known. The treasures were found in 1939 during excavations of ancient burial mounds close to the River Deben near the town of Woodbridge in Suffolk, a site which, before the construction of sea walls, lay just 200 yards (185m) from the high-water level. The **Mildenhall Treasure**, an important collection of 4th-century Roman silverware, was found at Mildenhall, in Suffolk, just a few years later. Some mystery still surrounds the discovery of the treasure, which was not immediately declared to the authorities. Its centrepiece is the 18-pound (8kg) Great Dish, decorated with images of Neptune, the sea god, with a beard of seaweed and dolphins leaping from his hair.

TAKING A BREAK

The **Coffee Gallery** (23 Museum Street, WC1, tel: 020 7436 0455) is a good place to stop for a light lunch.

BRITISH MUSEUM: INSIDE INFO

Top tips The museum has two entrances: the main one on Great Russell Street and a quieter one on **Montague Place**.

• Video and still photography is generally allowed.

• **Guided tours** of the museum's highlights (60 and 90 mins; charge) or individual galleries (50 mins; free) are available. For further information, or to sign up, ask at information points in the Great Court. Audio-guides are also available.

In more detail The **Mexican Gallery (Room 27)** contains several impressive displays, the loveliest of which are the turquoise mosaic statues from the Mixtec–Aztec era (1400–1521).

• If you have time, admire the craftsmanship of the gold and silver **Oxus Treasure (Room 51)**, a collection of Persian artefacts dating from the 5th or 4th century BC.

One to miss The famous **Portland Vase**, a piece of Roman blown glass, is actually rather small and unimpressive. Repairs carried out after it was smashed into a couple of hundred pieces by a drunken visitor in 1845 are all too clearly visible.

② British Library

The British Library ranks alongside the National Library of Congress in Washington and the Bibliothèque Nationale in Paris as one of the three greatest libraries in the world. Its contents include some of the world's most incredible printed treasures. Exhibits span almost three millennia, from the Buddhist Diamond Sutra of AD 868, the world's oldest printed book, up to the modern manuscripts of Paul McCartney and John Lennon. Along the way they take in Shakespeare's First Folio, the Gutenberg Bible, the Magna Carta and the notebooks of Leonardo da Vinci.

The purpose-built, modern library buildings, grouped around an attractive central plaza, provide an airy, attractive, user-friendly space in which to enjoy the collection.

The **John Ritblat Gallery: Treasures of the British Library** contains the library's most valuable items, including maps, religious texts, letters and literary and musical manuscripts. The gallery is remarkable for the fame, age, breadth and quality of its collection. The light is kept low to protect the material and the atmosphere is almost hallowed – as indeed it should be in the presence of the Lindisfarne Gospels and Bedford Hours, two of the loveliest early English illuminated manuscripts. Among the other treasures on display are original manuscripts by Jane Austen and Charlotte Brontë, scores by Mozart and Handel, including that of the *Messiah*, letters from Gandhi, and Lord Nelson's last (unfinished) love letter to Lady Hamilton.

The binding of the Lindisfarne Gospels (*c* AD **698**)

For an interactive experience head for **Turning the Pages**, a unique computer-based system (just off the John Ritblat Gallery) that allows visitors to "browse" through some of the treasures a page at a time.

✠ 197 F5 ✉ 96 Euston Road, NW1 ☎ 020 7412 7332; www.bl.uk
🕐 Mon–Fri 9:30–6 (also Tue 6–8), Sat 9:30–5, Sun and public holidays 11–5
🍴 Restaurant, coffee shop and café Ⓢ King's Cross
🚌 10, 30, 73, 91 Free

The library's two other galleries offer a more practical look at books. The **Pearson Gallery** interprets and enlivens the library's great collections and is the location for special exhibitions. The **Workshop of Words, Sounds and Images** investigates the technology of book production, printing and sound recording. It offers an interactive, computer-based chance to design a book page – there are demonstrations of calligraphy, book-making and printing on Saturdays.

TAKING A BREAK

Visit the library's café or restaurant (▶ Inside Info, below). Alternatively, try **Patisserie Deux Amis** (63 Judd Street, WC1, tel: 020 7383 7029), a simple café serving filled baguettes and delicious cakes.

Edouard Paolozzi's statue of Newton (1995) in the British Library's piazza depicts him measuring the universe with a pair of dividers

---

VITAL STATISTICS

❑ The library basement is equivalent to over five storeys and holds 500 miles (300km) of shelving.

❑ Some 12 million books are stored in the basement, but the library's total collection numbers more than 150 million items.

❑ The library receives a free copy of every book, comic, newspaper, map and magazine published in the United Kingdom. This means it receives an average of 3 million items annually.

❑ The library building was mooted in the 1950s, but opened only in 1998, by which time it had cost three times its original budget.

BRITISH LIBRARY: INSIDE INFO

Top tips Visit the **café or restaurant**, as you can enjoy some of the best views of the central glass tower that houses the 65,000 leather-bound volumes of King George III's library from here.

In more detail Guided tours provide an introduction to the history and workings of the library (1 hour, moderate charge, Monday, Wednesday and Friday at 3 pm, Saturday 10:30 am and 3 pm. Tours on Sunday at 11:30 am and 3 pm include a visit to one of the reading rooms. For reservations tel: 020 7412 7639.

6 Madame Tussaud's

One of London's most popular tourist attractions, Madame Tussaud's offers you the chance to meet James Bond, see how tall actor Arnold Schwarzenegger really is and have your photograph taken with boxing legend Mohammad Ali – or at least waxwork models of these and more than 400 other famous people. A visit provides a fun-packed couple of hours' entertainment for adults and children alike.

Film actor Brad Pitt is one of the many A-list stars you can see

The displays proper start with **Blush** where you are in with the A-list. You can give Brad Pitt a squeeze or make J-Lo blush (you'll have to visit to find out how!) and you may even be interviewed on Madame T's TV.

Next comes the glitz of **Premiere Night** with a lavish production of screen stars past and present.

Upstairs on the **World Stage** there are models of religious leaders, members of the Royal Family, politicians and world leaders as well as figures from the arts including Picasso, Beethoven and The Beatles.

From here you plunge into the **Chamber of Horrors**, the most ghoulish section (unsuitable for children under 12). Torture, execution and murder are dealt with, together with lots of

The green copper dome of Madame Tussaud's Auditorium	✚ 196 B4 ✉ Marylebone Road, NW1 ☎ 0870 400 3000; www.madame-tussauds.com 🕐 Daily 10–5:30; closed 25 Dec 🍴 Café Tussaud's for snacks, but a	better choice in Baker Street near by 🚇 Baker Street 🚌 13, 18, 27, 30, 74, 82, 113, 139, 159, 274 💷 Expensive

gruesome sound effects, the subject matter, portrayed in graphic detail with live actors to add to the fear factor. There is an additional charge for this area.

More wholesome family entertainment is provided by the **Spider-Man** exhibition, where your task is to capture him on camera. In the **Spirit of London** section, you can take a ride through colourful tableaux of 400 years of London's history.

The stars of the **Auditorium**, formerly known as the London Planetarium, are of the astronomical variety. Projected onto the domed ceiling, they take viewers on a dramatic journey across the universe. Entrance to the Auditorium is included in the entry fee to Madame Tussaud's.

TAKING A BREAK

Try the dim sum at the hugely popular **Royal China** (40 Baker Street, W1, tel: 020 7487 4688).

As if it were yesterday – John, Paul, George and Ringo, as they appeared at the start of their career

MADAME TUSSAUD'S: INSIDE INFO

Top tips The exhibition is hugely popular and you may have to wait up to two hours during peak season to get in. To avoid the wait, **book tickets by credit card**, which allows you to enter by the ticket holders' entrance. There is a small booking fee for tickets bought in this way.

• The exhibition space opens half an hour earlier in **school holidays** (ring for details), but avoid visiting at this time, if possible. The exhibition is quieter later in the afternoon: if you arrive by 4 pm you'll still have time to see everything.

9 Covent Garden

When London's wholesale fruit and vegetable market moved out of Covent Garden in the 1970s the scene was set for its

transformation into one of the city's most lively, entertaining and popular districts. Weekends are best for exploring the superb shopping, market and entertainment area, with plenty of excellent bars, cafés and restaurants. There are some excellent museums, top London theatres and the world-renowned Royal Opera House.

The district's heart is the Piazza, the square surrounding the restored 19th-century market building that now houses small shops and the crafts stalls of the Apple Market. Close by is the revamped Royal Opera House and the indoor Jubilee Market (clothes, crafts and leather goods), while the Theatre Museum (➤ 155) and London's Transport Museum (➤ 155) will provide a good couple of hours' diversion.

One of the Piazza's highlights is the variety of street entertainers who congregate here, embracing everything from Chinese orchestras and South American pan pipe musicians to acrobats, mime artists and didgeridoo players. They generate much of the buzz and atmosphere of the place. The many small streets, especially Neal Street and the area north of the Covent Garden Underground station, are also worth exploring for their individual and unusual shops (➤ 159) and tucked-away cafés, bars and restaurants.

Acrobats in Covent Garden

Right: Fruit and vegetables in Covent Garden have given way to a wide variety of cafés, bars and craft vendors

✛ 200 B3 🚇 Covent Garden 🚌 Along Strand 6, 9, 11, 13, 15, 23, 77A, 91, 176

COVENT GARDEN: INSIDE INFO

Top tips Don't leave Covent Garden without wandering down **Neal Street**. Interesting shops here include **The Kite Store** (48 Neal Street, WC2, tel: 020 1666 6252), which also sells rockets and frisbees, and **The Tea House** (15 Neal Street, WC2, tel: 020 7240 7539), selling a huge range of teas and tea pots.
• Don't miss **Neal's Yard Remedies** (15 Neal's Yard, WC2, tel: 020 7379 7222), where you can buy herbal remedies, top-quality oils and toiletries. The shop also has a good selection of books on herbal and alternative medicine.
• For delicious English cheeses, try **Neal's Yard Dairy** (17 Shorts Gardens, WC2, tel: 020 7240 5700). Or stop at **Monmouth Coffee Company** (➤ 157), for one of the best cups of coffee in London.

Hidden gem Take time to go inside **St Paul's Church**, which dominates the western side of the Piazza, and pause in the delightful garden. It is known as the Actor's Church because of the many memorials of film and stage actors it holds.

At Your Leisure

3 Camden Markets

This conglomeration of markets, spreading out from Camden Lock along Chalk Farm Road and Camden High Street, draws many visitors to Camden Town. Sunday, when all the markets are open, is the best day to visit, though individual markets listed below are open on other days. The whole area is usually extremely crowded, especially in the summer. The market is particularly good for modern clothing, jewellery and crafts.

➕ Off map 197 E5

Camden Lock

Renovated warehouses beside the canal are packed solid with stalls selling arts, crafts, old and new clothing, and CDs, plus food and drink.

🕐 Tue–Sun 10–6

Camden Canal Market

This market is located to the north of the canal between Chalk Farm Road and Castle Haven Road. The entrance is small, but the place is packed with

collectable items such as books and clothes – even bicycles.

🕐 Sat–Sun 10–6

Stables Market

This is the most northerly of the markets (off Chalk Farm Road). It sells pretty much the same range of items as Camden Lock but with some furniture and antiques as well.

🕐 Sat–Sun 8–6; Mon–Fri 9–5, reduced number of stalls

Electric Market

Selling second-hand clothes, plus some new items, this market has an emphasis on the weird and way out.

✉ Camden High Street, just north of Camden Town Underground
🕐 Sun 9–5:30

Camden Market

Look here for old and new clothing, jewellery and audio cassettes.

✉ Camden High Street 🕐 Thu–Sun 9–5:30

4 Regent's Park

Regent's Park ranks alongside St James's Park as one of central London's loveliest green spaces (➤ 14). Fringed by the glorious Regency architecture of John Nash, it is loved by locals and visitors alike for its rose garden, its open-air theatre, boating lake and London Zoo (➤ 153).

An oft-overlooked park attraction is a trip on the Regent's Canal. Built in 1820, it runs for 8 miles (13km) between chic Little Venice in west London to Limehouse in the Docklands, where it eventually joins the Thames. Little Venice is a particularly attractive enclave; the stretch of canal that runs through it is dotted with decorated houseboats awash with potted plants and flowers in summer.

Regent's Canal, a peaceful backwater

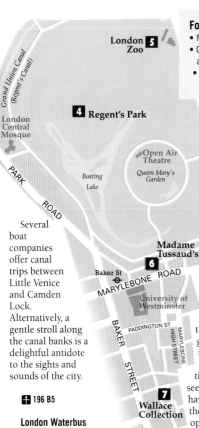

For Kids
- Madame Tussaud's (► 148–149)
- Covent Garden street entertainers and puppet show (► 150–151)
- London Zoo (► 153)

London Zoo 5

Regent's Park 4

Open Air Theatre
Queen Mary's Garden

Boating Lake

London Central Mosque

PARK ROAD

Madame Tussaud's 6

Baker St

MARYLEBONE ROAD

University of Westminster

BAKER STREET

PADDINGTON ST

MARYLEBONE HIGH STREET

Wallace Collection 7

Grand Union Canal (Regent's Canal)

Several boat companies offer canal trips between Little Venice and Camden Lock. Alternatively, a gentle stroll along the canal banks is a delightful antidote to the sights and sounds of the city.

➕ 196 B5

London Waterbus Company
☎ 020 7482 2660 🕐 Daily 10–5, Apr–Sep. Hourly departures.

Jason's Trip
☎ 020 7286 3428 🕐 Three times daily Apr–Oct

Walkers Quay (*Jenny Wren*)
Sightseeing trips from Camden Town to Little Venice and return (90 min)
☎ 020 7485 4433 🕐 Daily Mar–Oct (2 trips per day, 4 trips at weekends and during school holidays)

5 London Zoo

Opened in 1828 as the world's first institution dedicated to the scientific study of animals, London Zoo was once the most fashionable place to be

seen in the capital and in its heyday in the 1950s attracted more than 3 million visitors per year. Today conservation and study take preference over public display and changing fashions mean that the zoo is a much quieter place. Nonetheless, it is still a very popular and important visitor attraction offering the chance to see around 5,000 animals from 650 species, many of which are endangered in the wild. Plan your tour around the daily events and get up close to reptiles, spiders and pelicans or see the keepers interacting with the giraffes and gorillas. Aside from these creatures, visitor favourites are the big cats – Asian lions, tigers and leopards. If you want to see elephants and rhinos you will have to travel 30 miles (50km) up the motorway to the zoo's sister operation at Whipsnade where they enjoy more space.

➕ 196 B5 ✉ Regent's Park, NW1
☎ 020 7722 3333;
www.londonzoo.co.uk 🕐 Daily 10–5:30, Mar to late Oct; 10–4:30, Feb and late Oct; 10–4, rest of year
💷 Very expensive

7 Wallace Collection

This remarkable collection of *objets d'art* is made all the more alluring by its setting, Manchester House, a beautiful 18th-century mansion acquired in 1797 by the 2nd Marquess of Hertford. Its collection of artefacts was bequeathed to the nation on condition it should never be sold, loaned or removed from central London.

Every room is filled with treasures, though most people's favourite is

Room 22, where a wonderful collection of works by Titian, Rubens, Murillo, Van Dyck and others is on display. The collection's best-known work, Frans Hals's *The Laughing Cavalier*, is also here. The portrait of an unknown young man was painted in 1624. While obviously a figure of substance, the man in question is neither laughing nor a cavalier: the title was coined in 1888 when the picture was lent to the Royal Academy Old Masters Exhibition. Near by is

Hertford House provides an elegant backdrop to the Wallace Collection's many *objets d'art*

another portrait of an unknown sitter, Velázquez's *Lady With A Fan*.

The collection's sheer variety is its principal charm, providing the opportunity to admire things you might normally overlook, be it Sèvres porcelain, fine furniture, detailed miniatures or 18th-century paintings. The displays of armour are some of the best in the country outside the Tower of London.

➕ 196 B3 ✉ Hertford House, Manchester Square, W1 ☎ 020 7563 9500; www.wallacecollection.org
🕐 Daily 10–5, closed 24–26 Dec
🍴 Courtyard restaurant 🚇 Bond Street
🚌 2, 10, 12, 13, 30, 74, 82, 94, 113, 137, 274 🎫 Free

Left: Gerrard Street, at the heart of London's Chinatown, is crammed with restaurants

8 Chinatown

The few blocks around Gerrard Street provide a magnet for London's 60,000-strong Chinese community. Many live elsewhere, but flock here on Sundays when the area is most lively. The streets are full of Chinese signs, restaurants (► 156), grocers and bookshops. Even the telephone booths resemble pagodas.

197 F2 Around Gerrard Street, W1 Leicester Square 14, 19, 24, 29, 38, 176

10 Theatre Museum

The museum has a wide range of artefacts from some 400 years of British theatre history and is unmissable for anyone who enjoys the performing arts. Younger visitors should enjoy the museum's programme of activities, especially the costume workshops and stage make-up demonstrations. Most of the museum guides are "resting" actors, and use their professional skills to entertain visitors.

The museum's displays embrace every aspect of theatre: Gilbert and Sullivan and the Music Hall (vaudeville), for example, have their own sections, and many theatrical characters are featured, including actors Sir Henry Irving and Ellen Terry and playwright/actor Nöel Coward. Other sections look at the technical aspects of the theatre. Families should visit on Saturdays and Thursday afternoons when Stage Truck offers creative activities designed to engage young (4–12 year old) visitors.

Dramatic props at the Theatre Museum

200 B4 Russell Street, Covent Garden, WC2 020 7943 4700; www.theatremuseum.org Tue–Sun 10–6 (last admission 5:30) Covent Garden Along Strand 6, 9, 11, 13, 15, 23, 77A, 91, 176, RV1 Free

11 London's Transport Museum

This museum portrays the history of London over the last 200 years by looking at the way in which transport has affected the lives of people in the city. It also shows what it takes to shift millions of travellers around the capital daily. Visitors can see how the Underground and bus systems were built and operate and its interactive exhibits include the chance to drive an Underground train simulator. There are also displays illustrating current transport issues, such as the impact of increasing car ownership on the capital's roads. The museum is closed until early 2007 while it undergoes expansion and redevelopment.

200 B3 Covent Garden, WC2 020 7565 7299; www.ltmuseum.co.uk Sat–Thu 10–6, Fri 11–6. Last admission 5:15pm Café Covent Garden Along Strand 6, 9, 11, 13, 15, 23, 77A, 91, 176 Moderate; under 16s free

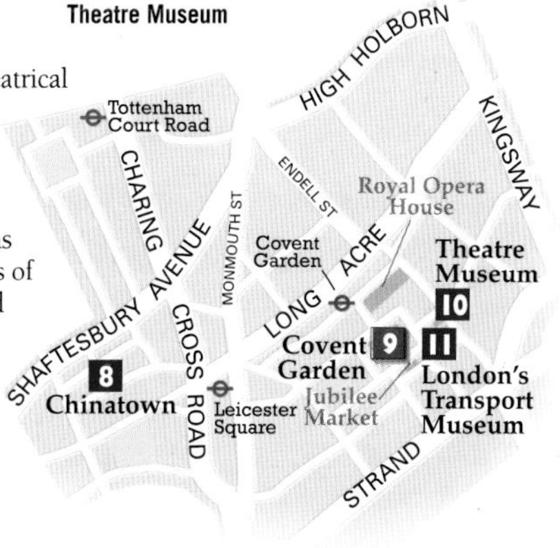

Where to...
Eat and Drink

Prices

Expect to pay per person for a meal excluding drinks and service

£ up to £25   ££ £25–£50   £££ more than £50

Alastair Little Soho ££

Everything about Alastair Little's eponymous restaurant is understated – from the bare aquamarine walls and stripped floorboards, to the casual but informed service and the fresh, deceptively simple food. An Italian influence sits well with the refreshingly seasonal ingredients, the quality of which shines through in every dish. The *prix-fixe* menus (there is no a la carte) are very good value for money.

➕ 197 E2 ⊠ 49 Frith Street, W1
☎ 020 7734 5183 ⏰ Lunch: Mon–Fri noon–3. Dinner: Mon–Sat 6–11
🚇 Leicester Square

Bank ££

An enormous contemporary brasserie, this is one of the most colourful of London's large-scale restaurants, where there's something for everyone at any time of the day. The menu combines classic brasserie favourites with new metropolitan ideas. All dishes are highly enjoyable and of a consistently good standard.

➕ 200 B4 ⊠ 1 Kingsway, WC2
☎ 020 7379 9797;
www.bankrestaurants.com
⏰ Mon–Fri 7:30 am–11:30 am, noon–3, Sat 11:30–3:30, 5:30–11:30, Sun 11:30–5, 5:30–9 🚇 Holborn

Christopher's ££

Set on two floors in a grand Victorian building, this lively restaurant serves some of the best classic American food in London. The steaks, specially imported from the United States, Maine lobsters, tasty grills and Maryland crab cakes are unmissable; portions are ample. Christopher's is popular: reservations are recommended. The café-bar has greater informality and a menu of salads and sandwiches.

➕ 200 B3 ⊠ 18 Wellington Street, WC2 ☎ 020 7240 4222;
www.christophersgrill.com ⏰ Lunch: Mon–Fri noon–3, Sat–Sun 11:30–4 (brunch). Dinner: Mon–Sat 5–midnight am 🚇 Covent Garden

Floridita ££

On the site of Terence Conran's old Mezzo restaurant, Floridita is his latest London venture, bringing the taste, excitement and sassy attitude of Cuba to W1. The food, Cuban and Latin American, is sensational with langosta (crayfish) the signature dish, but Floridita is as much about the cigars (separate cigar bar), the hot rhythms (with bands flown over from Havana), the daiquiris and late-night clubbing, as the dining experience.

➕ 197 E2 ⊠ 100 Wardour Street, W1 ☎ 020 7314 4000;
www.floriditalondon.com
⏰ Mon–Wed 5:30–2, Thu–Sat 5:30–3 🚇 Piccadilly Circus

Fung Shing ££

Chinatown may be wall-to-wall with Chinese restaurants, and Lisle Street in particular a crowded, run-down part of it, but the long-standing Fung Shing remains one of the best places to eat. The high quality, authentic Cantonese food that it serves further distinguishes it from its neighbours. The staff are adept and patient at explaining the menu.

➕ 197 F1 ⊠ 15 Lisle Street, WC2
☎ 020 7437 1539;
www.fungshing.co.uk ⏰ Daily noon–11:30 🚇 Leicester Square

The Ivy ££

The Ivy ranks as one of London's most fashionable eating places, with an almost cult status; regulars return again and again for their favourite dishes. What they enjoy is best described as classic brasserie food. Traditional British ideas are tempered by modern European and oriental additions. More than a dozen wines are available by the glass. Reserve well in advance.

➕ 197 F2 ✉ 1 West Street, Covent Garden, WC2 ☎ 020 7836 4751; www.caprice-holdings.co.uk ◉ Daily noon–3 (also Sun 3–3:30), 5:30–midnight Ⓤ Leicester Square, Covent Garden

J Sheekey ££

One of the oldest and best-known seafood restaurants in the capital, Sheekey's has been around since 1896. Run by the team responsible for such gastronomic temples as The Ivy and Le Caprice, this is the place to go for traditional British

fish dishes. A selection of modern creations add an extra dimension to the menu.

➕ 197 F1 ✉ 28–32 St Martin's Court, WC2 ☎ 020 7240 2565; www.caprice-holdings.co.uk ◉ Daily noon–3 (also Sun 3–3:30), 5:30–midnight Ⓤ Leicester Square

Lindsay House ££

Visitors to this lovely Georgian house have to ring the bell in order to be admitted. The cream colour scheme is enhanced by some stylish modern touches. Owner-chef Richard Corrigan has won great accolades for his cooking. His Celtic roots are still very evident in his gutsy, almost robust style, but his creations also incorporate a delicate touch. His fish dishes in particular are imaginative.

➕ 197 E2 ✉ 21 Romilly Street, W1 ☎ 020 7439 0450; fax: 020 7437 7349 ◉ Lunch: Mon–Fri noon–2.30. Dinner: Mon–Sat 6–10.45. Closed last 2 weeks Aug Ⓤ Leicester Square

Monmouth Coffee Company £

This is one of Soho's best-kept secrets. From the front it is nothing more than a shop selling bags of coffee beans, but at the back are eight tables. It's the perfect place to stop, relax and sample some great coffees and a delectable selection of pastries from the wide-ranging stock.

➕ 197 F2 ✉ 27 Monmouth Street, WC2 ☎ 020 7379 3516 Ⓤ Mon–Sat 8–6:30 Ⓤ Covent Garden

Orrery ££–£££

This is one of the most prestigious restaurants in the Conran group, with just 80 seats, plus a shop and food store. However, the family design traits are all there: arched windows, lots of natural lighting, blond wood; a classy, stylish look. The short menu explores French classics, giving them a modern twist. The food bears many of Conran's trademark Modern European characteristics; raw ingredients especially have a

true freshness and are of the best quality.

➕ 196 B3 ✉ 55–7 Marylebone High Street, W1 ☎ 020 7616 8000; www.conran.com ◉ Lunch: daily noon–2.45. Dinner: Mon–Sat 7–10.45, Sun 7–10:15 Ⓤ Baker Street, Regent's Park

Le Palais du Jardin ££

This large, popular brasserie right at the heart of Covent Garden has a strong Parisian feel, especially with the all-day seafood counter at the front, and the hustle and bustle of waiters traditionally clad in long white aprons. It is the seafood – lobster in particular – that those in the know come here for, but there is also a varied selection of meat dishes. This is a good place for a pre-theatre meal.

➕ 200 A4 ✉ 136 Long Acre, WC2 ☎ 020 7379 5353; fax: 020 7379 1846 ◉ Daily noon–3, 5:30–1 am Ⓤ Covent Garden, Leicester Square

Pâtisserie Valerie £

This cramped but cosy old-fashioned tea room is a Soho institution with shared tables and motherly waitresses. The patisserie is superb (just checkout the window display), but there are also good salads, breakfasts, *Croque Monsieur* and savoury quiches to go.

✚ 197 E2 ⬚ 44 Old Compton Street, W1 ☎ 020 7437 3466; www.patisserie-valerie.co.uk ⬤ Mon–Sat 7:30–8, Sun 9–6 Ⓔ Leicester Square

La Porte des Indes ££

La Porte des Indes is a spectacular Indian restaurant filled with lush, tropical greenery and decked out in rich colours. The kitchen explores the relationship between France and its Indian colonies through such dishes as *beignets d'aubergines* – slices of aubergine (eggplant) filled with cheese and herb pâté. Lunch consists of a spectacular buffet, which offers one of the best-value deals in the area.

✚ 196 A2 ⬚ 32 Bryanston Street, W1 ☎ 020 7224 0055; www.pilondon.net ⬤ Mon–Fri noon–2:30, Mon–Sat 7–11:30, Sun noon–3, 7–10:30 Ⓔ Marble Arch

Quo Vadis ££

This contemporary restaurant is the epitome of London style, where the talents of Marco Pierre White merge: his artworks can be seen on the walls, and his influence as a chef is evident in the kitchen – the menu is a blend of classic and modern Italian, and dishes are often works of art themselves.

and in particular in its fish and seafood. Inside the bold pink exterior are bright silks and richly coloured oil paintings. Try crab *varuthathu* (fresh crabmeat stirfried with coconut, ginger and mustard seeds), accompanied by rice tossed in lemon juice, fresh curry leaves and mustard seeds.

✚ 197 D3 ⬚ 5 Charlotte Street, W1 ☎ 020 7637 0222; www.rasarestaurants.com ⬤ Lunch: noon–3. Dinner: 6–10.45. Closed Sun lunch, two weeks in Dec Ⓔ Tottenham Court Road

Soho Spice £

Remodelled in late 2004, Soho Spice is the exciting fresh new face of Indian dining in the capital. They offer a short menu of around ten starters, ten kebabs and ten curries. The kebabs are the house speciality with unusual but winning choices such as quail, halibut and piccata of lamb. The presentation and style, from furnishings to what arrives on your plate,

maintains the cool, modern approach. Downstairs is a late-night bar with DJ and dance floor.

✚ 197 E2 ⬚ 124–6 Wardour Street, W1 ☎ 020 7434 0808; www.sohospice.co.uk ⬤ Mon–Thu 11:30 am–12:30 am, Fri–Sat 11:30 am–3 am, Sun 11:30–10:30 Ⓔ Piccadilly Circus

Vasco & Piero's Pavilion ££

Dining out in Soho tends to be an overwhelmingly trend-driven affair, so it's heartening that this much-loved Italian restaurant is still going strong. The small space is nothing special in itself: peach-coloured walls hung with modern art, somewhat cramped tables and hard metal chairs. The daily changing menu is brief and reflects the owners' Umbrian heritage. Service is speedily efficient without rushing diners.

✚ 197 D2/E2 ⬚ 15 Poland Street, W1 ☎ 020 7437 8774; www.vascosfood.com ⬤ Mon–Fri noon–3, 6–11, Sat 7–11. Closed lunch Sat, all Sun Ⓔ Oxford Circus

Rasa Samudra ££

Meaning a "taste of the ocean", this colourful venue for authentic Indian home cooking specialises in the cuisine of the coastal state of Kerala in the southwest of India,

✚ 197 E2 ⬚ 26–9 Dean Street, W1 ☎ 020 7437 9585; www.whitestarline.org.uk ⬤ Lunch: Mon–Fri noon–3. Dinner: Mon–Sat 5:30–11:30 Ⓔ Leicester Square

Where to... Shop

This central part of London acts as a visitor-magnet and shopping here takes in both extremes of tourist clichés and sophisticated specialist goods.

COVENT GARDEN

Covent Garden's pedestrian-only Piazza (Tube: Covent Garden) is popular with visitors (▶ 150–151). Traders here are keen to capitalise on the crowds and many shops stay open till 7 or 8 pm.

The Market itself is a good starting point. Stand and watch street performers or meander the arcades. The Candle Shop (30 The Market, WC2, tel: 020 7379 4220) sells all styles, perfumes and colours of candle. Culpeper Herbalists (8 The Market, WC2, tel: 020 7379 6698) stocks English herbs, oils, bath salts, pot-pourri and toiletries that make superb gifts. Benjamin Pollock's Toy Shop (44 The Market, WC2, tel: 020 7379 7866) is an amazing emporium of hand-made puppets, puppet theatres and other toys.

If you're looking for clothes, British designer Paul Smith (43 Floral Street, WC2, tel: 020 7836 7828) sells superb casual wear, sharp suits, and unusual socks, ties and cufflinks. Robot (37 Floral Street, WC2, tel: 020 7836 6156) is stocked with trendy shoes and foot-gear, hats and cool clothing.

BLOOMSBURY

The British Museum's shop (Great Russell Street, WC1, tel: 020 7323 8000. Tube: Holborn, Tottenham Court Road, Russell Square) sells Egyptian artefacts and Michelangelo mementos, and hundreds of other historical replicas.

Bloomsbury is also the traditional home of London's publishing houses, so there are bookshops galore. Charing Cross Road (Tube: Leicester Square) is the place for bookworms: Foyles, Books etc, Blackwell's and Waterstone's are the big four. Any Amount of Books (62 Charing Cross Road, WC2, tel: 020 7836 3697. Tube: Tottenham Court Road) sells second-hand books and has a bargain basement. Ulysses (40 Museum Street, WC1, tel: 020 7831 1600. Tube: Tottenham Court Road) specialises in first editions.

SOHO

Chinatown lies at the heart of Soho, and Gerrard Street is at the heart of Chinatown. It is the cultural and financial centre of Britain's Chinese community, with an amazing choice of restaurants and Chinese shops.

Soho is better known for its restaurants than for conventional shopping. Food, however, is a serious draw. Berwick Street Market (Berwick Street), a Monday to Saturday fruit and vegetable extravaganza, is worth a visit. On Old Compton Street there are I Camisa & Son (61 Old Compton Street, W1, tel: 020 7437 7610. Tube: Leicester Square), which sells Italian deli foods, the Algerian Coffee Store (52 Old Compton Street, W1, tel: 020 7437 2480. Tube: Leicester Square) for a range of fresh coffees, and the wonderful Pâtisserie Valerie for delicious French cakes (▶ 158).

American Retro (35 Old Compton Street, W1, tel: 020 7734 3477. Tube: Leicester Square) is a great source of funky accessories. In Brewer Street check out the Vintage Magazine Shop (39–43 Brewer Street, W1, tel: 020 7439 8525. Tube: Piccadilly Circus), a good place to search out an old movie poster or rare film and music magazines.

London's clubbers help to keep places open later in Soho than in other parts of the capital.

Where to...
Be Entertained

This part of London is crammed with theatres, clubs, cinemas and bars, and on a Saturday night it can seem as if the whole metropolis has squeezed itself into taxis or travelled on the Tube to surface at Leicester Square and Covent Garden. Late on a Friday or Saturday night the streets are still thronged with people and the atmosphere is lively. There is much to take in when considering the choice of entertainment.

THEATRE

The choice ranges from the long-running blockbusters of Shaftesbury Avenue to Off-West End at the **Donmar Warehouse** (tel: 0870 060 6624. Tube: Covent Garden). Although you can go directly to the individual theatre's box office, you might be able to pick up a half-price ticket from The Society of London Theatres' ticket booth, **tkts**, in the clocktower building on the south side of Leicester Square (open Mon–Sat noon–6:30, Sun noon–3:30). There is a service charge and tickets are for a performance on that day only. For a popular show, this is often your only chance of getting a ticket: be prepared to get there before noon to be as close to the front of the queue (line) as possible. There are other more expensive ticket booths in the square, so be careful to join the right queue. Also, never buy tickets offered by people who may approach you while waiting. They are working illegally and the tickets could well be fakes.

Ticketmaster (tel: 0870 534 4444) or **Keith Prowse/First Call** (tel: 0870 906 3838) may also help you find seats. However, there is a hefty service charge.

Another option is the charity ticket hotline **Theatre Cares** (tel: 020 7539 3880). Tickets for popular West End shows, for example *Miss Saigon*, *Les Misérables*, *The Phantom of the Opera*, are available and the price includes a donation to AIDS charities.

CLUBS

London is king of the hill as far as the music scene is concerned and its clubs cater for a wide spectrum of tastes, from mainstream rock acts, country and jazz, to techno, indie and hip hop sounds. The listings magazine *Time Out* (published every Tuesday) is the most authoritative and comprehensive of all the London magazines. As music and themes vary from night to night, it is essential to check for up-to-date information.

Heaven (Under The Arches, Villiers Street, WC2, tel: 020 7930 2020. Tube: Charing Cross), a huge gay club with a laid-back, friendly atmosphere, is also popular with straight men and women.

Other popular club venues worth checking out:

The Astoria (157 Charing Cross Road, WC2, tel: 020 7434 9592. Tube: Tottenham Court Road), a brilliant venue for up-to-the-minute sounds as well as rock and reggae.

Café de Paris (3 Coventry Street, W1, tel: 020 7734 7700. Tube: Piccadilly Circus), a glam dance hall, overlooked by a galleried restaurant.

The Rock Garden (6–7 The Piazza, Covent Garden, WC2, tel: 020 7240 3961. Tube: Covent Garden), a restaurant-cum-nightspot noted for showcasing new talent in a variety of musical areas.

Excursions

Kew

Kew is an excellent day out. Not only is it convenient – just a short boat or train ride from central London – but its highlight, the Royal Botanic Gardens, is the world's foremost botanical garden and one of the loveliest spots in the capital.

The Royal Botanic Gardens' 300 acres (121ha) contain around 30,000 species of plants, including 13 species extinct in the wild. Keen botanists and gardeners will revel in the floral diversity, but non-experts can also easily savour the gardens' overall beauty. Visits outside the summer months can be especially rewarding – September to November produces wonderful autumn colours, camellias bloom in January, and February to May sees the first blooms of spring. It would be easy to wander here for days, but to see the highlights visit the glasshouses in the order below. Their display boards offer entertaining information about some of the plants.

The **Princess of Wales Conservatory** features ten computer-regulated climate zones. Wander from orchids in the humid tropical zone to cacti in the dry tropical zone to appreciate the huge influence

The famous landmark Kew Pagoda, completed in 1762 for Princess Augusta, mother of George III

Hidden Gem

Tucked away within the gardens are Queen Charlotte's Cottage Grounds, named after George III's queen, who had a rustic "cottage" built here in the 1770s. The gardens are now a woodland nature reserve, specialising in British species.

Previous page: The moat at Windsor Castle has been transformed into lovely gardens

Kew Gardens

☎ 020 8940 1171 (24-hour recorded information); www.kew.org ⏰ Daily 9:30–dusk (telephone for exact closing times). The glasshouses and galleries close earlier. Closed 24–25 Dec 🍴 Several cafés and restaurants in the gardens and other options near by 🚇 Kew Gardens 🚆 Kew Bridge 65, 391. For information on river trips to Kew from central London ➤ 102–103 💷 Expensive (children free)

of climate on floral types. The most bizarre plants are the "living stones" lithops of Namibia, indistinguishable from stones until they produce brilliantly coloured flowers.

The **Palm House** is a masterpiece of Victorian engineering, constructed between 1844 and 1848 with some 16,000 sheets of glass. Climb one of the wrought-iron spiral staircases to the raised walkways to view its lush rainforest interior containing tropical species such as coconut, banana and rubber from across the globe, and don't miss the basement with its marine plants and habitats, in particular the coral reef. Kew is one of the few places in Britain with living coral, something that is notoriously difficult to cultivate in captivity.

The **Temperate House** is the largest of the glasshouses (590 feet/180m by 138 feet/42m). An elegant structure, it was begun in 1860, but work was stopped after the central block was finished and the building was not completed until almost 40 years later. Today its highlights are a Chilean wine palm, planted in the mid-19th century and now one of the world's largest indoor palms, and subtropical plants such as citrus trees, tea trees and Himalayan rhododendrons.

Just behind the Temperate House is the **Evolution House**, which traces the development of the most ancient plants. A bubbling primordial sludge has been re-created, replicating – it is thought – the earliest "soil". From here plant evolution is traced from the first bacteria through algae, mosses and ferns to conifers and flowering plants.

The ten-storey **Pagoda** is, sadly, not open to the public. During World War II it was used in research into how accurately bombs would drop. Holes were drilled in all ten floors and models dropped from top to bottom.

Top: The Palm House at Kew incorporates 16,000 panes of glass and took four years to build

Above: Luxuriant tropical plants thrive in its controlled climate

Windsor

A visit to Windsor Castle is the obvious highlight of a trip to Windsor, but the town is attractive in its own right. There is also the chance to visit historic Eton College, traditionally a school for the sons of the rich and famous, and – a treat for the children – the modern theme park of Legoland.

Top tips

- The Changing of the Guard takes place at 11 am daily (except Sundays) from April to July and on alternate days for the rest of the year.

- Buy a guidebook on the way in, as very little is labelled.

Visitor Information Centre

✉ 24 High Street, Windsor
☎ 01753 743900
🕐 Daily including most bank holidays; times vary throughout the year

Windsor Castle

☎ 01753 831118 (24 hour); 020 7766 7304; www.royalresidences.com 🕐 Daily 9:45–5:15 (last admission 4), Mar–Oct; 9:45–4:15 (last admission 3) rest of year. Closed Good Fri, Easter Sun morning, Service for the Order of the Garter in mid-Jun, 25–26 Dec. St George's Chapel closed to visitors Sun. Subject to full or partial closure at other times 🖐 Very expensive

Eton College

☎ 01753 671177;
www.etoncollege.com
🕐 Daily 2:30–4:30 school term time, 10:30–4:30 school holiday time, Apr–Sep
🖐 Moderate; tours moderate

Legoland Windsor

✉ Winkfield Road
☎ 08705 040404; www.legoland.co.uk
🕐 Daily 10–7 mid-Jul to early Sep; 10–6 (or dusk if earlier) rest of year;
🖐 Very expensive (2-day tickets available)

Windsor Castle

Windsor Castle looks the part of a castle to perfection, with towers, turrets, battlements and even uniformed soldiers on guard. It possesses a grandeur that far outshines that of Buckingham Palace (► 50–51). The world's largest inhabited castle, Windsor was founded by William the Conqueror in about 1080, when it formed part of the defences around London. In time it became a royal residence, partly because of the opportunities for hunting afforded by the surrounding countryside. Henry I had quarters in the castle in 1110, and almost 900 years later the sovereign is still resident. Queen Elizabeth II spends most weekends here, as well as much of April and June.

A fire on the night of 20 November, 1992, probably started by the heat of a spotlight too close to a curtain, destroyed much of the castle's interior. Several State Rooms, including St George's Hall, the Grand Reception Room, the State Dining Room and the Crimson Drawing Room were damaged. The fire burned for 15 hours and it took 1.3 million gallons (6 million litres) of water to extinguish it. Restoration took five years and cost £38 million, most of which was met by the Royal Family with money earned from the annual opening of Buckingham Palace and visitor admissions to the precincts of Windsor Castle.

Left: Windsor Castle is an imposing sight, especially from the Thames

Above: Henry VIII's gate

Areas of the castle open to the public include the State Rooms (all year except 11–14 June), Semi-State Rooms (late September to March only) and St George's Chapel (daily, all year except Sundays). Their vast array of treasures includes fabulous Gobelins tapestries, ornate antique furniture and paintings by artists such as Van Dyck, Rubens, Gainsborough, Dürer, Rembrandt, Reynolds and Canaletto.

The castle tour follows a set route, the key highlights of which are as follows:

Queen Mary's Dolls' House is an entire house built on a scale of 1:12. Look especially for the tiny leather-bound books in the library, and the vacuum cleaner, crockery, kitchen equipment, the miniature works of art on the walls, and a sewing machine that actually works.

The **Grand Staircase** and **Grand Vestibule** provide a magnificent introduction to the State Rooms. Both are lined with statues, firearms, armour and huge cases filled with miscellaneous treasures – among them, in the Grand Vestibule, the bullet that killed Admiral Lord Horatio Nelson at the Battle of Trafalgar in 1805 (currently on display at the National Maritime Museum in Greenwich ► 179).

The opulent **Grand Reception Room** was designed for King George IV, a monarch with a passion for ornate French design, which is why everything from walls and ceiling to furniture and chandeliers is intricately gilded and adorned.

St George's Chapel, the burial place of ten British monarchs, including the executed Charles I

St George's Hall – superbly restored since the 1992 fire – is the grandest of the castle's rooms. More than 180 feet (55m) long, it is impressive for its size alone, but is also remarkable for its decoration – crests, busts and suits of armour – and the wonderful oak hammerbeam roof.

Ten monarchs are buried in **St George's Chapel**, a beautifully decorated space distinguished, among other things, by its choir stalls, altar and gilded vaulting. It also contains Prince Albert's Memorial Chapel, built in memory of Victoria's beloved husband who died at Windsor in 1861. It's a startling piece of work laden with statues, Venetian mosaics and inlaid marble panels.

Windsor

Almost next door to the castle on the High Street is the 17th-century **Windsor Guildhall**, where Prince Charles married Camilla Parker-Bowles in April 2005. It is open only on Mondays from 10 am to 2 pm (closed public holidays).

If you've more time to spend in the area, **Eton College** lies a 15-minute walk across the river from Windsor. One of Britain's oldest private schools, Eton was founded in 1440, and pupils still wear formal dress. Today it is still highly prestigious; most pupils come from rich and influential families. More than 18 of Britain's prime ministers were educated here. The school yard, oldest classroom, museum and chapel are open to the public, and afternoon guided tours are available.

Legoland Windsor, a popular theme park just 2 miles (3.2km) from the town centre, is ideally suited to those with younger children. It mixes rides and displays with constructions made from the popular Lego bricks together with live-action shows. A half-hourly shuttle bus operates to Legoland from stops close to Windsor and Eton Central and Riverside railway stations (tickets including admission, shuttle bus and rail travel are available from most major railway stations in Britain).

Getting There

Windsor is 21 miles (34km) west of London.

Train (☎ 0845 748 4950) Direct trains to Windsor and Eton Riverside from Waterloo Station, every 30 min. Journey time approximately 55 min.

From Paddington Station to Windsor and Eton Central, changing trains at Slough, every 30 min. Journey time approximately 40 min.

Bus (☎ 0870 608 7261) Greenline service from Victoria Coach Station, journey time 57 min. Telephone for times.

Walks & Tours

1 MAYFAIR SQUARES

Walk

DISTANCE 3 miles (5km) **TIME** 2 hours. Allow extra time for window-shopping, refreshment stops and visiting churches **START POINT** Piccadilly Circus Underground station ⊞ 197 E1 **END POINT** Oxford Circus Underground station ⊞ 197 D2

Amid the noise and bustle of the surrounding streets, Mayfair (▶ 46–61) is an enclave of luxury and elegance. Originally laid out in the early 18th century by wealthy families such as the Grosvenors and Berkeleys, the area is the most expensive in London and retains evidence of past glories, including fine houses, both grand and humble, leafy squares, elegant shopping arcades and the old-fashioned alleyways and cobbles of Shepherd Market.

As you walk, look out for commemorative blue plaques, indicating that a famous person is associated with the building, and for shop fronts carrying royal crests; the companies awarded crests supply a member of the Royal Family – read the small print to find out which one.

1–2

Leave Piccadilly Circus Underground station by the Piccadilly (South Side) exit and walk straight

Elegant Burlington Arcade, off Piccadilly

along Piccadilly past St James's Church, designed by Wren, Princes Arcade, lined with quality shops, and Hatchards, booksellers since 1797. You'll soon reach the high-class grocery and department store Fortnum & Mason, which was founded by a servant of Queen Anne in 1707. The store is very exclusive – some of the sales assistants even wear tailcoats.

2–3

Cross Piccadilly to Burlington House, an 18th-century mansion, now home to the Royal Academy of Arts (▶ 58). Just beyond is Burlington Arcade, built in 1819. This is the best known of the

REGENT

OXFORD
STREET

HANOVER
SQ

PRINCES
STREET

ST

🚇 Oxford
Circus

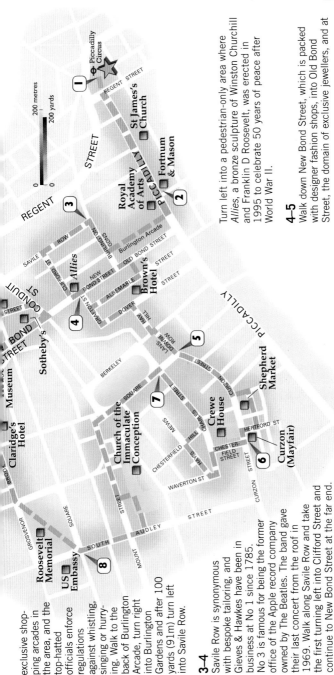

Turn left into a pedestrian-only area where *Allies*, a bronze sculpture of Winston Churchill and Franklin D Roosevelt, was erected in 1995 to celebrate 50 years of peace after World War II.

4–5

Walk down New Bond Street, which is packed with designer fashion shops, into Old Bond Street, the domain of exclusive jewellers, and at

exclusive shopping arcades in the area, and the top-hatted officials enforce regulations against whistling, singing or hurrying. Walk to the back of Burlington Arcade, turn right into Burlington Gardens and after 100 yards (91m) turn left into Savile Row.

3–4

Savile Row is synonymous with bespoke tailoring, and Gieves & Hawkes have been in business at No 1 since 1785. No 3 is famous for being the former office of the Apple record company owned by The Beatles. The band gave their last concert from the roof in 1969. Walk along Savile Row and take the first turning left into Clifford Street and continue to New Bond Street at the far end.

No 28 Old Bond Street turn right through the Royal Arcade to Albemarle Street. Turn right and you'll see Brown's Hotel on the left: in 1876, Alexander Graham Bell made his first successful telephone call from here. At the top of Albemarle Street turn left into Grafton Street, and after a short distance, left into Dover Street, then right into Hay Hill. Cross the road at the bottom into pedestrianised Lansdowne Row and walk through from here to Curzon Street.

5–6

Walk straight along Curzon Street and after 200 yards (183m), you'll come to G F Trumper, Court Hairdresser and Perfumer, established in 1875. The building is considerably older,

however, and with its original dark wood, glass and light fittings is one of London's finest 18th-century shops. Turn left through the covered entrance into Shepherd Market, built in 1735. Today its lanes are filled with outdoor cafés, small shops and restaurants; everything here is older and on a smaller scale than the surrounding area.

At Ye Grapes pub, at the far end of the passageway, turn immediately right through a pedestrian-only area. Cross cobbled Trebeck Street and turn right up Hertford Street past the Curzon Mayfair Cinema to Curzon Street. Across Curzon Street stands Crewe House (now the Saudi Arabian Embassy), which Shepherd built in 1730 as his own home.

6–7

Turn left into Curzon Street and then right into elegant Chesterfield Street, left at the top into Charles Street, right at the Red Lion pub on to Waverton Street and right again into Hay's Mews, originally the

Shepherd Market, with narrow streets, shops and pubs

stables for the coach horses of the wealthy, now converted into highly desirable homes. Take the next right into Chesterfield Hill and at the end turn left, back into Charles Street. Follow this road to its end at Berkeley Square.

7–8

Berkeley Square was made a household name through the song "A Nightingale Sang in Berkeley Square". It was originally laid out in the mid-18th century and retains its attractive, leafy feel, though these days the traffic roaring along the surrounding roads detracts from the prettiness and pollutes the air. Walk up the left (west) side of the square, which has retained the most character.

At the top left (northwest) corner turn left into Mount Street; after about 200 yards (183m) turn left into peaceful Mount Street Gardens where there is an entrance to the solemn Church of the Immaculate Conception (open daily 7–6:30). Continue to the other side of the gardens and then turn right into South Audley Street. This leads to Grosvenor Square, one of London's largest squares, with the modern United States Embassy to the left – it's certainly assertive, although hardly in keeping with the square's period style. There are statues here of United States presidents Roosevelt and Eisenhower.

8–9

Walk diagonally right across the square and leave from the far (northeast) corner along Brook Street. Continue straight ahead past Claridge's (▶ 37), one of London's finest hotels, which is often patronised by visiting royalty. No 25 Brook Street is where George Frederick Handel lived and died. Music lovers can visit the Handel House Museum, dedicated to the composer and his work, on the upper floors. Guitarist Jimi Hendrix lived next door at No 23 from 1968 to 1969.

9–10

At the next intersection turn right into New Bond Street. Along on the left is Sotheby's, the prestigious auction house – anyone can view the often fabulous articles waiting to be sold. Take the next turning left into Conduit Street and turn immediately left into St George Street, where the imposing bulk of St George's Church is ahead on the right. Built in 1724 it has long been a fashionable society wedding venue.

10–11

Carry on to the top of St George Street where the statue of William Pitt, who became prime minister in 1783 at the age of only 24, marks the entrance to Hanover Square. Take Princes Street

Berkeley Square is a green oasis in an exclusive area

from the top right (northeast) corner of the square out to Regent Street. Turn left and you soon reach Oxford Circus Underground station.

Taking a Break

Stop at one of the coffee shops or snack bars on Lansdowne Row or try one of the outdoor cafés or pubs in Shepherd Market.

When?

Weekdays are best, as on Sundays the shops are closed and on Saturdays weddings are often scheduled at the churches.

Places to Visit

Handel House Museum

🚇 196 C2 ☎ 020 7495 1685 🕐 Tue–Sat 10–6, Thu 10–8, Sun noon–6 💰 Moderate

St James's Piccadilly

🚇 197 E1 ☎ 020 7734 4511 🕐 Open to visitors daily 8–6:30. Free lunchtime concerts (1:10) Mon, Wed, Fri. Concerts most evenings Thu–Sat

St George's

🚇 197 D2 ✉ Hanover Square ☎ 020 7629 0874 🕐 Mon–Fri 8–4

2 THE CITY
Walk

The City of London (▶ 67–88), also known as the Square Mile, is a major world financial centre bursting with banks, corporations, financial institutions and trading centres. The wheeling and dealing takes place behind closed doors, and security concerns mean that most buildings are closed to the public.

However, the streets have a real buzz during the week (they're dead at weekends) and this walk takes in towering landmarks, city churches, an art gallery and a Roman amphitheatre.

DISTANCE 2 miles (3.2km) **TIME** 2 hours. Allow more time for visits **START POINT** Monument Underground station ➕ 202 A3 **END POINT** Bank Underground station ➕ 202 A4

1–2

Leave Monument Underground station via the London Bridge/King William Street (South) exit. Walk straight ahead on to London Bridge for sweeping views up and down river; Tower Bridge to the east with HMS *Belfast* moored across to your right.

The Romans first bridged the River Thames at this point almost 2,000 years ago and there has been a succession of bridges here since. The one you're on dates from 1973, the previous bridge having been sold to American businessman Robert P McCulloch Sr for display in Arizona. Londoners joke that he thought he was buying Tower Bridge.

St Lawrence Jewry 7

Guildhall

St Mary-le-Bow 8

CHEAPSIDE

KING STREET

GRESHAM STREET

Bank of England & Museum 6

LOTHBURY

BARTHOLOMEW LANE

Stock Exchange

Tower 42

OLD BROAD STREET

THREADNEEDLE ST

Royal Exchange 10

BISHOPSGATE

GREAT ST HELEN'S

St Helen Bishopsgate

Swiss Re-Insurance Tower 5

Lloyd's

LEADENHALL ST

Leadenhall Market 4

LIME STREET

Mansion House 9

St Stephen Walbrook

WALBROOK

BUCKLERSBURY

QUEEN VICTORIA ST

CANNON

WATLING STREET

BOW LANE

KING WILLIAM STREET

GRACECHURCH ST

PHILPOT LANE

FENCHURCH STREET

EASTCHEAP

Monument

3–4

Walk up Fish Street Hill to Eastcheap at the top and turn right; the next road on the right is Pudding Lane, now lined with modern office buildings.

Cross Eastcheap into Philpot Lane and look ahead for a view of the dramatic Lloyd's Building. Designed by Sir Richard (now Lord) Rogers, it houses the world centre of insurance for over 200 years since it was founded in the coffee houses of the City. You'll either love or hate the steel-and-glass giant with the entrails of pipes and shafts exposed on the outside – it looks especially dramatic at night.

Towering above the Lloyd's building, just behind it, is the Swiss Re Tower, home to Swiss Re re-insurance company, designed by Sir Norman

(now Lord) Foster and nicknamed The Gherkin.

At the end of Philpot Lane, cross Fenchurch Street into Lime Street and take the first street left, the cobbled Lime Street Passage, which leads into Leadenhall Market (▶ 82).

4–5

Leave the market through Whittington Avenue and turn right into Leadenhall Street by Lloyd's. Cross the road and head north across an open square to St Helen Bishopsgate, one of the few churches to survive the Great Fire of London. There are 38 churches within the Square Mile, many of them designed by Wren; with almost no resident parishioners and insufficient weekday worshippers to justify this number of buildings, the threat of closure hangs over many.

5–6

Turn left at the church and along Great St Helen's to Bishopsgate. Look directly ahead to Tower 42. At 604 feet (184m) it is the City's tallest building.

HMS *Belfast*

Tower Bridge and HMS *Belfast*

2–3

Walk back towards the Underground station and take the first road to the right, Monument Street, to the Monument. It was co-designed by Sir Christopher Wren, architect of St Paul's Cathedral, in the 1670s as a memorial to the Great Fire in 1666. It is 203 feet (62m) tall – the distance on the ground from its base to the place where the fire started in Pudding Lane – and there are 311 steps up to the viewing platform.

The Monument recalls the Great Fire

Thames

LONDON BRIDGE

2

0 — 200 metres

0 — 200 yards

Turn left in Bishopsgate and cross at the traffic lights into Threadneedle Street. At the intersection with Old Broad Street a small sign proclaims the London Stock Exchange; electronic dealing has replaced its old trading floor where deals used to be done in person.

Continue along Threadneedle Street and turn right down Bartholomew Lane where you will find the Bank of England. The bank's museum (➤ 82) gives an insight into its processes.

6–7

Carry on to the end of Bartholomew Lane, then turn left along Lothbury and into Gresham Street. To your right, behind St Lawrence Jewry Church, is the Guildhall, the symbolic heart of the City. The original 15th-century building has undergone many reconstructions but the main hall remains the high-light, decked with shields and banners and displaying figures of the legendary giants Gog and Magog.

Within the Guildhall complex is a curious Clock Museum, which includes a skull-shaped pocket watch that once belonged to Mary Queen of Scots; the Guildhall Art Gallery, where important paintings from the Corporation of

London's 300-year-old collection are on display, and below ground, London's only Roman amphitheatre, discovered in 1988 and opened to the public in 2003.

7–8

With your back to Guildhall, cross Gresham Street into King Street and continue down to Cheapside where you turn right towards the huge steeple of St Mary-le-Bow. The church's original Norman crypt still exists while the

spacious elegance of Wren's work is obvious both in the fine lines of the spire and in the elegant arches and vaulted roof of the interior. Traditionally, only those born within the sound of Bow bells can call themselves true Cockneys (native Londoners).

Walk through Bow Churchyard next to the church where there is a statue of Sir John Smith (1580–1631), who married Native American princess Pocahontas and was a parishioner here. Walk around the back of the church and turn right into Bow Lane, where you will see Williamson's Tavern on the right. Turn left into Watling Street; Ye Olde Watling pub, at the bottom, dates from 1666 and, by tradition, Sir Christopher Wren used it as an office while building St Paul's Cathedral.

8–9

Walk along Watling Street to a large intersection and cross into Queen Victoria Street. Turn right into Bucklersbury to St Stephen Walbrook Church, built by Wren (1672–79); the dome is thought to have been a trial run

Guildhall, the symbolic heart of the City, is where the Lord Mayor of London is inaugurated

is the Royal Exchange, first granted a charter to trade in all kinds of commerce by Queen Elizabeth I in the 16th century, although this particular building dates from 1844. Until recently, it was the centre of futures trading, though this has now closed. The gardens in front are a good place for a rest, and if you stand with your back to the giant statue of the Duke of Wellington

The Royal Exchange, founded in 1571

9–10

From the church turn along Walbrook and then right at the end towards the huge, temple-like building at the far side of the intersection. This

you will see a plaque that details the nearby buildings: the Mansion House, official residence of the Lord Mayor of London, is across to the left, and the solid bulk of the Bank of England, surrounded by its windowless walls, is on the right.

The walk ends here – Bank Underground station is near by.

Taking a Break
The Place Below, in the Crypt of St Mary-le-Bow, (tel: 020 7329 0789) serves top-quality vegetarian food 7:30–3:30.

Places to Visit

Monument
🕂 202 A3 ⊠ Monument Street, ☎ 020 7626 2717 ◉ Daily 9:30–5:30 💷 Inexpensive

St Helen Bishopsgate
🕂 202 B4 ⊠ Great St Helen's, EC3 ☎ 020 7283 2231 ◉ Mon–Fri 9–12:30. Afternoons by appt 💷 Free

Bank of England Museum
🕂 202 A4 ⊠ Bartholomew Lane, EC3 ☎ 020 7601 5545; www.bankofengland.co.uk/museum ◉ Mon–Fri 10–5 💷 Free

Guildhall
🕂 201 F4 ⊠ Gresham Street, EC2 ☎ 020 7606 3030; www.cityoflondon.gov.uk ◉ Guildhall: Mon–Sat 10–4:45, Sun noon–4. Clock Museum: Mon–Fri 9:30–4:45. Art Gallery and amphitheatre: Mon–Sat 10–5, Sun noon–4 💷 Guildhall and Clock Museum free: Art Gallery and amphitheatre (same ticket) inexpensive; free on Friday and after 3:30 daily

St Mary-le-Bow
🕂 201 F4 ⊠ Cheapside, EC3 ☎ 020 7248 5139 ◉ Mon–Wed 6:30–6, Thu 6:30–6:30, Fri 6:30–4. Free lunchtime concert Thu 1:05 💷 Free

St Stephen Walbrook
🕂 202 A4 ⊠ 39 Walbrook, EC4 ☎ 020 7626 8242 ◉ Mon–Thu 10–4, Fri 10–3 💷 Free

for that of St Paul's. The telephones on display in the church commemorate the founding in the rector's study, on 2 November, 1953, of the first telephone helpline for the despairing, which eventually became the Samaritans organisation.

3 GREENWICH
Walk

Greenwich, 8 miles (13km) down the River Thames from central London, overflows with royal, maritime and astronomical associations – and is known across the globe for Greenwich Mean Time and the Greenwich Meridian where East meets West. Add to that the rolling parkland, superb views and lively weekend markets (Fri–Sun), and Greenwich begins to look unmissable.

DISTANCE 2 miles (3.2km) **TIME** 2 hours. Allow additional time for visits – you could easily spend a day here **START POINT** Greenwich Pier. Allow an hour from Westminster Pier to Greenwich by boat **END POINT** Greenwich Pier

The Chapel of St Peter and St Paul at the Old Royal Naval College, which was redesigned after a fire in 1779

1–2
From Greenwich Pier walk straight ahead to the tall-masted ship *Cutty Sark*. Built at Clydeside in Scotland in 1869, this handsome ship was the fastest tea clipper of its time, ferrying tea from China and wool from Australia, on occasion covering over 360 miles (580km) in one day. The exhibitions show what conditions were like aboard, and

Sleek masts and intricate rigging: the 19th-century tea clipper *Cutty Sark*

illustrate the ship's history. There is also an interesting display of ships' figureheads.

Walk back past the entrance to Greenwich Pier and east along the footpath beside the river. The Old Royal Naval College is on the right, built on the site of the old Greenwich Palace where Henry VIII and his daughter Queen Elizabeth I were born. The college was built by architect Sir Christopher Wren, assisted by Nicholas Hawksmoor and Sir John Vanbrugh, starting in 1696. Generations of sailors, including Prince Charles, learned their trade here until its closure in 1995. The chapel and Grand Hall are open to the public and the latter contains the largest painting in the country, *The Triumph of Peace and Liberty* (a tribute to King William and Queen Mary). It was executed between 1707 and 1727 by James Thornhill (and several assistants) and measures 105 feet by 49 feet (32m by 15m). For this Thornhill was paid £6,685, a massive sum at the time. From the central gates there is a lovely view through the college to Queen's House, the elegant white building behind, and beyond to the Royal Observatory on the hill above. There are also excellent views down the river to the Millennium Dome, the beleaguered focus of London's Millennium celebrations, and across the river to the stainless steel and glass bulk of Canary Wharf – at 797 feet (243m), it is London's, and indeed the UK's, tallest skyscraper.

Continue along the river path to Park Row and the Trafalgar Tavern.

Royal Observatory

General Wolfe's Statue

Park Café

BLACKHEATH AVENUE

Reservoir

Ranger's House

CROOM'S HILL

The Old Royal Naval College in Greenwich, where generations of sailors learned seamanship

2–3

The Trafalgar Tavern was built in 1837 and frequented by writer Charles Dickens: sample its fare or turn away from the river and walk along Park Row and cross the main road (Romney Road). There is an entrance to the National Maritime Museum and Queen's House on the right.

The National Maritime Museum is a treasure trove of naval instruments, charts, models,

The Royal Observatory at Greenwich was founded by Charles II in 1675

paintings and memorabilia; there's even a royal barge. The history of seafaring (exploratory as well as the military) is comprehensively illustrated in state-of-the-art exhibits and interactive displays. One whole gallery is devoted to Admiral Lord Horatio Nelson, victor of the Battle of Trafalgar in 1805. Exit back into Park Row and enter Greenwich Park.

3–4

Follow the first path in front of the Queen's House until you can turn right, then take the second path to the left, which climbs steeply up One Tree Hill. Queen Elizabeth I often came here to enjoy the fine view, a custom commemorated in verse on the benches.

4–5

From One Tree Hill either follow the paths or cut across the grass towards the Royal Observatory, the regal red-brick-and-white building with the green dome on the next hill. You'll arrive at the statue of General James Wolfe; he was a local man who in 1759 commanded the British army during the capture of Quebec, in which he was killed. There's another good view of London from here: look for St Paul's Cathedral, with the distinctive black bulk of Tower 42 (formerly called the NatWest Tower) close to it.

The Royal Observatory was founded in 1675 by King Charles II, with the aim of solving the problem of finding longitude at sea. Astronomers now study the skies away from the bright distracting lights of London, but the exhibits illustrate the history of astronomy and the challenges of measuring position and time. You can straddle the Prime Meridian, the line at 0° longitude from which all other longitudes are reckoned, and see the revolutionary chronometers with which John Harrison (1693–1776) solved the longitude problem.

5–6

With your back to General Wolfe, walk along Blackheath Avenue, with the Park Café on the left. At the small roundabout turn right on to a path that follows a line of trees to a gate in the park wall. Turn left along the gravel drive to Croom's Hill.

The 17th-century Ranger's House, a 200-yard (183m) detour to the left, houses a splendid collection of medieval and Renaissance works of art.

6–7

As you walk down the hill, admire the 17th- and 18th-century houses. Towards the bottom of Croom's Hill, you will find the Fan Museum, the only one of its kind in the world, located in two 18th-century houses. Founded in 1989 by Helen Alexander, whose personal collection of more than 3,500 fans is the basis of the exhibition, the museum displays stunning examples of the fan-maker's craft.

7–8

From the Fan Museum continue straight to the bottom of Croom's Hill, then walk ahead into Stockwell Street (the Village Market is on the right) and turn right into Greenwich Church Street with the Fountain Food Court on the bend. Continue along Greenwich Church Street and cross Nelson Road. The entrance to the main craft market, offering a varied selection of goods, is through a small alleyway to the right. Return to Greenwich Church Street, turn right, cross College Approach, and after 100 yards (91m) you'll be back at the *Cutty Sark*.

8–9

You can either return to central London by boat, or take the Docklands Light Railway (DLR) (▶ 34). There is a DLR station close to the *Cutty Sark*. Trains run on an elevated track, and you get some panoramic views of the futuristic landscape of Docklands on your way back into the city centre.

Taking a Break

Trafalgar Tavern, fast food in the Fountain Food Court, afternoon tea in the Orangery of the Fan Museum (Tue and Sun) and restaurants in Greenwich Church Street.

When?

Friday, Saturday or Sunday when the markets are open.

Places to Visit

Old Royal Naval College

⌖ Entrance from King William Walk, SE10
☎ 020 8269 4747;
www.greenwichfoundation.org.uk ⊛ Mon–Sat
10–5 ⦿ Free

National Maritime Museum, Queen's House and Royal Observatory

⌖ Greenwich Park, SE10 ☎ 020 8858 4422
information line: 020 8312 6565; www.nmm.ac.uk
⊛ Daily 10–6 (last admission 5:30), in summer;
10–5 (last admission 4:30), in winter; closed
24–26 Dec ⦿ Free

Ranger's House

⌖ Chesterfield Walk, Greenwich Park, SE10
☎ 020 8853 0035; www.english-heritage.org.uk
⊛ Wed–Sun 10–5, late Mar–Sep. Closed late
Dec–Feb. Open other times by appointment only
⦿ Moderate

Cutty Sark

⌖ King William Walk, SE10 ☎ 020 8858 3445;
www.cuttysark.org.uk ⊛ Daily 10–5. Closed
24–26 Dec ⦿ Moderate

Fan Museum

⌖ 12 Croom's Hill, SE10
☎ 020 8305 1441; www.fan-museum.org
⊛ Tue–Sat 11–5, Sun noon–5
⦿ Moderate

HAMPSTEAD
Walk

DISTANCE 3.5 miles (6km)
TIME 3 hours. Allow more for refreshment stops and visiting the houses
START POINT Golders Green Underground station **END POINT** Hampstead Underground station

This walk through the charming village of Hampstead and across Hampstead Heath, 4 miles (6.5km) to the north of central London, offers some of the most rural scenery in the capital, a spectacular view from Parliament Hill, historic houses and delightful lanes. Hampstead has been a popular residential area, particularly with writers and artists, since the 18th century, when visitors flocked to drink the restorative spa waters; famous inhabitants have included artist John Constable, poet John Keats, writers Ian Fleming and Agatha Christie, and actors Peter O'Toole, Elizabeth Taylor and Emma Thompson.

1–2

Catch the No 210 bus from outside Golders Green Underground station to Kenwood House – ask the driver to tell you where to alight. On the way look out for Jack Straw's Castle. There was an inn on this site for more than 500 years until the latest pub (dating from 1962) was converted to apartments. Still serving pints of beer, however, is the 16th-century Spaniard's Inn, associated with the highwayman Dick Turpin and literary figures Dickens, Keats, Shelley and Byron.

There are two entrances to Kenwood House a few hundred yards after Spaniard's Inn on the right – West Lodge and East Lodge; both lead to the house.

2–3

Kenwood House dates from the 18th century and is famed for the work of the Scottish architect Robert Adam. The highlight of the interior is the fabulously ornate library and the Iveagh Bequest art collection which includes a Rembrandt self-portrait, the *Guitar Player* by Vermeer and

HAMPSTEAD LANE

East Lodge

Kenwood House **2**

West Lodge

3

Spaniard's Inn

1

0   300 metres

works by J M W Turner, Joshua Reynolds and Thomas Gainsborough.

With your back to the house, looking across the lake from the elegant south front, turn right and follow the wide gravel path as it passes in front of a row of wooden benches. Walk through the first wooden gate to the right – just opposite a field containing a splendid Henry Moore sculpture entitled *Two Piece Reclining Figure No 5* (1963–4).

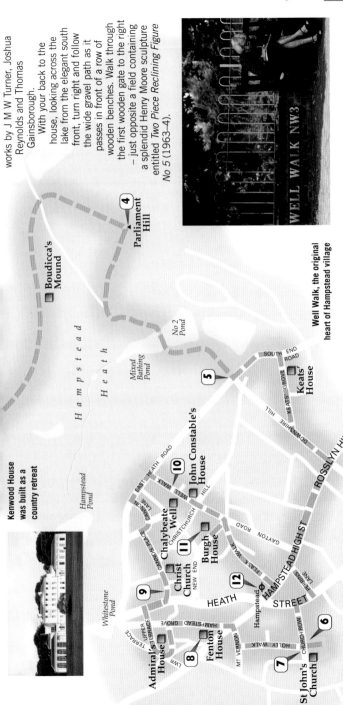

Kenwood House was built as a country retreat

Well Walk, the original heart of Hampstead village

From Parliament Hill there are panoramic views across the capital

3–4

Take the gravel path to the left and stay on it as another path joins from the right. After 300 yards (274m) you'll pass through an iron gate. Fork left and you'll descend through the trees to a large gravel area where you continue straight across. At the next intersection, marked by a wooden post, go straight across and after 50 yards (46m), at the next intersection, again marked by a wooden post, turn left. You'll descend gradually and to the right you'll see Boudicca's Mound, planted with trees and enclosed by a fence. Boudicca, Queen of the Iceni tribe, led her people against the Romans in the 1st century AD. Local legend claims this as her burial place. Follow the path straight through the next intersection of paths then take the next path to your right and you'll spot Parliament Hill directly ahead, bare of trees and with benches on the skyline.

4–5

On Parliament Hill look for the plaque identifying the London landmarks laid out below. Facing the plaque, turn right and walk straight along the path that leads you between two of the many ponds on the Heath; the Mixed Bathing Pond is on the right and Hampstead Number Two pond on the left. Follow the path left along the side of Hampstead Number Two pond and out to the main road, East Heath Road.

5–6

Cross East Heath Road at the pedestrian crossing and walk left down South End Road. Take the third turning right into Keats' Grove, with Keats' House along on the left. This is where the poet John Keats (1795–1821) lived for two years, wrote some of his best-known work and fell in love with the girl next door. The house contains many of his possessions and manuscripts.

Continue along Keats' Grove and turn left into Downshire Hill and then right into Rosslyn Hill. Turn left just after the King William IV pub into Perrins Lane, right at the end into Heath Street and then take the first turning left into elegant Church Row.

6–7

At the far end of Church Row enter the left gate of St John's Church and turn immediately left along the rough path. At the bottom of the churchyard on the left, behind a small iron fence, is the grave of Hampstead's most famous resident and artist John Constable (1776–1837), together with his wife and their eldest son.

Walk up to the church, which has a pleasantly proportioned interior, fine stained glass and, at the front to the right of the choir, a memorial to John Keats.

7–8

Leave the church and, with your back to the church door, turn left and cross the churchyard. Now cross the road into Holly Walk to start the stretch of the walk through the back lanes of

Hampstead village. On the right, the row of quaint cottages in Benhams Place dates from 1813. At the end of Holly Walk turn right into Mount Vernon, follow the path to the left of the last house and take the lower path to the left as it swings around to the left on to Holly Bush Hill. At the top of Holly Bush Hill, the black-and-gold gates across the grass belong to Fenton House, one of the oldest and grandest Hampstead houses, with a large collection of early musical instruments.

8–9

Walk along the right side of Fenton House into Hampstead Grove and turn left into Admiral's Walk. Along on the right, the startling Admiral's House was turned into a facsimile of a ship by a former owner – who also used to fire cannons to commemorate naval victories. Continue along Admiral's Walk to Lower Terrace, turn right and then right again into Upper Terrace, and head straight across a small crossroads to the main road (Heath Street). Turn right and take the first left, a small lane, into Hampstead Square.

9–10

Walk straight across the top of the square, with Christ Church on the right, continuing straight into Cannon Place. At the end of the road turn right down the hill, left into Cannon Lane and you'll reach East Heath Road. Turn right and take the second road on the right, Well Walk.

10–11

To your right is the now defunct Chalybeate Well, where the spring water, rich in iron salts, was discovered in the 18th century. Just opposite the well is 40 Well Walk, one of the Hampstead homes of John Constable. Cross Christchurch Hill and at the end turn right into New End Square, where you will see historic Burgh House on the right. Built in 1703, it now houses the local history museum and art gallery.

11–12

From Burgh House head back down New End Square and take the first turning right into Flask Walk. This leads up to Hampstead High Street, where a right turn leads to Hampstead Underground station.

Taking a Break

The Brew House Café at Kenwood House and the Buttery at Burgh House.

When?

Weekends are the best time to see kite-flying on Parliament Hill (shops are closed Sunday).

Places to Visit

Kenwood House
Hampstead Lane, NW3
020 8348 1286; www.english-heritage.org.uk
Mon, Tue, Thu, Sat 10–5, Wed, Fri 10.30–5, Apr–Oct; closes 4 pm, rest of year; closed 24–25 Dec Free

Keats' House
Keats' Grove, NW3
020 7435 2062
Tue–Sun 1–5, May–Oct Moderate

Fenton House
20 Hampstead Grove, NW3
020 7435 3471; www.nationaltrust.org.uk
Wed–Fri 2–5, Sat–Sun and bank holidays 11–5, Easter–Oct; Sat–Sun 2–5, Mar Moderate

Burgh House
New End Square, NW3 020 7431 0144
Wed–Sun noon–5 (closed some Sats)
Free

5 Number 15 Bus Trip

From Marble Arch to the Tower of London

This bus trip takes in many of the major London sights including Marble Arch, Piccadilly Circus, Trafalgar Square and St Paul's Cathedral, plus well-known thoroughfares – Oxford Street, Regent Street, Haymarket and the Strand. Sit upstairs on the bus and as close to the front as possible for the best views.

TIME 1 hour depending on traffic
START POINT Marble Arch Underground station ✚ 196 A2
END POINT Tower Hill Underground station ✚ 202 C3

BUS STOP		
Marble Arch		
Towards Oxford Circus		
6	12	15
23	94	159
N3	N6	N12
N15	N16 N23	N9A N96

1–2

Leave Marble Arch Underground station by the Subway 1 underpass, Marble Arch and Oxford Street North. Look across to the right to the huge marble edifice in the middle of the one-way system – this is the Marble Arch that gives the area its name. Built for the forecourt of Buckingham Palace it was moved to its current incongruous site in 1851 when the front of the palace was remodelled.

Turn left out of the underpass and catch the No 15 bus at the second stop you come to, stop L. Ask for the Tower of London.

Hop on the bus at Marble Arch

The bus goes along Oxford Street, one of London's busiest shopping streets, lined with department stores. Much of Oxford Street is now shabby but look out for the grand frontage of Selfridges on the left. The store was built by an American, Gordon Selfridge, early in the 20th century and certainly rivals Harrods for contents, if not fame and exclusivity.

2–3

At Oxford Circus the bus turns right into Regent Street, and a different world architecturally. Grand and unified, it is one remnant of the "Nash Sweep", a processional route running from St James's Park, through Trafalgar Square to

MARBLE ARCH

Marble Arch ⊖ Marble Arch

1

OXFORD **Selfridges** STREET

REGENT ST OXFORD CIRCUS **2**

NT STREET

GRE MA S

Left: Regent Street
Below: The Law Courts

Regent's Park, designed by architect John Nash (1752–1835). Most distinctive of the shops is Liberty (▶ 65) – look along Great Marlborough Street for the black-and-white mock Tudor entrance of this exclusive department store.

At the end of Regent Street neon advertisements announce your arrival at Piccadilly

Circus, with the fountain and Eros to the right (▶ 60).

3–4

The bus turns right down Haymarket, named for the market which sold hay for the royal horses stabled in the area until 1830, and then left and around the south side of Trafalgar Square. The National Gallery (▶ 54–57) is on the left, as Nelson on his column and the fine spire of St Martin-in-the-Fields rises ahead (▶ 53).

4–5

As the bus turns right along Duncannon Street, look towards the Charing Cross railway station forecourt with its highly ornate reproduction of an Eleanor Cross. In 1290, King Edward I built 12 crosses along the funeral route of his wife, Eleanor of Castile, from Nottinghamshire to Westminster Abbey, each cross marking the spot where her body rested on the 12-day journey.

The bus passes along the Strand, once famed for its music halls (Vaudeville) and theatres, and arches around Aldwych, rejoining the Strand at St Clement Danes church in the centre of the road, with the Royal Courts of Justice on the left. In the centre of the road, the griffin statue marks the boundary of the City of London – the sovereign stops here on ceremonial occasions to ask the permission of the Lord Mayor of London to enter the City.

PICCADILLY
CIRCUS — Trocadero Centre

REGENT ST — Eros

HAYMARKET

LEICESTER SQUARE

PALL MALL

National Gallery **(4)**

St Martin-in-the-Fields

TRAFALGAR SQUARE — DUN-CANNON ST

Nelson's Column

Charing Cross Station

STRAND

STRAND

ALDWYCH

St Clement Danes

Royal Courts of Justice **(5)**

Temple

STRAND

FLEET STREET

St Bride's Church

LUDGATE CIRCUS

(6)

Thames

0 — 200 metres
0 — 200 yards

5–6

The road now becomes Fleet Street, which was once the publishing centre for the British national press – the newspapers have now moved to modern premises in Docklands. On the left is Ye Olde Cheshire Cheese pub, dating from the mid-17th century. Dr Samuel Johnson, compiler of the first English dictionary, was a regular customer here, and it became popular with later authors, including Dickens, Thackeray and Mark Twain. Look on the right for the white spire of St Bride's Church, one of Sir Christopher Wren's most distinctive creations – it is said that soon after it was built a baker copied the design for a tiered wedding cake and an enduring tradition was born.

6–7

The bus crosses Ludgate Circus into Ludgate Hill, heading straight towards the dramatic West Front of St Paul's Cathedral, then it passes to the right of the cathedral, into Cannon Street. Look to the left for Tower 42 and the new Swiss Re Tower. A few hundred yards later, just after Monument Underground station, look to the right down Fish Hill Street to see the Monument (▶ 173). The bus then heads along Eastcheap, along Great Tower Street, and into Byward Street, where it passes the church of All Hallows-by-the-Tower with its distinctive green roof. It then continues along Tower Hill to the Tower of London. The bus stops just outside the Tower Hill Memorial which was built to honour the 24,000 men in the merchant navy and fishing fleets who lost their lives in World War I with "no grave but the sea".

Either cross the road and catch a No 15 bus back to Marble Arch or follow signs to Tower Hill Underground station, a few yards away.

When?

Any time, but avoid rush hours (8–9.30 am, 4:30–6 pm weekdays).

St Paul's comes into view on the number 15 bus route

St Paul's Cathedral

LUDGATE HILL

ST PAUL'S CHURCHYARD

CANNON STREET

EAST-CHEAP

KING WILLIAM ST

The Monument

Thames

All Hallows by-the-Tower Church

BYWARD ST

GREAT TOWER ST

Tower of London

TOWER HILL

 Tower Hill

7

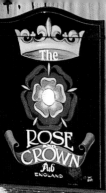

Practicalities

Websites
- British Tourist Authority
  www.visitbritain.com
- UK Travel Guide
  www.londontown.com
  www.visitlondon.com
- London Tourist Board
  www.LondonTown.com
- London Travel Service
  www.bridge-travel.co.uk

In the UK
Britain and London Visitor Centre
1 Regent Street
London SW1Y 4XT
☎ 0870 156 6366

BEFORE YOU GO

WHAT YOU NEED

- ● Required
- ○ Suggested
- ▲ Not required

Some countries require a passport to remain valid for a minimum period (usually at least six months) beyond the date of entry – check before you travel.

	UK	Germany	USA	Canada	Australia	Ireland	Netherlands	Spain
Passport/National Identity Card	▲	●	●	●	●	▲	●	●
Visa (regulations can change – check before you travel)	▲	▲	▲	▲	▲	▲	▲	▲
Onward or Return Ticket	▲	○	○	○	○	○	○	○
Health Inoculations (tetanus and polio)	▲	▲	▲	▲	▲	▲	▲	▲
Health Documentation (► 192, Health)	▲	●	●	●	●	●	●	●
Travel Insurance	○	○	○	○	○	○	○	○
Driving Licence (national)	●	●	●	●	●	●	●	●
Car Insurance Certificate	▲	●	n/a	n/a	n/a	●	●	●
Car Registration Document	▲	●	n/a	n/a	n/a	●	●	●

WHEN TO GO

High season   Low season

JAN	FEB	MAR	APR	MAY	JUN	JUL	AUG	SEP	OCT	NOV	DEC
43°F	43°F	46°F	50°F	55°F	61°F	66°F	66°F	61°F	55°F	48°F	45°F
6°C	6°C	8°C	10°C	13°C	16°C	19°C	19°C	16°C	13°C	9°C	7°C

☀ Sun   Sun/Showers   Wet   Very wet

The chart above shows **average daily** temperatures for each month.
London experiences defined seasons. **Spring** (March to May) has a mixture of sunshine and showers, although winter often encroaches on it. **Summer** (June to August) can be unpredictable; clear skies and searing heat one day followed by sultry greyness and thunderstorms the next. **Autumn** begins in September, but clear skies can give a summery feel. Real autumn starts in October and the colder weather sets in during November. **Winter** (December to February) is generally mild and snow is rare, but expect the occasional "cold snap".
Be prepared for the **unpredictability** of the British climate – dress in layers and carry rainwear or an umbrella.

In the USA	In Australia	In Canada
Visit Britain	Visit Britain	Visit Britain
7th Floor	Level 2	5915 Airport Road
551 Fifth Avenue	15 Blue Street	Suite 120
New York	North Sydney NSW 206	Mississauga
NY 10176-0799	☎ (02) 9021 4400	Ontario L4V 1T1
☎ 1-800-462-2748		☎ (905) 405 1720

GETTING THERE

By Air Heathrow and Gatwick are London's two principal **airports**, handling worldwide scheduled flights. Charter flights also operate from Gatwick. Luton, Stansted and London City (Docklands) airports are increasingly busy, handling mainly European charter and business flights.

There are **direct flights** to London from most European, US and Canadian cities. Flights from Australia and New Zealand stop *en route* in either Asia or the US.

Approximate **flying times** to London: Dublin (1.25 hours), New York (7.5 hours), Los Angeles (11 hours), Vancouver (10 hours), Montréal (7 hours), Toronto (7 hours), east coast of Australia (22 hours), New Zealand (24 hours).

Ticket prices are lower from November to April, excluding Easter and Christmas. Check with the airlines, travel agents, flight brokers, travel sections in newspapers, and the Internet for current special offers.

All **airport taxes** are usually included in the price of a ticket.

By Train An alternative option for travellers from Europe is the train. The Channel Tunnel offers a direct link between London and Paris or Brussels for foot passengers aboard "Eurostar" trains (tel: 08705 186186), while the car-carrying train, "Eurotunnel" (tel: 08705 353535), operates between Calais (France) and Folkestone (England).

By Ferry Passenger and car ferries operate from Ireland, France, Belgium, Netherlands, Germany, Scandinavia and Spain.

TIME

 London is on Greenwich Mean Time (GMT) in winter, but from late March until late October British Summer Time (BST, i.e. GMT+1) operates.

CURRENCY AND FOREIGN EXCHANGE

Currency Britain's currency is the pound (£) sterling. There are 100 pennies or pence (p) to each pound. **Notes (bills)** are issued in denominations of £5, £10, £20 and £50. **Coins** come in denominations of 1p, 2p, 5p, 10p, 20p, 50p, £1 and £2. An unlimited amount of British currency can be imported or exported.

Sterling **travellers' cheques** are a safe way to carry money. They may be accepted as payment by some hotels, restaurants and large department stores.

Credit cards (MasterCard, VISA and American Express) are widely accepted.

Exchange You can exchange foreign currency and travellers' cheques at banks and bureaux de change. There are exchange facilities at larger travel agents, in large department stores and hotels, at most main post offices or at dedicated bureaux de change. Be sure to check the rate of exchange and the commission charged before any transaction as they do vary. It is possible to obtain local currency through automated cash machines (ATMs) using a debit or credit card. ATMs are found everywhere in Central London. Your bank will provide details of where your cards will be accepted in London.

| GMT 12 noon | London 12 noon | USA (NY) 7AM ← | USA (West Coast) 4AM ← | Sydney 10PM → | Germany 1PM → |

WHEN YOU ARE THERE

CLOTHING SIZES

Australia/UK	Rest of Europe	USA	
36	46	36	**Suits**
38	48	38	
40	50	40	
42	52	42	
44	54	44	
46	56	46	
7	41	8	**Shoes**
7.5	42	8.5	
8.5	43	9.5	
9.5	44	10.5	
10.5	45	11.5	
11	46	12	
14.5	37	14.5	**Shirts**
15	38	15	
15.5	39/40	15.5	
16	41	16	
16.5	42	16.5	
17	43	17	
8	34	6	**Dresses**
10	36	8	
12	38	10	
14	40	12	
16	42	14	
18	44	16	
4.5	38	6	**Shoes**
5	38	6.5	
5.5	39	7	
6	39	7.5	
6.5	40	8	
7	41	8.5	

NATIONAL HOLIDAYS

1 Jan	New Year's Day
Mar/Apr	Good Friday
Mar/Apr	Easter Monday
First Mon May	May Day Holiday
Last Mon May	Spring Bank Holiday
Last Mon Aug	Late Summer Bank Holiday
25 Dec	Christmas Day
26 Dec	Boxing Day

Almost all attractions close on Christmas Day. On other holidays some attractions open, often with reduced hours. There are no general rules regarding the opening times of restaurants and shops, so check before making a special journey. Bear in mind that public transport services are likely to be less frequent on public holidays.

OPENING HOURS

○ Shops ● Offices ● Banks
● Post Offices ● Museums/Monuments ● Pharmacies

8 am 9 am 10 am noon 1 pm 2 pm 4 pm 5 pm 7 pm

☐ Day ☐ Midday ☐ Evening

Shops Many shops in central London open for longer hours and also on Sunday.
Banks High Street banks are also open Saturday morning and bureaux de change are open daily until late.
Museums Smaller museums may close one day or more a week.
Pharmacies When pharmacies are closed a sign in the window gives details of the nearest one that operates extended hours or is on 24-hour duty.

POLICE 999

FIRE 999

AMBULANCE 999

PERSONAL SAFETY

London is generally a safe city and police officers are often seen on the beat (walking the streets) in the central areas. They are usually friendly and approachable. To help prevent crime:

- Do not carry more cash than you need.
- Do not leave a bag unattended in public places.
- Beware of pickpockets in markets, on the Underground, in tourist sights or crowded places.
- Avoid walking alone in parks or dark alleys at night.

Police assistance:
☎ **999** from any phone

ELECTRICITY

The power supply in Britain is 230/240 volts.
Sockets accept only three-

 (square)-pin plugs, so an adaptor is needed for continental European and US appliances. A transformer is also needed for appliances operating on 110–120 volts.

TELEPHONES

The traditional red phone booths are now rare; instead they come in a wide variety of designs and colours. Coin-operated phones take 10p, 20p, 50p and £1 coins (20p is the minimum charge), but phones taking British Telecom (BT) phonecards or credit cards are often more convenient. BT phonecards are available from post offices and many shops. Calls from hotel phones are expensive. To call the operator dial 100.

International Dialling Codes
Dial 00 followed by

Ireland:	353
USA:	1
Canada:	1
Australia:	61
New Zealand:	64
Germany:	49
Netherlands:	31
Spain:	34

POST (MAIL)

Post offices are open Mon–Fri 9–5:30, Sat 9–1. The only exception is Trafalgar Square Post Office, 24–8 William IV Street, open Mon–Fri 8–8, Sat 9–8. *Poste restante* mail may also be collected here.

TIPS/GRATUITIES

Yes ✓   No ✗

Restaurants (if service not included)	✓	10%
Bar service	✗	
Tour guides	✓	£1–2
Hairdressers	✓	10%
Taxis	✓	10%
Chambermaids	✓	50p–£1 per day
Porters	✓	50p–£1 depending on number of bags
Usherettes	✗	

EMBASSIES AND CONSULATES

USA	Ireland	Australia	Canada	New Zealand
020 7499 9000	0870 005 6725	0870 005 6701	020 7258 6600	0870 005 6962

HEALTH

Insurance
Nationals of EU countries, Australia and New Zealand can get free or reduced-cost medical treatment in Britain with the European Health Insurance Card (EU nationals) or a passport. Medical insurance is still advised, and is essential for all other visitors.

Dental Services
Visitors qualifying for free or reduced-cost medical treatment (see Insurance above) are entitled to concessionary dental treatment, providing the treatment is by a National Health dentist. Private medical insurance is still recommended, and is essential for all other visitors.

Weather
The sun can shine a lot in July and August. Some sights involve being outdoors for prolonged periods when you should "cover up", apply sunscreen and drink plenty of water.

Drugs
Prescription and non-prescription drugs are available from pharmacies. Pharmacists can advise on medication for common ailments. Pharmacies operate a rota so there will always be one open 24 hours; notices in all pharmacy windows give details.

Safe Water
Tap water is safe to drink. Mineral water is widely available but is often expensive.

CONCESSIONS

Students Holders of an International Student Identity Card may obtain concessions on travel, entrance fees and some goods and services. Information can be found at the National Union of Students' website (www.nus.org.uk).
Senior Citizens Senior citizens (usually over 60) will find discounts on travel, entrance fees and some events and shows. Proof of age may be required.
Visitor Attractions Pass The London Pass (www.londonpass.com) covers around 60 attractions, restaurants and shops.

TRAVELLING WITH A DISABILITY

Provision is generally good for visitors with disabilities. Many of the capital's sights have access for wheelchair users but transport can be a problem; not all Underground stations have lifts (elevators) and ramps. Most public houses are not adapted for wheelchairs.
Visit www.visitlondon.com for more information.

CHILDREN

London offers a great deal of child-centred entertainment. Details of activities are given in *Kids Out* magazine.
Baby-changing facilities are available in most family-orientated attractions.
Under 16s pay half fare on public transport, while under 5s travel free.

LAVATORIES

The cleanest public lavatories (restrooms) are usually found in department stores, hotels and restaurants.

CUSTOMS

The import of wildlife souvenirs from rare and endangered species may be either illegal or require a special permit. Before purchase you should check customs regulations.

Streetplan

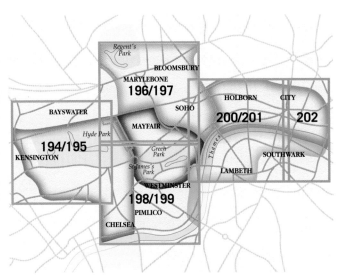

To identify the regions see the map on the inside of the front cover

Key to Streetplan

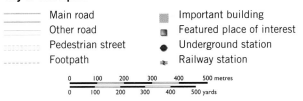

Main road		Important building	
Other road		Featured place of interest	
Pedestrian street		Underground station	
Footpath		Railway station	

0	100	200	300	400	500 metres
0	100	200	300	400	500 yards

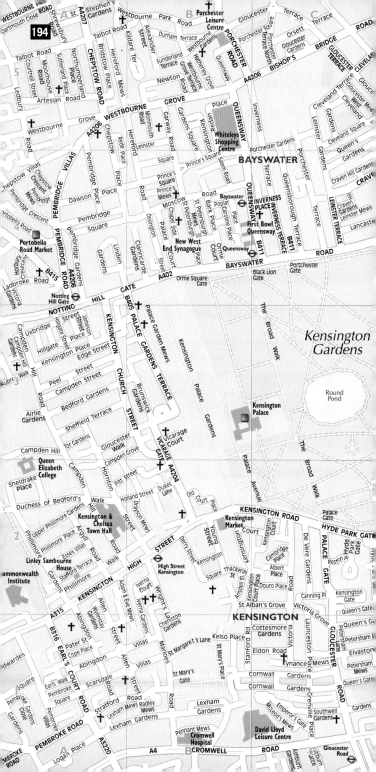

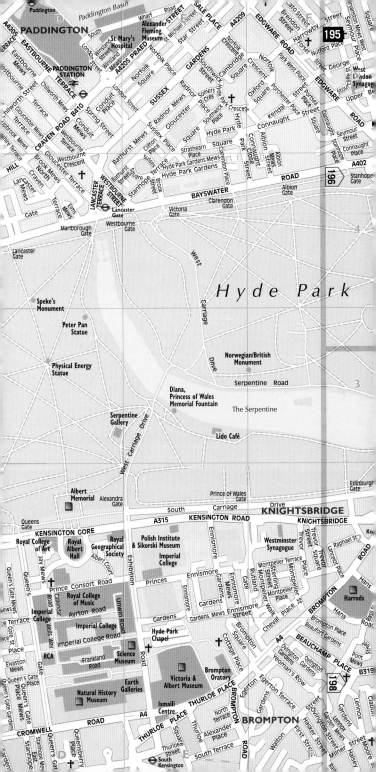

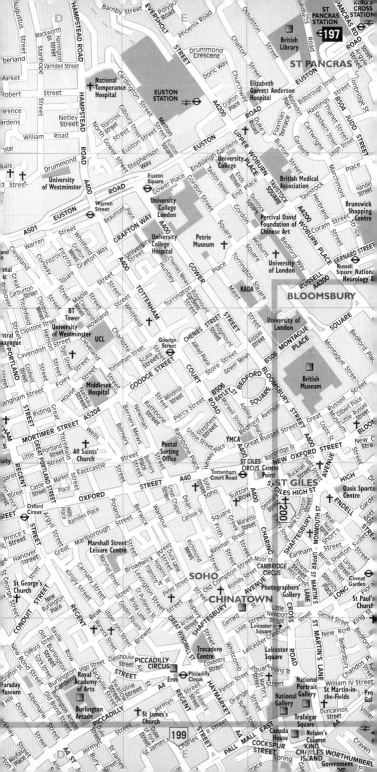

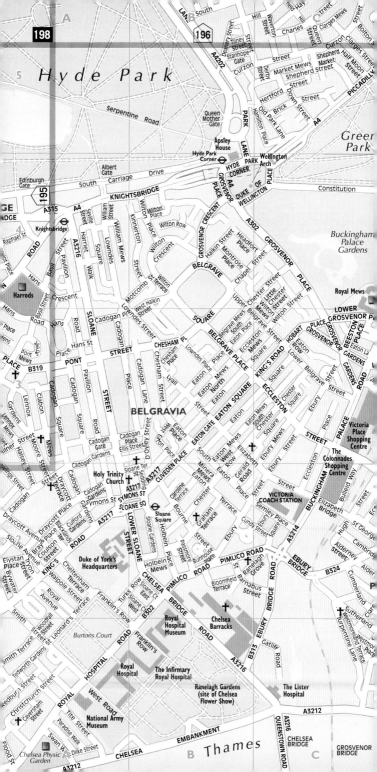

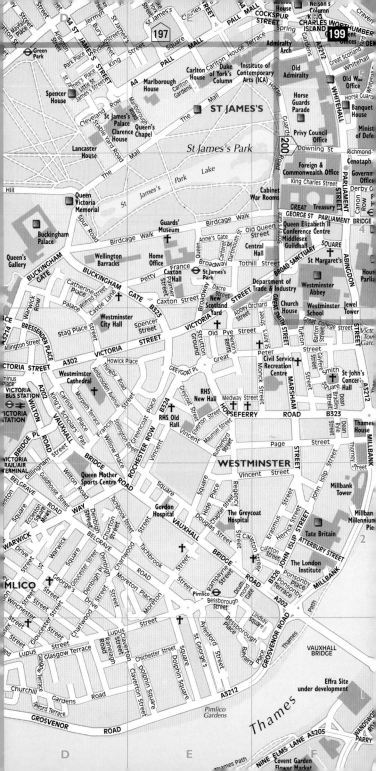

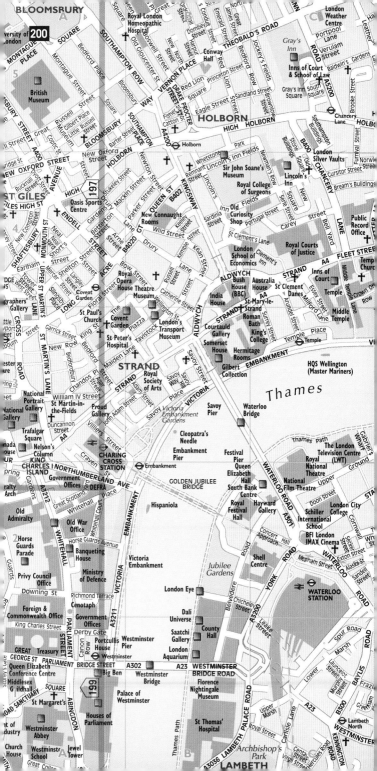

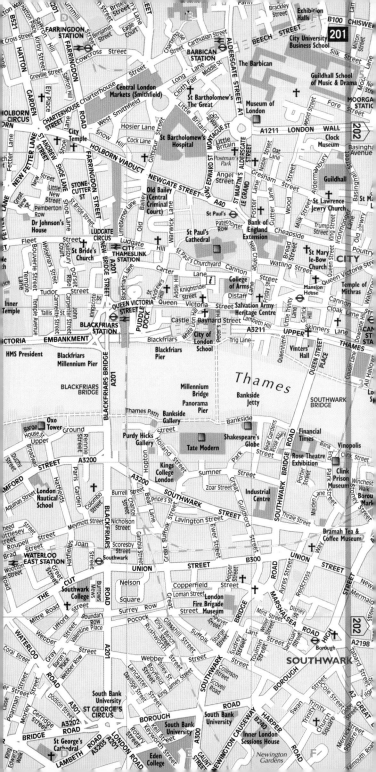

210   **Street Index**

Picture credits

Front and back covers (t) AA Photo Library/Stuart Bates, (ct) AA Photo Library/
J McMillan, (cb) AA Photo Library/Clive Sawyer, (b) AA Photo Library
The Automobile Association wishes to thank all the photographers, libraries and associations for their assistance with the preparation of the this book.
ALAMY 176 (Michael Booth); BRIDGEMAN ART LIBRARY, LONDON 6/7 Great Fire of London, 1666 by Lieve Verschuier (1630–86) Museum of Fine Arts, Hungary, 55 The Virgin and Child with SS Anne and John the Baptist, c1499 (charcoal, chalk on paper) by Leonardo de Vinci (1452–1519) National Gallery, 56 Bathers at Asnieres, 1884 (oil on canvas) by George Pierre Seurat (1859–91) National Gallery, 128b Kensington Palace: The Kings Staircase (photo), 146 Binding of the Lindisfarne Gospels. Lindisfarne Gospels, (c698 AD) Private Collection; THE BRITISH MUSEUM 140t, 142/3, 143, 145; CORBIS 11t (Adam Woolfitt), 15t (Eric Crichton), 26 (Peter Aprahamian); CROWN COPYRIGHT: HISTORIC ROYAL PALACES 128t; CROWN COPYRIGHT: THE ROYAL COLLECTION © 2005, Her Majesty Queen Elizabeth II 72; DACS © ARS, NY and DACS, London 2001 100/1;
E T ARCHIVE 25; MARY EVANS PICTURE LIBRARY 7, 12t; HULTON GETTY 8t, 8b, 11c, 77; IMAGES COLOUR LIBRARY 117b; KEW GARDENS 163t, 163b; MADAM TUSSAUDS 148t, 149; THE NATURAL HISTORY MUSEUM 126t; POWERSTOCK/ZEFA 2cb, 45; REX FEATURES LTD 10, 11b, 16, 18, 22; THE SCIENCE MUSEUM 121, 122b, 123b; SPECTRUM COLOUR LIBRARY 96t; TATE GALLERY, LONDON 1999 100 Jackson Pollock, Summertime, 102 Millais, Ophelia ; TONY STONE IMAGES 14b, 51, 151, 154t COURTESY OF THE TRUSTEES OF THE V&A PICTURE LIBRARY 119t, 119b.
The remaining photographs are held in the Association's own photo library (AA PHOTO LIBRARY) and were taken by the following:
Peter Baker 49t; Stuart Bates 70b; Malc Birkitt 13t; Caroline Jones 161; Max Jordan 10, 18/19, 19, 53, 54, 93b, 150t; Paul Kenward 2t, 3ct, 5, 49b, 59l, 59r, 107, 111, 114t, 116, 120, 127b, 131b, 141t, 148b, 155, 177l, 177r, 179; Jenny McMillan 48, 50, 52t, 60b, 141b; Michael Moody 17t; Robert Mort 2ct, 2b, 31, 67, 70t, 115, 124, 150b, 171, 181r; Clive Sawyer 17b; Barrie Smith 97, 152; Rick Strange spine, 9t, 9b, 20br, 24, 29r, 59, 92b, 96b, 96c, 114b, 117t, 125b, 126b, 127t, 131t, 164, 165, 191t, 191r; James Tims 3cb, 3b, 13b, 14t, 15b, 19b, 20l, 20tr, 21tl, 21bl, 21r, 27, 28, 28/9t, 28/9b, 57, 79, 81, 85, 92t, 94, 98/9, 118, 122t, 123t, 125t, 129, 137, 140b, 147, 154b, 167, 170, 173t, 173b, 174, 175, 181l, 182, 184l, 184r, 185t, 185b, 186, 187; Martin Trelawny 144; Richard Turpin 60t, 93t, 104, 105, 106, 178; Roy Victor 3t, 74b, 76, 89, 103, 191l; Wyn Voysey 23, 73, 74t, 95, 162, 166 (The Dean and Canons of Windsor Castle); 176; Peter Wilson 99, 168; Tim Woodcock 52b, 80, 83, 130t; Gregory Wrona 142.
Illustrations on pages 71 and 78 by Maltings Partnership
Abbreviations for terms appearing above (t) top; (b) bottom; (l) left; (r) right; (c) centre.

Acknowledgements

Extract on page 30 from *Success* by Martin Amis reproduced by kind permission of Crown Publishers Inc. Extracts by Ian Parker, Dale Peck and Will Self from *Granta 65: London, The Lives of the City* on page 30 reproduced with kind permission of Granta.

Questionnaire

Dear Traveler

Your comments, opinions and recommendations are very important
to us. So please help us to improve our travel guides by taking a few
minutes to complete this simple questionnaire.

Send to: Spiral Guides, MailStop 66, 1000 AAA Drive,
Heathrow, FL 32746–5063

Your recommendations…
We always encourage readers' recommendations for restaurants, nightlife or shopping –
if your recommendation is added to the next edition of the guide, we will send you a
FREE AAA Spiral Guide of your choice. Please state below the establishment name,
location and your reasons for recommending it.

_____

_____

_____

_____

_____

Please send me AAA Spiral _____
(see list of titles inside the back cover)

About this guide…
Which title did you buy?

_____ **AAA Spiral**

Where did you buy it? _____

When? m m / y y

Why did you choose a AAA Spiral Guide? _____

_____

_____

_____

Did this guide meet your expectations?

Exceeded ☐   Met all ☐   Met most ☐   Fell below ☐

Please give your reasons _____

_____

_____

_____

continued on next page…

Were there any aspects of this guide that you particularly liked?

Is there anything we could have done better?

About you…

Name (Mr/Mrs/Ms)

Address

Zip

Daytime tel nos.

Which age group are you in?

Under 25 ☐   25–34 ☐   35–44 ☐   45–54 ☐   55–64 ☐   65+ ☐

How many trips do you make a year?

Less than one ☐   One ☐   Two ☐   Three or more ☐

Are you a AAA member? Yes ☐   No ☐

Name of AAA club

About your trip…

When did you book? ☐ ☐ / ☐ ☐   When did you travel? ☐ ☐ / ☐ ☐

How long did you stay?

Was it for business or leisure?

Did you buy any other travel guides for your trip?   ☐ Yes   ☐ No

If yes, which ones?

Thank you for taking the time to complete this questionnaire.